Rancière Now
Current Perspectives on Jacques Rancière

Theory Now

Series Editor: Ryan Bishop

Rancière Now

Current Perspectives on Jacques Rancière

EDITED BY
OLIVER DAVIS

polity

First published in 2013 by Polity Press

Polity Press
65 Bridge Street
Cambridge CB2 1UR, UK

Polity Press
350 Main Street
Malden, MA 02148, USA

ISBN-13: 978-0-7456-6256-5 (hardback)
ISBN-13: 978-0-7456-6257-2 (paperback)

A catalogue record for this book is available from the British Library.

Typeset in 10.5 on 12 pt Sabon by
Servis Filmsetting Ltd, Stockport, Cheshire
Printed and bound in Great Britain by Berforts Information Press Ltd

For further information on Polity, visit our website: www.politybooks.com

Contents

Acknowledgements

I would like to thank all of the contributors for their dedicated and timely work on this volume. On behalf of us all I would like to thank David Winters and Emma Hutchinson from Polity for their interest in the project and for the invaluable practical and intellectual support they have provided. I am grateful to Adrian Rifkin for his counsel at various stages and to the anonymous readers of the draft manuscript for their suggestions. I would like to thank everyone with whom I have had occasion to discuss Jacques Rancière's work over the last few years and in particular the members of the TBLR Seminar at the University of Bergen and Gabriel Rockhill, whose incisive responses to a paper based on my chapter came at just the right moment. Finally, I am grateful to the University of Warwick for a term of sabbatical leave.

Contributors

Jackie Clarke is Senior Lecturer in French at the University of Glasgow. She is the author of *France in the Age of Organization: Factory, Home and Nation from the 1920s to Vichy* (Berghahn, 2011) and has published widely on twentieth and twenty-first century French history, society and culture. She is currently working on a project about work, consumption and subjectivity in France from the 1950s to the present, taking the history and memory of the domestic appliance manufacturer Moulinex as a focal point.

Tom Conley is Abbott Lawrence Lowell Professor of Romance Languages and Literatures and of Visual and Environmental Studies at Harvard University. He is the author of numerous influential books, book chapters and articles and is one of Rancière's leading interpreters and interlocutors.

Oliver Davis is Associate Professor of French Studies and Programme Director of the Centre for Research in Philosophy, Literature and the Arts at Warwick University. He is the author of, among other works, the critical introduction *Jacques Rancière* (Polity, 2010).

Geneviève Fraisse is a leading French philosopher and author of some fourteen books, many of which approach what she terms the controversy of the sexes from epistemological, political and historical perspectives. Her most recent book is a collection of interviews and shorter texts entitled *La Fabrique du féminisme, Textes et entretiens* (Le Passager Clandestin, 2012). She worked alongside Jacques Rancière in the collective responsible for the journal *Les Révoltes Logiques* (1975–81). She has served as a member of the European Parliament (1999–2004) and makes frequent appearances on French television and radio.

Tim Jarvis holds a PhD in creative writing from the University of Glasgow, awarded for a thesis which took the form of a novel interwoven with theoretical material. He has published several short stories of his own, as well as critical articles on Borges and Ishiguro. He has facilitated creative writing workshops and presented theoretical papers on the pedagogy of this process.

Jeremy F. Lane is Associate Professor of French at the University of Nottingham and author of *Bourdieu's Politics: Problems and Possibilities* (Routledge, 2006), *Pierre Bourdieu: A Critical Introduction* (Pluto, 2000) and numerous articles on topics ranging from Bourdieu to jazz. His latest book is *Jazz and Machine-Age Imperialism* (University of Michigan Press, forthcoming).

Bill Marshall is Professor of Comparative Literary and Cultural Studies at Stirling University and Director of the Institute of Germanic and Romance Studies at the University of London. He is the author of numerous books and articles, including *Guy Hocquenghem* (Duke University Press, 1997), *Quebec National Cinema* (McGill University Press, 2001), *André Téchiné* (Manchester University Press, 2007) and most recently *The French Atlantic: Travels in Culture and History* (Liverpool University Press, 2009).

Jean-Luc Nancy is Emeritus Professor of Philosophy at Strasbourg University and author of over fifty books, most recently *L'Équivalence des catastrophes (Après Fukushima)* (Galilée, 2012).

Caroline Pelletier teaches in the Institute of Education at the University of London. She has published numerous articles and book chapters which look at education from the perspective of social and cultural theory, several of which involve Rancière's work.

Sabine Prokhoris is a practising psychoanalyst based in Paris and the author of numerous works including *La Cuisine de la sorcière (La Psychanalyse prise au mot)* (Aubier, 1988), *Le Sexe prescrit: la différence sexuelle en question* (Aubier, 2002), *Fabriques de la danse*, with Simon Hecquet (Presses Universitaires de France, 2007), *La Psychanalyse excentrée* (Presses Universitaires de France, 2008) and, most recently, *Le Fil d'Ulysse – Retour sur Maguy Marin* (Les Presses du Réel, 2012).

Jacques Rancière is Emeritus Professor in the Department of Philosophy at Paris 8. He is the author of numerous articles and over twenty books, including *Aisthesis: scènes du régime esthétique de l'art* (Galilée, 2011).

Carolyn Steedman is Professor of History at Warwick University and a leading British social historian. She is the author of, among many other works, *Dust* (Manchester University Press, 2001), *Master and Servant. Love and Labour in the English Industrial Age* (Cambridge University Press, 2007) and *Labours Lost. Domestic Service and the Making of Modern England* (Cambridge University Press, 2009). She has just finished writing her latest book, *The Stockingmaker, the Magistrate and the Law. How to Frame Everyday Life*, a study of Joseph Woolley, a Nottinghamshire framework knitter, and the local magistrate. She hopes it will be published in 2013.

Joseph J. Tanke is Assistant Professor in the Department of Philosophy at the University of Hawaii. He is the author of *Foucault's Philosophy of Art: A Genealogy of Modernity* (Continuum, 2009), of *Jacques Rancière: An Introduction – Philosophy, Politics, and Aesthetics* (Continuum, 2011) and most recently the co-editor (with Colin McQuillan) of *The Bloomsbury Anthology of Aesthetics* (Bloomsbury, 2012).

Abbreviations

References to Rancière's major works have been given in parentheses in the main body of the text and in the Notes with the abbreviations below. English translations have been referenced wherever they exist; occasionally the French edition has also been referenced. For example (D1, M19) refers to *Disagreement: Politics and Philosophy*, trans. Julie Rose (Minneapolis: University of Minnesota Press, 1999), p. 1 and to *La Mésentente: Politique et philosophie* (Paris: Galilée, 1995), p.19. Where no published English translation is available the French text alone has been referenced; for example (A30) refers to *Aisthesis: scènes du régime esthétique de l'art* (Paris: Galilée, 2012), p. 30. Wherever the English translation has been modified this is signalled with '[TM]'.

Rancière in English translation

AD   *Aesthetics and Its Discontents*, trans. Steven Corcoran (Cambridge: Polity, 2009).

AL   *Althusser's Lesson*, trans. Emiliano Battista (London: Continuum, 2011).

AU	*The Aesthetic Unconscious*, trans. Debra Keates and James Swenson (Cambridge: Polity, 2010).
CC	*Chronicles of Consensual Times*, trans. Steven Corcoran (London: Continuum, 2010).
D	*Disagreement: Politics and Philosophy*, trans. Julie Rose (Minneapolis: University of Minnesota Press, 1999).
DIS	*Dissensus: On Politics and Aesthetics*, ed. Steven Corcoran (London: Continuum, 2009).
ES	*The Emancipated Spectator*, trans. Gregory Elliott (London: Verso, 2009).
FF	*Film Fables*, trans. Emiliano Battista (Oxford: Berg, 2006).
FW	*The Flesh of Words: The Politics of Writing*, trans. Charlotte Mandell (Stanford: Stanford University Press, 2004).
FI	*The Future of the Image*, trans. Gregory Elliott (London: Verso, 2007).
HD	*Hatred of Democracy*, trans. Steven Corcoran (London: Verso, 2006).
IS	*The Ignorant Schoolmaster: Five Lessons in Intellectual Emancipation*, trans. Kristin Ross (Stanford: Stanford University Press, 1991).
M	*Mallarmé: The Politics of the Siren,* trans. Steven Corcoran (London: Continuum, 2011).
MS	*Mute Speech*, trans. James Swenson (New York: Columbia University Press, 2011).
NaH	*The Names of History: On the Poetics of Knowledge*, trans. Hassan Melehy with a Foreword by Hayden White (Minneapolis: University of Minnesota Press, 1994).
NL	*Nights of Labor: The Workers' Dream in Nineteenth-Century France*, trans. John Drury, introduced by Donald Reid (Philadelphia: Temple University Press, 1989). Republished by Verso as PN, below.
PhP	*The Philosopher and His Poor*, trans. John Drury, Corinne Oster and Andrew Parker (Durham: Duke University Press, 2003).
PA	*The Politics of Aesthetics: The Distribution of the Sensible*, translated and introduced by Gabriel Rockhill, with an Afterword by Slavoj Žižek (London: Continuum, 2004).

PoL   *The Politics of Literature*, trans. Julie Rose (Cambridge: Polity, 2011).

SP   *On the Shores of Politics*, trans. Liz Heron (London: Verso, 1995).

StP   *Staging the People: The Proletarian and His Double*, trans. David Fernbach (London: Verso, 2011).

PN   *Proletarian Nights: The Workers' Dream in Nineteenth-Century France* (London: Verso, 2012). A new edition of NL, above.

SV   *Short Voyages to the Land of the People*, trans. James Swenson (Stanford: Stanford University Press, 2003).

Rancière in French

A   *Aisthesis* (Paris: Galilée, 2011).

BP   *Aux Bords du politique* (Paris: La Fabrique and Gallimard, 1998).

BT   *Béla Tarr, le temps d'après* (Paris: Capricci, 2011).

CT   *Chroniques des temps consensuels* (Paris: Seuil, 2005).

CV   *Courts Voyages au pays du peuple* (Paris: Seuil, 1990).

DI   *Le Destin de l'image* (Paris: La Fabrique, 2003).

EC   *Les Écarts du cinéma* (Paris: La Fabrique, 2011).

EmS   *L'Empire du sociologue*, with the other members of the *Révoltes Logiques* collective (Paris: La Découverte, 1984).

EP   *Esthétiques du peuple*, with the other members of the *Révoltes Logiques* collective (Paris: La Découverte/Presses Universitaires de Vincennes, 1985).

FC   *La Fable cinématographique* (Paris: Seuil, 2001).

LGG   *Louis-Gabriel Gauny, le philosophe plébéien*, texts by Gabriel Gauny selected and introduced by Rancière (Paris: La Découverte/Maspero and Presses Universitaires de Vincennes, 1983).

H   *La Haine de la démocratie* (Paris: La Fabrique, 2005).

IE   *L'Inconscient esthétique* (Paris: Galilée, 2001).

LA   *La Leçon d'Althusser* (Paris: Gallimard, 1974).

MI   *Le Maître ignorant: cinq leçons sur l'émancipation intellectuelle* (Paris: Fayard, 1987).

PS	*Mallarmé: La politique de la sirène* (Paris: Hachette, 1996).
M	*La Mésentente: Politique et philosophie* (Paris: Galilée, 1995).
ME	*Malaise dans l'esthétique* (Paris: Galilée, 2004).
MEG	*La Méthode de l'égalité*, an interview with Laurent Jeanpierre and Dork Zabunyan (Paris: Bayard, 2012).
MP	*Moments politiques: Interventions 1977–2009* (Paris: La Fabrique, 2009).
NH	*Les Noms de l'histoire: essai de poétique du savoir* (Paris: Seuil, 1992).
NP	*La Nuit des prolétaires: archives du rêve ouvrier* (Paris: Fayard, 1981).
PM	*La Parole muette: essai sur les contradictions de la littérature* (Paris: Hachette, 1998).
PS	*Le Partage du sensible: esthétique et politique* (Paris: La Fabrique, 2000).
PP	*Le Philosophe et ses pauvres* (Paris: Flammarion, 2nd edn, 2007).
PL	*Politique de la littérature* (Paris: Galilée, 2007).
SP	*Les Scènes du peuple (Les Révoltes logiques, 1975–1985)* (Lyon: Horlieu, 2003).
SE	*Le Spectateur émancipé* (Paris: La Fabrique, 2008).
TP	*Et tant pis pour les gens fatigués: entretiens* (Paris: Amsterdam, 2009).

Editor's Introduction

What does Jacques Rancière's work have to say about the 'now' evoked in the title of this volume and series? The worker-artists and worker-intellectuals of *Proletarian Nights*, to the archives of whose writings Rancière had repaired in the 1970s after parting company with Althusser, stayed up late into the short night set aside for them to rest before starting work again the following morning. The artisans' working day in the early nineteenth century was so long and their pay so meagre that these workers should have had no time for anything other than their work and the rest needed to resume that work again in the early morning. They 'should' have had no time according to a logic of domination first articulated in Plato's *Republic*, although as Jeremy F. Lane notes in his contribution to this volume, the social hierarchy of castes Plato outlined there was not justified in rational terms but founded instead on what Plato confessed was a myth, or 'noble lie'. When Rancière's workers stayed up to write poetry or set up political, or philosophical, magazines their revolt against the rigours of the working day was directly a revolt against domination, its rationality, its particular division and distribution of time and space and against the monolithically restrictive identity which it sought to impose upon them: the order of domination stipulated that these workers could only be workers. As Lane shows, Rancière's unique insight into Pierre Bourdieu's sociology was to reveal how, in spite of its most strenuous and vocal efforts, it remained in significant respects complicit with Plato's lie.

In his 2012 preface to *Proletarian Nights*, which makes much of the similarities between these worker-intellectuals and those on the precarious fringes of working life today, Rancière writes:

> In this world, the question is always to subvert the order of time prescribed by domination, to interrupt its continuities and transform the pauses it imposes into regained freedom. It is to unite what [it] separates and to divide what it ties together by asserting, against the rationality imposed by its managers, their governments and experts, a capacity for thought and action that is common to all. (PNxi–xii)

Often at great personal cost this handful of worker-intellectuals took it upon themselves to revolt against the temporality of domination. Most of them did so without prior political or intellectual training or direction; they did not wait to be instructed but acted in the 'now', which first of all meant wresting that 'now' from the reproductive cycle of the working day. In *Proletarian Nights* Rancière is concerned to salvage these 'logical revolts' – revolts which were 'logical' both in the colloquial sense of 'only to be expected' and 'logical' because framed in words – from two kinds of condescension.[1] From the condescension of those historians who would dismiss such worker-intellectuals as causally insignificant figures in the pre-history of organized labour and also from the condescension of the Althusserian Marxism in which he had been schooled and which, according to Rancière's critique, viewed the dominated as trapped in a 'perfect circle' of incapacity: they were 'maintained in their place by ignorance of the laws of domination' but 'the place in which they found themselves prevented them from understanding the laws of this domination' (PNviii). Althusserian Marxism promised to break the circle which it had imposed by dispensing *instruction* to the dominated yet what Rancière claimed he found in the archives was that these artisans of the 1820s and 1830s had no need of such instruction in the secret mechanism of domination. However, Geneviève Fraisse, in her contribution to this volume, will suggest that Rancière's wholesale rejection of any *science* of domination must be seen as a reactive overcorrection and one which poses particular problems for feminist politics.

Althusserian Marxism, according to Rancière's critique of it, promised to supply the dominated, or their political representatives, with the knowledge they lacked in order to end domination by revolution. Despite this expressly revolutionary objective, Rancière characterized Althusserian Marxism as a pedagogy of inequality and unending deferral which, under the pretence of hastening the moment of revolution by its teaching was, in fact, premised on the idea that this moment would never come. In the meantime, Althusserianism perpetuated inequality by distinguishing between the knowledge of the master explicator (and the Party) and the ignorance of the unschooled masses. Althusser and the other prominent figures on the Left whom Rancière likened to him in these respects in *The Philosopher and his Poor* [1983], Bourdieu and the later Sartre in particular, spoke of the need for dramatic change while offering only a self-serving pedagogy which reproduced the inequality of Plato's *Republic* in which intellectuals, as latter-day philosopher-kings, ruled over the social hierarchy.

In *The Ignorant Schoolmaster* [1987] Rancière went further, suggesting that pedagogy in general, or as generally practised, was an unending deferral of the moment of equality. What made this a radical critique was that it applied even and perhaps especially to two kinds of education usually regarded in the French context as exemplars of enlightened, 'progressive', pedagogy: the system of mandatory primary education established by Jules Ferry in the 1880s and the 'rational pedagogy' advocated by Bourdieu and his policy-making disciples in the French Socialist Party in the 1980s. Bourdieu saw reformed pedagogy as the path to social justice because it would equip all children without exception with the 'softer' skills and implicit knowledge that children from more privileged backgrounds tended to arrive at school already possessing, skills and knowledge which his research had led him to believe played a major role in determining career and earning potential later in life.[2] What Rancière realized about the sociologist's work on the French school system was that, despite its indignantly critical tone, it presented both diagnosis and remedy in such a way that politicians keen to be seen to be 'doing something' about social inequality could easily draw upon it, all to the benefit of Bourdieu himself. More significant, however, for Rancière, than the accrual of personal and disciplinary prestige was the idea that Bourdieu's plans for reform of the education system were in effect a roundabout justification of the legitimacy of schooling and the existing social order. Rancière was not offering rival proposals for reform of the French school system in *The Ignorant Schoolmaster* but he was insinuating that education, even of the most concertedly progressive kind, is all too often mainly preoccupied with establishing, justifying and preserving the hierarchies of its own institutions, disciplines, qualifications and methods (foremost among these explanation) and, in turn, with justifying the rationality of the existing social order:

> Joseph Jacotot's singularity, his *madness*, was to have sensed this: his was the moment when the young cause of emancipation, that of the equality of men, was being transformed into the cause of social progress. And social progress was first of all progress in the social order's ability to be recognized as a rational order. This belief could only develop to the detriment of the emancipatory efforts of reasonable individuals, at the price of stifling the human potential embraced in the idea of equality. An enormous machine was revving up to promote equality through instruction. This was equality represented, socialized, made unequal, good for being *perfected* – that is to say, deferred from commission to commission, from report to report, from reform to reform, until the end of time. Jacotot was alone in recognizing the effacement of equality under progress, of emancipation under instruction. (IS134)

The 'presumption of equality', which Rancière salvages from the worldly failure of Jacotot's endeavours, is a way of blocking progressive-pedagogical deferral by insisting on intellectual equality in the 'now', as the immediate point of departure rather than the distant end result of education. What Jacotot's (anti-) method, as re-described and re-cathected by Rancière, could mean for teaching practice is explored, in the context of creative writing pedagogy, by Caroline Pelletier and Tim Jarvis in their co-authored chapter in this volume. They consider, but ultimately dismiss, what they see as mainly superficial similarities between creative writing pedagogy and Jacotot's universal teaching. They are right to do so, for Jacotot and Rancière were dreaming not just of a different kind of education but first and foremost of a radically different world.[3] Rancière calls Jacotot's egalitarian pedagogy his '*madness*' because it implies a vision of the social order which is so different from the status quo as to threaten despair and ruin – indeed sometimes real madness – for those brave and foolish enough to seek to put it into practice. The change of optic in *The Ignorant Schoolmaster* reveals the educational apparatus to be that which produces and justifies social inequality. For it takes in students of equal potential but instead of verifying their equality contrives to churn out finished products who are more or less 'qualified'. And it produces more than these differentially qualified, hierarchically classified, students; in the process it also produces the very idea of inequality and thereby rationalizes every form of hierarchical social arrangement. Rancière's fidelity to his own break with Althusser would not have allowed him to put matters in quite these terms but what Jacotot's egalitarian folly allowed him to apprehend, in *The Ignorant Schoolmaster*, is the education system as the site par excellence of the ideological production of inequality.

Rancière's radical conception of equality, drawn in part from Jacotot, is thus of equality which is presumed in the 'now'. In a valuable attempt to articulate its originality, Todd May has described this as 'active' equality, to distinguish it from more established philosophical and economic conceptions of distributive equality.[4] It can also be characterized as 'declarative' equality because, when it re-appears in a central role in the mature politics of *Disagreement* [1995], the process of political subjectivation typically begins with a *declaration* of equality, that is of their own equality, by the dominated, whom Rancière terms, in French, the *sans-part* because they are without (*sans*) a share or part (*part*), in the political process. This foundational speech act initiates the emancipatory process, or performance, which Rancière calls political subjectivation and which he conceives as simultaneously the coming into being of a new political subject and the emergence into audibility and visibility of their grievance.[5]

In Rancière's account of subjectivation there is no causal necessity leading to such moments in which equality is declared, these being construed instead as fleeting interruptions of the order of domination by an incommensurable order of thinking – and, I would also want to add, of feeling. While Rancière realizes that the *sans-part* will often refer back to earlier emancipatory movements and sometimes to legal and constitutional principles enshrined as the codified memory of those uprisings, those moments and principles only have purchase to the extent that they are re-animated by the declaration of equality in the present; in themselves they are mere traces without the foundational power to institute equality, or indeed democracy, as enduring forms of social arrangement. The 'now' of equality – or of true politics, or democracy, in the very closely interrelated senses in which Rancière understands these three terms in *Disagreement* – is always unmotivated, anachronistic, disruptive or disjunctive; it is always, as Kristin Ross has astutely observed, 'untimely'.[6] In creating the 'now' of politics the declaration of equality breaks open the saturated temporal order of domination; it shatters that 'consensus' and moves to reconfigure the world along more egalitarian lines.

Rancière's political thought undoubtedly has more to say about the 'now' of egalitarian upsurge than its 'inscription' over time. This has irked some on the left because it implies that no single such democratic-egalitarian uprising is capable of instituting an enduringly just social order. To some it has seemed that his formalist account of democracy – in which the *sans-part* intermittently breaks open the closed spatial and temporal order of domination – is a complacently non-committal redescription of the way the world already operates. In other words, some have felt that Rancière's political thought was already too much like aesthetics in its emphasis on the *form* of revolt. Yet if there is no historical necessity to the 'now' of equality then the fact that it need never happen also means, by the very same token, that it can always happen. In other words, the *sans-part* need never wait (for progress, for concessions, for the instruction which purports to give them an adequate understanding of domination) before declaring and 'staging' their equality.[7] Yet the effect of this, I would argue, is doubly to precipitate the moment of action. Doubly because *both* the thought that things could go on like this forever *and* the feeling that they could pivot in an instant are, under conditions of domination, incentives to act. It is not, of course, the mere abstract possibility but rather the reflective awareness that things could continue as they are forever which is an incentive to the *sans-part* to act in the now and herein lies much of the efficacy of Rancière's thought as a catalyst for emancipatory political struggle. To the extent that it fosters a becoming-conscious of the contingency of domination it is an incitement to revolt.

The availability of Rancière's thought for egalitarian political struggle is enhanced by its staunch and longstanding resistance initially to schemes of explanation of a teleological or historicist persuasion and subsequently to all forms of explanation which presuppose the inherently superior insight of the explainer. Whether in his early political writings, as part of the collective behind *Les Révoltes Logiques*, by questioning the New Philosophers' assertion that Marxism made the Gulag inevitable, or by resisting Fukuyama's doctrine of the 'end' of 'history' and politics, or in his historiographical writing, by debunking the scientistic historicism of the *Annales* School, or in his writing on art, by questioning the teleologies of modernism and postmodernism, Rancière has consistently resisted styles of explanation which suggest that things could not have been otherwise. Such reasoning is complacent, he suggests; every teleological 'fable' it generates is a 'rampart' against 'disorder' (AD68). Such fables may well be the stock-in-trade of academic institutions, policy think-tanks and their qualified experts; they may even be an inevitable feature of any collective, intersubjective, attempt to understand the world. Yet he insinuates that they are also self-protective falsifications which shield the individual and the community from an encounter with the originary disorder on which they rest. *Sous les pavés, la plage.*[8] Thus in the preface to *Proletarian Nights* Rancière asserts that the book and its author dissent from

> the belief, shared equally by modernism and postmodernism, in a straight line of history on which ruptures in the course of time are conceived as the work of time itself, of an overall temporal process that generates and suppresses successive forms of life, consciousness, and

action. It rejects this idea of time, seeing it as always, beneath its apparent objectivity, a manner of putting things and beings in a hierarchical order, in their proper place. (PNviii)

What happens to scholarship when you dispense with teleology and subsequently with explaining in the way Rancière suggests? In *Proletarian Nights* what you get is a reconstruction, without hierarchizing explanatory mediation, of the *brouillage* of its subjects' inner lives. A churning vat, endlessly fascinating and impossibly inconclusive. As Rancière's new preface acknowledges and Carolyn Steedman confirms in this volume, nobody really knew what to make of the book when it first appeared in the early 1980s. In its rejection of teleological explanation Rancière's work is forever throwing its reader back onto shifting sands – *sous les pavés, la plage* – forever returning him or her to the ordeal of an encounter with that disorder, an ordeal that is also an opportunity for autonomous meaning-making. Like Jacotot before him, Rancière can seem at times to be an intractable master: 'Don't try to fool me or fool yourself. Is that really what you saw? *What do you think about it?* Aren't you a thinking being?' (IS23)

In its corrosive analytical resistance to the joined-up thinking first of historicism and then of explanation as it is usually practised his work repeatedly beaches the reader on the shores of disorder, goading him or her to exercise freedom by making something of the wreckage, be that subjectivation or the enjoyment of aesthetic form. While there may indeed be, as Steedman suggests, a certain hectoring menace in the refusal to accept "I can't" for an answer, the intention, as she acknowledges, is emancipatory. It says that with the disorder of this wreckage anyone can do anything . . . provided of course s/he still has the fortitude. In its insistence on the radical contingency of the social order, the irrational arbitrariness of history and the element of delusional self-aggrandizement in every attempt at explaining, Rancière's work has not only remained faithful to May '68 but has sheltered, concretized, intensified and relayed its elusive spirit.

The impossible – unbearable – teaching of May '68 was that any and every sociopolitical and pedagogical order is contingent. Nothing has subsequently been proven by the collapse of

Communist regimes, any more than it had been by the demise of those utopian workerist communities founded in North America in the nineteenth century. We may live in the 'time after' Communism, as Rancière calls it in his book on Hungarian film-maker Béla Tarr, but this *temps d'après* is no more than simply a time which just happens to come after. 'The time after is not the morose and uniform time of those who no longer believe in any-thing' (BT15–16). When contemplated with a cold enough eye and in the absence of the reassuring ramparts of teleological expla-nation this 'time after' is neither the inevitable result of historical process nor a determining moment for the future shape of things. It is, rather, a beach-like horizontal plane on the shores of which numerous possibilities and virtualities, of domination and eman-cipation alike, have been washed up and coexist in their radical contingency.

Overview of this Volume

This volume has been conceived and arranged in three sections: (i) politics; (ii) history, reading, writing; (iii) literature, film, art, aesthetics.

In the politics section Jackie Clarke asks whether Rancière's work can help frame an understanding of social movements and phenomena, including the riots which gripped France in 2005 and the United Kingdom in 2011. Rancière's is first and fore-most a non-identitarian understanding of politics and this is the source of much of the friction between it and the work of social scientists; in his contribution Jeremy F. Lane offers an account of the vexed relationship between Rancière and Bourdieu and the social sciences more generally. In the following chapter the former collaborator of Rancière's, philosopher and historian Geneviève Fraisse, asks whether Rancière's decision to turn away from social-scientific knowledge of domination limits the usefulness of his emancipatory politics, particularly for feminist struggle.

In the section on history, reading and writing, British social historian Carolyn Steedman examines the mixed reception of

Rancière's work among her colleagues and casts valuable new light on Rancière's particular use of Jacotot's method of teaching reading and writing in *The Ignorant Schoolmaster*. The teaching of creative writing is the focus of Caroline Pelletier and Tim Jarvis's contribution, which draws both on Rancière's critical reflections on pedagogy and his work on literature as a specific manifestation of the art of writing in the aesthetic regime. Psychoanalyst Sabine Prokhoris rounds off the second section with a sceptical reflection on the difficulties of reading Rancière's own work.

The third section opens with Joseph J. Tanke's account of *Aisthesis*, in particular of the chapter or 'scene' devoted to Stendhal's *The Red and the Black* and also of the logic of the 'scene' itself. Tom Conley's contribution is a parallel exploration of *Les Écarts du cinéma* and *Aisthesis* which illuminates Rancière's particular conception of the aesthetic surface and explores his practice of the 'écart'. My own chapter strives to elaborate a synthetic account of the politics of art in the aesthetic regime in terms of aesthetic contingency and the aesthetic affect. Bill Marshall's chapter then probes the 'entangled' relationship between the film theory of Rancière and that of Deleuze. Jean-Luc Nancy, in the penultimate chapter, questions Rancière on what he sees as the suppression of 'metaphysics' from *Aisthesis* and advances a critique of *le partage du sensible*; Rancière responds with a robust defence of his approach and Nancy rounds off the dialogue with a lucid account of what divides and unites the two philosophers. In the final chapter, an interview with me, Rancière elaborates on some of the methodological choices implicit in *Aisthesis* and discusses his ongoing work on the aesthetic regime of art.

I
Politics

1

Rancière, Politics and the Social Question

Jackie Clarke

To consider Rancière's thought from the point of view of 'the social question' might be considered a perverse enterprise. While his thinking is fundamentally concerned with equality, he does not conceive of equality in social terms. Indeed, it might be said that much of his intellectual effort has been devoted to disentangling the political from the social and to critiquing conceptions of politics that appeal to the existence of a community (at least in the sense that that term is normally understood).[1] At the same time the centrality of this divorce from the social in Rancière's thinking is part of what makes it worth revisiting in the context of this reflection on *Rancière Now*. If social equality had fallen from favour somewhat as a political objective in the 1990s, when Rancière published his most important works on politics and the political, the advent of the economic crisis since 2007 has brought the question of social and economic inequality back into sharp focus. It has also given rise to new social movements. It is in relation to the changing shape of the social question since the 1980s that I wish to reflect on Rancière's political thought. I will begin by outlining some key elements of his thinking and considering the insights it offers into contemporary politics and social movements. I will then raise two principal reservations, the first relating to what I see as a kind of inverted materialism in Rancière's thinking and the second to his reluctance to think about the problem of political organization.

In a series of writings in the late 1980s and 1990s Rancière developed a conception of politics which distinguished between two processes commonly understood as political: on the one hand, the exercise of power and the organization of collective life; on the other, emancipation. Retaining the term 'the political' for the latter type of activity, Rancière designated the former as 'policing'. What is implied in the term 'police', as Rancière uses it, is not necessarily a repressive force, but an order, a distribution of roles. The police order rests on and enacts a set of assumptions about who counts in the collectivity: it is 'the law, generally implicit, that defines a party's share or lack of it . . .; it is an order of the visible and the sayable that sees that a particular activity is visible and another is not, that this speech is understood as discourse and another as noise' (D29). Thus, the police order is always hierarchical, even if it claims otherwise, as is typically the case in democracies. Politics is what happens when this allocation of roles is disrupted and revealed as contingent, when the contradictions of a supposedly democratic order are exposed by an action which demonstrates that not everyone is taken account of equally.

The social world is conceived here in terms of what Rancière calls the 'division of the sensory' – not a distribution of wealth (though this plays a part), so much as an allocation of time and space. The division between a masculine public sphere and feminine domestic sphere, which disqualified women from voting until the twentieth century, would be one example of this. Similarly, the assumption that intellectual and aesthetic pursuits are the preserve of the formally educated – an idea disputed by the nineteenth-century worker-poets that Rancière studied in *Proletarian Nights* – operates, in this account, in the form of an allocation of the worker to the space of the factory and to the activity of manual work, condemning him or her to be unheard. In this way, the social world figures in Rancière's analysis primarily as an obstacle to emancipation – it is always part of the police order. As a number of critics have observed, Rancière's suggestion that some distributions – and some forms of police – are better than others, is not followed up with much exploration of how one might distinguish these, let alone a discussion of what a better social order would look like.[2] For reasons that will be discussed more later, Rancière considers this to be the wrong question. He has attended instead to the ways in which policing tends to foreclose politics and to the emancipatory acts which disrupt the police order.

When Rancière talks about equality, therefore, he is not talking about social and economic redistribution as such, but about intellectual capacity and the recognition of that capacity – he asserts the equality of any speaking being with another (D30). Speech is central here in that inequality is seen to manifest itself as a refusal to consider someone as a being capable of thinking and speaking like any other, while politics consists in a particular kind of emancipatory speech act which challenges this. For Rancière, political speech acts take the form of a disagreement over who counts, over the status of the interlocutors as fully reasoning (speaking) subjects. By way of illustration he offers the case of the French feminist Jeanne Deroin, who presented herself at a polling station in 1849 (nearly a century before women would finally have the right to vote in France), and in doing so highlighted the gap between the rhetoric of universalism ('universal suffrage' had been proclaimed the previous year) and the reality of women's continuing disqualification from the public sphere (D41–2). It is important to note that while such disagreements may invoke the name of a particular social category ('women'), it is an error in Rancière's view to understand this name as a reference to a prior community or social body. Rather, he argues, the names invoked in such speech acts serve to articulate a wrong and expose an inequality. If they express some sense of political community, this exists only in a rather abstract sense in the speech act itself. Politics, for Rancière, is never 'the enactment of the principle, the law or the self of the community'.[3] Its logic is rather to pose the question: 'Do we or do we not belong to the category of men or citizens or human beings, and what follows from this?' – the second part of the question performing the crucial calling to account.[4] It is the police order, he argues, which purports to act as an expression of the community, thereby naturalizing the power of governments.[5] One implication of this association between policing and the idea of community is that Rancière has questioned the emancipatory potential of identity politics, suggesting that it always leads back to the classificatory logic of policing in which everyone has an allocated place.

While Rancière developed these ideas as part of a reflection on politics in general, drawing on chronologically disparate examples, the questions that preoccupied him in the late 1980s and 1990s were also prompted by the particular political realignment that took place in that period. This was a moment when the end of politics and the end of history were being loudly proclaimed, when what was previously understood as a terrain of ideological conflict was being redefined as one of management.[6] In the space formerly known as politics, depoliticization became the new language of governmental legitimacy.[7] Politicians now contested elections on the basis of who could best embody this new 'post-politics'. Hence, while Jacques Chirac sought to paint François Mitterrand as the embodiment of the old order in the 1988 presidential elections in France (SP7), the British Labour Party was involved in a similar effort to reframe political differences as a temporal gap – the question was no longer whether one was on the left or the right, but whether one was 'old' or 'new'.

This remapping of the space of electoral politics also involved a reconfiguration of the social question. As Rancière has observed, consensus politics, which was supposed to spell the end of utopian politics, actually ushered in a new 'utopia of the centre': 'the utopia of a social realm capable of setting its own house in order, of cancelling both its own division and the divisions deriving from the passions that seek to appropriate the political centre' (SP19). In France this was particularly apparent in the emergence of a media and political discourse about 'social exclusion'. As the language of class and inequality receded in public debate, social disparities came to be imagined in spatialized terms, as a problem of whether one was included or excluded, inside or outside. This was in part a recognition of the acute geographical marginalization of multi-ethnic communities in peripheral housing estates around French cities, although the identification of these spaces as a 'social problem' has also served to reinforce their stigmatization. To this extent, the language of inclusion and exclusion is symptomatic of an ethnicization as well as a spatialization of the social question in

France.[8] But it also reflects transformations in the world of work and welfare, as the social gains and relative stability that had characterized the postwar era have been eroded and growing numbers of people find themselves caught in long-term unemployment or precarious work situations.[9] As French sociologist Robert Castel has observed:

> All this seems to indicate that our society has rediscovered with surprise the presence within itself of a kind of population thought to have long since vanished, the 'useless of the world', who exist in society without really belonging to it. They occupy the position of *supernumeraries,* floating in a kind of social no man's land, not integrated and perhaps unintegrateable, at least as Durkheim spoke of integration as belonging to a society formed by a collection of interdependent elements.[10]

Two connected features of this reconfiguration of the social question stand out. Firstly, in contrast with the class analysis that had informed public debate about social inequality in France, at least on the left, in the 1960s and 1970s, it tends to pathologize the dispossessed – the excluded are not a class, they are a problem.[11] Secondly, it implies that the solution to this problem lies not so much in social change but in integration – or, to use a revealingly objectifying phrase common in French discussions of unemployment and homelessness, 'social insertion'. While this formulation of the social question does not necessarily preclude the possibility of a political claim (in Rancière's sense) being made in the name of the excluded, it does tend to promote a functionalist understanding of the social in which the objective is cohesion rather than justice.

It has been widely recognized that the interest of Rancière's thought lies partly in the way it works against the logic of consensus politics.[12] Against the view that conflict can and should be relegated to the past, Rancière proposes a conception of politics that puts dissensus (of a particular kind) at its heart. Although he has been accused of reproducing elements of 'endism'[13] – of accepting that government and electoral politics are now about management and that the space for politics has been largely foreclosed – it is clear that Rancière is fundamentally preoccupied with what happens in moments when that foreclosure is resisted. Indeed,

Kristin Ross has argued that his interest in the event – in politics *as* event – rather than in structure and space offers a welcome foil to the functionalist logic of consensus politics and spatialized social theory.[14] One might also suggest that in a context in which social movements seemed to have receded and in which the radical left was being discussed primarily in terms of its defeat, the figuration of politics as an interruption or a sporadic moment of rupture, rather than a long march towards social justice, appeared to speak to the needs of the moment. Moreover, while Rancière has not dwelt much on the remapping of the social question per se, he has certainly viewed the discourse of 'the fight against social exclusion' with an illuminating anti-functionalist eye, denouncing the ideal of a society made whole – a society in which the struggle against exclusion can be won – as an illusion of the police order.[15] Ever since the fifth century BC, he argues (in one of many references to ancient Athens), the police order has sought to foreclose politics by claiming that everyone has a share in the community (D14); the claim that everyone has been counted 'including the excluded' (to use Oliver Davis's neatly paradoxical phrase) can be seen as one more manifestation of this.[16]

Rancière's analysis also seems to illuminate some important features of the new social movements that have developed since the 1990s. No sooner had the fight against social exclusion been declared in France than a new movement emerged to dispute its claims. Or rather a series of movements emerged which became collectively known as the Le Mouvement des sans – literally, the movements of those who are without, the 'have nots'. This was a heterogeneous group of actors which included associations representing the homeless, the unemployed and undocumented migrants. They emerged on the public stage through a series of actions whose high points included an occupation on the rue du Dragon in Paris in 1994 launched by the association Droit au logement (Right to Housing), the occupation of the Église St Bernard in Paris by undocumented migrants in summer 1996, and a wave of occupations and demonstrations by the unemployed in winter 1997. On the face of it, these movements represented rather disparate social groups. Mobilized along the lines of what might have appeared to be single issue politics, they emerged outside or on

the margins of the labour movement.[17] Some of their demands –
such as that for improved unemployment benefits – related to the
material interests of specific groups. Others were more explicitly
about having a voice: the 1997 movement for the unemployed, for
example, demanded a seat at the table alongside the other 'social
partners' (employers and organized labour) who managed the
French unemployment insurance scheme. What was most striking about these movements, however, was the way in which they
were able to make common cause, something that was perhaps
most clearly exemplified when the various associations issued a
collective manifesto, the Call of the Have Nots (*Appel des Sans*) in
December 1995.

This articulation of a new political subjectivity – that of the
'have nots' – was arguably what gave the movement much of its
political force, particularly if one understands politics in Rancierian
terms. If we consider the name 'sans' or 'have nots' as the representation of a social group, we might question the coherence of
the group and hence its ability to represent a clearly defined set of
interests. But, as we have seen, for Rancière, political subjectivity
is not about the representation of a pre-existing identity or community. Rather subjectivity is conceived in terms of a *process* of
subjectivation. This consists not in the expression of a self but in
the articulation of a relation to another or in an interrogation of
how a category relates to the universal. In this way it is conceived
as a kind of dis-identification or declassification which opens
up the question of who counts.[18] When the Movement of the
Unemployed spoke in solidarity with undocumented workers, it
refused to subscribe to a logic of social classification and economic
competition which set the interests of one group against the other.
Instead, the social actors who participated in the Mouvement des
sans forged a name for themselves that laid bare the contradictions
of language of the fight against social exclusion. That discourse
simultaneously pronounced the existence and non-existence of the
excluded and did so in terms that evoked an absence rather than a
group.[19] The Mouvement des sans chose a different name, one that
spoke not of presence and absence, belonging and not belonging,
but of deprivation and hence inequality.

Moreover, if one subscribes to a Rancierian view of politics, the question of whether movements like the Mouvement des sans authentically represent a coherent social group is not so much an irrelevance, as a depoliticizing gesture – a form of interpretive policing. This has been most apparent recently in responses to the Occupy Movement which began in New York in September 2011 and which mobilized around the slogan 'We are the 99%.'[20] This proposition encapsulated the idea that the majority was paying for the financial crisis, while the wealthiest in society (symbolized by the bankers and investors of Wall Street) were able to avoid tax and cash in on the misfortunes of others on the financial markets. The power of the slogan lies in the way it disputes the claim made by governments in a period of austerity that (to use the words adopted by British Prime Minister David Cameron), 'We are all in it together.' Or as US Republican Presidential Candidate, Newt Gingrich put it 'There is no such thing in America as 99%. We are 100% American. We are all part of America.'[21] If one way of claiming there was no 99 per cent was to assert the national whole, another was to insist on the division of the 99 per cent into groups with separate interests. Conservative commentator Erick Erickson launched 'We are the 53%', a blog which set 'those of us who pay' – the 53 per cent of Federal income tax payers – against 'those of you who whine', implying that the Occupy movement was in the latter camp.[22] In an article in *Forbes* magazine Todd Henderson, a Professor of Law at the University of Chicago, argued that there was no single 99 per cent, but rather a series of vested interests which differed depending on the policy area under consideration – so that in education, for example, students and parents were the 99 per cent while teachers were the one per cent.[23] What this has in common with Erickson's response is that it evaluated the statement 'We are the 99%' as a description of a socio-economic group. What such objections do is shift our attention from politics to sociology – they parcel people back into their assigned socio-economic identities and thus, Rancière would argue, reassert the police order.

What is useful therefore in thinking about social movements with Rancière is the insight that his perspective offers into political subjectivities and the politicizing or depoliticizing potential of certain kinds of speech acts. After a period when anglophone interest in 'French theory' was driven notably by a political and intellectual interest in the question of difference, the current vogue for Rancière in the English-speaking world is perhaps symptomatic of a search for ways of thinking about equality which avoid the pitfalls of social determinism. Yet what Rancière offers ultimately is a politics of moments, rather than a politics of movements. As other critics have noted, there is little sense in his writing of how one gets from one moment of political disagreement to another, and little interest in social change – in *how* a better order might be established.[24] While the decision not to start from these questions is part of what constitutes the strength and originality of Rancière's philosophy of the political, the questions remain.

Rancière's suspicion of the social can be understood in the context of his break with Marxism after 1968. As a student in Paris in the 1960s, he was part of a generation that distanced itself from Stalinism and from the French Communist Party which was seen to have lost its revolutionary potential by becoming part of the parliamentary establishment. Prior to 1968, as a student of Louis Althusser, he had subscribed to Althusser's distinctive brand of Marxism, which insisted on the scientific nature of historical materialism and on the role of intellectuals in discerning and explaining the theoretical implications of Marx's writing. However, the revolts of 1968, which developed spontaneously in university campuses and factories, saw students and workers throw off organizational and intellectual hierarchies, in favour of ad hoc 'bottom-up' organization and self-management (*autogestion*). Rancière's trajectory is similar in that his post-'68 work is marked by a repudiation of Althusser and by a marked hostility towards social determinism, pedagogical hierarchies and institutionalization.[25]

By the 1980s these tendencies were apparent in Rancière's polemics against Bourdieusian sociology, which was highly influential in France at the time, notably in debates about the democratization of culture and education. In *The Ignorant Schoolmaster*, Rancière argued that the ostensibly progressive educational ideas associated with the sociologist reproduced the hierarchies they claimed to undermine. To conceive of education as a means of achieving the end-goal of social equality was, in his view, to reassert the power of those who know to emancipate those who don't know (just as Althusser had done) and in doing so to defer rather than enact equality. As he would later put it, 'anyone who starts out from distrust, who assumes inequality and proposes to reduce it, can only succeed in setting up a hierarchy of inequalities, a hierarchy of priorities, a hierarchy of intelligences – and will reproduce inequality ad infinitum' (SP52–3).[26] This is why Rancière is so reluctant to engage with the question of what a more egalitarian society would look like and how this might be achieved. His sidestepping of these questions is the product not of a mere disinterest in these issues, but of a conscious attempt to distance himself from modes of thinking that in his view can only lead to inequality and policing. This certainly creates a space for Rancière to develop an alternative view of equality but, in leaving aside questions that are crucial for activists if not philosophers, he also leaves himself open to a charge of excessive philosophical purism.

Moreover, for all its radical rejection of Marxist material-ism, Rancière's thinking seems to me to be marked by a form of inverted materialism in its conception of the social world. Although he rejects the idea that one's capacities are conditioned by one's social position, asserting the emancipatory potential of being 'out of place', Rancière also ascribes tremendous force to the social. This is apparent in the way the social world is figured in his writing as something that takes on a solidity, whereas politics is conceived in more abstract terms. For example, the logic of speech (which is the logic of politics or emancipation) is seen to differ from the logic of the social in that:

> the material arbitrariness of the social weight of things cannot be tra-versed by any subject for another subject. [. . .] Society is ordered in the same way as bodies fall to earth. What society asks of us is simply to acquiesce: what it demands is our consent. (SP83)

Thus the 'social bond' for Rancière is always a product of the 'weight of things'. The social is reified here, characterized as immovable or unbreachable, like a wall. So while the weight of things can certainly be momentarily escaped and resisted – for example by workers who refuse their social position by writing poetry – the social world itself appears fixed, allowing no possibility of change.

Rancière's contrast between the logic of speech and the logic of the social also positions speech rather strikingly outside the social. But what if we conceive of the social as something other than the 'weight of things'? What if social bonds could be constructed through emancipatory speech acts? In other words, what space is there in Rancière's account of politics for a sense of solidarity or camaraderie? This raises the question of the affective dimension of politics, something which does not figure in political subjectivity as Rancière envisages it.[27] Recognizing that dominant groups try to dismiss the speech acts of the dominated by characterizing them as noise or emotion, Rancière is concerned to demonstrate what is rational in such utterances.[28] Yet the police order's polarity between reason and sensibility remains operative here – it just changes sides. For where affect does appear in Rancière's thinking it is precisely on the side of the policing:

> What binds us all together prior to all community, prior to any equality of intelligence is the link that runs through all those points where the weight of things in us becomes consent, all those points *where acquiescence comes to be loved as inequality.* (SP83, my emphasis)

This alignment of affect with the police order is connected with Rancière's rejection of the idea, dear to much of the left, that community and equality go hand in hand while isolation and selfishness foster inequality (SP74). Tracing this conflation back to the French utopian socialists of the early nineteenth century, Rancière takes issue with their work-centred ideal of community in which 'moments of expansive cordiality' and conflict serve to solidify the social identity of workers *qua* workers (SP75). But this challenge to the idea of a *necessary* link between fraternity and equality in a community defined by work surely does not preclude the possibility of some sort of affective solidarity operating within the alternative form of politics that Rancière delineates.[29]

People who have participated in emancipatory social movements often speak of the sense of togetherness that comes with collective action but there is no reason to assume that this sentiment refers to a pre-existing community or social identity of the kind that Rancière rejects; on the contrary, one might argue that it is precisely the mingling that happens on the street in a demonstration that can give rise to the exhilaration of coming together. To return to the Mouvement des sans, for example, Daniel Mouchard cites the account of one group of trade union and association activists for whom the demonstrations of 1994 brought a significant encounter with those in much more precarious social situations, including homelessness. This encounter in which 'each person brought their own problems' was recounted as a 'revelation' for the activists. It was a moment remembered in terms of a solidarity constructed across social difference in the 'amiable' atmosphere of the demonstration.[30] Indeed the festive side of protest will be so familiar to anyone who has ever been on a demonstration, that an account of politics which leaves it out seems a rather impoverished one. In other words, it remains difficult to justify why love of inequality should be given space in Rancière's account while love of equality is not.

Like the affective togetherness that can come from shared action, the more organizational dimensions of coming together are the object of suspicion for Rancière. The 'community of equals' that he envisages is an 'insubstantial community of individuals engaged in the ongoing creation of equality' and can never take the form of an institution (SP84). Yet as Todd May has pointed out, certain kinds of institutionalization, such as cooperatives, surely manage to avoid the pitfalls of the organizations of the institutionalized left that Rancière is reacting against.[31] Moreover, if Rancière's conviction that institutionalization is the enemy of equality makes him reluctant to think about questions such as how one might organize to make politics happen, there are other kinds of questions we might ask which make his reticence around the question of organization troubling. For example, how does the police order work to undermine the organization of politics? When Rancière analyses the way in which consensus politics depoliticizes and forecloses the space in which political disagreement might emerge, he focuses essentially on the discursive work of foreclosure. Yet the development of his thinking coincided with a period in which consensus politics managed to establish itself not just by reimagining social space and shifting the discourse of electoral politics, but through the decline and dismantling of social movements. In France, trade union membership is estimated to have fallen by more than half between 1976 and 1988, as a result of factors such as economic restructuring and new management practices which circumvented unions.[32] The UK saw a head-on confrontation between government and trade unions in the 1980s which came to a head in the miners' strike of 1984. A wave of legislation through the 1980s and 1990s restricted the power of unions and the right to strike, narrowing the definition of a lawful trade dispute, outlawing secondary action, forcing unions to adopt postal ballots and give seven days' notice of a strike. Unions not adhering to the legislation risk punitive financial penalties. Of course one could debate the labour movement's complicity in its own decline, but if the aim of businesses and governments like that of Margaret Thatcher was to reduce social conflict in order to foreclose politics, then undermining organized labour was undoubtedly one of the ways in which this was achieved.

Community organizations have arguably been transformed too in the age of consensus politics. Paul Gilroy has contended that this was one of the major differences between the English riots of 2011 and those of the 1980s. The August 2011 events followed the shooting of Paul Duggan, a young black man from Tottenham in North London. Following a peaceful protest by local people, rioting broke out and spread rapidly to other neighbourhoods and cities, where it appeared to have little connection to the trigger event. A distinctive feature of the disturbances was the targeting of commercial premises and the high incidence of looting. This was followed by a major police and judicial clamp-down, as some unusually punitive sentences were handed down.[33] At a public meeting held against this backdrop, Gilroy lamented the impoverished nature of consensus politics and argued that the depoliticization of public debate was also the result of a process of privatization at a local level:

> When you look at the layer of political leaders from our communities, the generation who came of age during that time thirty years ago, many of those people have accepted the logic of privatization. They've

privatized that movement, and they've sold their services as consultants and managers and diversity trainers . . . And that means that, in many areas, the loss of experience, the loss of the imagination is a massive phenomenon.[34]

As a result, he suggested, it was more difficult to mount an effective defence campaign in the face of judicial repression.

Gilroy's intervention is interesting as it was part of a debate over the meaning of the riots that brought into sharp focus the question of what politics is and what part organizers or movements play in allowing politics to happen – questions that lie at the heart of Rancière's thinking. The composite nature of the riots as an event, along with their violent and acquisitive dimensions made it difficult to identify a clear politics in what was happening. While the peaceful protest outside the police station in Tottenham, which demanded that officers engage with local people as reasoning human beings (i.e. equals), might readily be seen as a political act in Rancierian terms, violence and looting sit uncomfortably with a theory of the political which centres on the rational speech act. But if violent revolt is considered somehow prior to the process of political subjectivization, it is surely left wide open to the kind of quasi-Althusserian reading that Rancière would reject. It is notable in this respect that Gilroy stops short of arguing that lack of community leadership was a cause of the riots – the argument is not that the rioters need an elite to teach them how to do politics. But what much of the left-wing commentary offered was a symptomatic reading of the events. Zygmunt Bauman, for example, saw the looting as a product of the particularly explosive combination of social inequality and rampant consumerism that characterizes contemporary English society.[35] For the Conservative-led government, on the other hand, it was a display of pure criminality by a 'feral underclass'.[36] This dehumanizing discourse set the tone for the judicial backlash and Labour politicians who sought to link the riots to social inequality were challenged to engage instead in the language of condemnation.[37] The question of the policing of London's black youth was thus occluded and when veteran campaigner Darcus Howe tried to raise it on the BBC News he found that he was dismissed as no better than a criminal himself.[38] Indeed, one might observe in this context that the interpretive policing of the event was rather more successful than its actual policing on the streets. In the light of all this, Gilroy's commentary stands out because it reformulates the question of the politics of the riots in terms which are less susceptible to these forms of interpretive policing: he asks not whether the riots constitute a political act, but 'is there politics in this country?'[39]

In conclusion, it seems to me that the questions raised here – those of organization and of the affective dimension of politics – are worthy of more attention than Rancière has been prepared to give them. In the light of the political experiences of his youth, Rancière is not wrong to caution against the dangers of institutionalization. But his solution to this problem is arguably so philosophically absolute as to be of little use to those who actually want to make politics happen. Activists such as those in the Occupy movement face the problem of how to make politics sustainable. One of the solutions they have adopted is the organization of alternative communities – the St Paul's occupation in London, for example, created its own quasi-institutional structure with a food tent, a library and the Tent City University. In other words, not all forms of organization look like the French Communist Party in 1968. At times Rancière's thinking seems so overdetermined by his past history with the left, that it seems to overlook the questions raised by the present. Taking a cue from Rancière's own attentiveness to the voices of the dispossessed, we might do well to think a bit more about the lessons of contemporary social movements, as well as the lessons that can be learned from the changing manifestations of what Rancière calls the police order.

2

Rancière's Anti-Platonism: Equality, the 'Orphan Letter' and the Problematic of the Social Sciences

Jeremy F. Lane

Perhaps the most common response to Rancière's work is to welcome the generosity of spirit that lies behind his presupposition of equality but to worry that such generosity betrays an unrealistic lack of attentiveness to the material conditions and historical contexts which act to limit such equality. Rancière's attentiveness to the possibilities of democratic emancipation may be admirable, it is suggested, but there is something hopelessly unrealistic about his account of political subjectivation. What is required is a greater measure of realism, an acknowledgement of 'the importance of material circumstances'[1] or an increased attentiveness to the 'conditions for the institution and durability of equality',[2] to quote two recent critics. In some cases, this leads commentators to argue that Rancière 'goes too far' in his critique of the sociologist Pierre Bourdieu, in particular.[3] Indeed, Charlotte Nordmann even suggests that some synthesis of Bourdieu and Rancière might leaven the deterministic tendencies of the former without uncritically embracing the idealism of the latter's alleged tendency to elevate equality to 'a form of transcendence'.[4]

In what follows, I want to suggest that such responses are fundamentally mistaken, manifesting a failure to grasp the radical nature of Rancière's critique of the social sciences. Firstly, there is no sense in which Rancière simply overlooks questions of historical context or material circumstance. In *Disagreement*, for example, he is explicit in his insistence that different political regimes, at different historical moments, offer radically different opportunities for enacting the logics of democracy, emancipation and equality (D30–1). The most cursory reading of *The Nights of Labor*, meanwhile, reveals Rancière's keen awareness of the material inequalities against which his worker-poets struggled. What he does refuse, however, is the slippage from registering such material inequalities to making the assumption that these must correspond to inequalities of inherent intellectual capacity, inequalities themselves seen as determining, *a priori*, corresponding inequalities of political capacity. For Rancière, such a slippage is characteristic of a range of approaches in the social sciences to questions of history, society and political agency. In short, Rancière's contention is that the social sciences typically seek to provide a positivist account of social or class identity, understood to be defined by a range of measurable, positive attributes relating to wealth, education, gender, ethnicity, historical circumstance, and so on. Behind that positivism, however, lurks a form of idealism rooted in Platonism, according to which those positive attributes are taken to form a kind of ideal core or essential identity determining in advance what people are and what they can and cannot do.

This slippage from positivism to idealism is no contingent mistake or accident, however. It is, rather, inherent to the *problematic* of the social sciences as a whole, to the manner in which those sciences construct the object of their enquiries, hence determining what can or cannot be thought within that given problematic. Rancière's criticism of the social sciences is thus not that they merely over-emphasize the weight of social determinations or the force of material circumstance and hence underestimate the possibilities for emancipation and political change. His criticism turns on questions neither of degree nor of the intentions, good or bad, of individual sociologists. His critique is far more radical and rests on the assertion that unless they work through the contradictions and blind spots inherent to their problematic, the social sciences will prove simply incapable of thinking the possibility of equality, emancipation, or political change at all. In such circumstances, the notion that the allegedly unrealistic nature of Rancière's account of political emancipation might be corrected by recourse to approaches borrowed unchanged from the social sciences is simply illogical. Further, simply to call upon Rancière to be more attentive to historical context or material circumstance, without further qualification, is to risk unwittingly reproducing the very pitfalls, contradictions and blind spots Rancière has identified as being inherent to the conventional social scientific problematic.

Rancière's critique of the Platonic problematic characteristic of the social sciences is extremely wide-ranging, at times apparently embracing sociology in its entirety, as well as significant amounts of work in the discipline of history, most notably that of the *Annales* school (in *The Names of History*). Assessing the validity of such a comprehensive critique would merit a book-length study of its own. For reasons of space, therefore, what follows will concentrate primarily on Rancière's critique of Bourdieu, since he has clearly come to epitomise all of the failings Rancière takes to be inherent to the problematic of social scientific thought more generally.

Bourdieu's and Plato's 'Polemical Complicity'

One of the key points of disagreement between Rancière and Bourdieu relates to their opposing assessments of Kantian aesthetics. Kant insists that if judgements of aesthetic taste are to claim universal communicability, then they must be 'disinterested', they must not be rooted in the narrowly subjective realm of personal tastes or partial interests. For Rancière, this notion of disinterested aesthetic contemplation contains a virtual democratic force, through its presumption of a capacity for aesthetic judgement and pleasurable contemplation shared by all. When the nineteenth-century carpenter Gabriel Gauny behaves for a moment 'as if' he were the owner of the house whose parquet floor he is laying, stepping back to contemplate his workplace as a site no longer of exploitation but of disinterested aesthetic contemplation, he enacts the founding gesture of Kantian aesthetics and lays claim to that shared humanity and equal capacity. This moment of pleasurable aesthetic contemplation may be based on an 'illusion' of material equality, but it is nonetheless rich in the emancipatory possibilities inherent to any such refusal to be defined absolutely by one's social condition or identity (NL81–2). From the point of view of Bourdieu's sociology of culture, on the other hand, the actions of a Gauny are unthinkable. For Bourdieu argues that to be able to adopt such a disinterested aesthetic gaze, to contemplate an object in turns of its form, with no concern for its function, presupposes an ability to achieve a leisurely distance from the realm of immediate material necessity that is contingent upon considerable material wealth. Misrecognized as a universal capacity, aesthetic disinterest can thus play its role in social reproduction. By passing off a socially determined capacity for disinterested aesthetic contemplation as a universal criterion of taste, Kantian aesthetics enables certain aptitudes and practices that are the preserve of the bourgeoisie to be misrecognized as objective measures of that class's inherent intellectual and moral worth. Thus, Kantian aesthetics formalizes that process whereby 'legitimate' aesthetic taste serves to naturalize and reproduce class divisions.[5] The actions of Gauny, or of the other worker-poets featured in *The Nights of Labor*, who were all determined to manifest their capacity for disinterested aesthetic contemplation *despite* their material impoverishment, are thus strictly unthinkable within the Bourdieusian problematic. Similarly, the possibility that Kant's aesthetic universal might contain a virtual democratic force, through its presumption of a universal capacity for aesthetic judgement, must be denounced as the misrecognized expression of class privilege.

For Rancière, this inability to think either the virtual democratic force contained in Kantian aesthetics or the possibility of individuals like Gauny ever existing is no oversight on Bourdieu's part; it is, rather, 'structural'. As he puts it:

> Bourdieu's polemic against aesthetics is not the work of one particular sociologist on a particular aspect of social reality; it is structural. A discipline, in effect, is not first of all the definition of a set of methods appropriate to a certain domain or certain type of object. It is first the very constitution of this object as an object of thought,

the demonstration of a certain idea of knowledge – in other words, a certain idea of the relation between knowledge and a distribution of positions.[6]

Rancière's argument is that Kant's concept of the universality of aesthetic judgement contains within itself a virtual democratic and egalitarian force that cannot be thought within the problematic of sociology, whether in the work of the discipline's founding fathers, such as Auguste Comte or Émile Durkheim, or in that of a more recent, apparently more politically radical sociologist such as Bourdieu.

The sociology of Comte and Durkheim was informed by the attempt to domesticate the disruptive democratic force of any such declaration of universality, 'to remake a body' for society in the wake of industrialization, urbanization and democratic revolution, by reconstituting 'the social fabric such that individuals and groups at a given place would have the *ethos*, the ways of feeling and think-ing, which corresponded at once to their place and to a collective harmony' (Disciplines, 7). In this, Comte and Durkheim reveal the extent to which 'social science' has been 'strangely contaminated by a problematic born of theocratic counterrevolutionary thought, which conceives the emergence of democracy as a loss of unity, a sundering of the social bond' (SP43). Counter-revolutionary thought conceived of the democratic revolution as a disruption of the natural order and hence insisted that claims as to the equal-ity of all citizens must be based on lies and dangerous falsehoods. The social sciences, even those committed to the most progressive political agendas, inherited this 'fantasy of a lost totality' in the form of a scepticism regarding the claims of democracy. Behind democracy's 'formal' claims to equality, the social sciences thus posited a 'hidden truth' of inequality, class division and exploita-tion, a hidden truth to which they enjoyed exclusive access. At this point, sociology drafted in the notion of 'misrecognition' to explain why the masses gave their allegiance to such an unjust regime (SP44). Unwittingly updating Plato's parable of the cave in the *Republic*, the social scientists set up a founding opposition between their objective knowledge, their *epistemè*, and the state of misrecognition, or *doxa*, in which the masses were assumed to languish. Bourdieu provides Rancière with a more recent example of a sociologist who, having failed to think through the implications of the problematic in which he works, is forced, despite his express intentions, to reproduce these Platonic assumptions.

As Rancière notes, more recent sociology, such as Bourdieu's, 'has certainly distanced itself from' the 'organicist vision of society' embraced by Comte and Durkheim (Disciplines, 7). Nonetheless, he insists that contemporary sociology remains in 'a polemical complicity with the Platonic ethical project' (Disciplines, 8). As Rancière acknowledges, at the level of its explicit intentions Bourdieu's sociology constitutes a wholesale critique and hence rejection of the kind of elitism and social inequality that Plato identifies as key to the maintenance of a just society in the *Republic*. Nonetheless, Bourdieu draws on Platonic concepts in order to elucidate the nature of the inequalities he is committed to challenging. As we have seen, Bourdieu argues that the capacity for disinterested aesthetic contemplation is anything but universal, being contingent on that leisurely distance from the realm of immediate material need that is the preserve of the moneyed classes. He extends this model from the realm of aesthetics to the realms of philosophical reflection, formal education and rational political deliberation, arguing in each case that what are in fact socially determined aptitudes are misrecognized as universal. Bourdieu maintains that each of these distinct domains, aesthetics, education, philosophy and politics, in fact requires of their participants what he terms 'the scholastic point of view', the *skholè*, that leisurely distance from immediate material need, which Plato claims to be the prerequisite for engaging in philosophical reflection or in the government of the city in the *Theatetus*.[7]

Plato is very happy with this state of affairs; for him, the fact that shoemakers or artisans lack the *skholè*, the leisure necessary to enable them to participate either in the realm of philosophical speculation or in the governance of the city is a good thing; it legitimates his conception of a society in which every class is allotted its 'natural' place, knows that place, and keeps to it. It is in this context that he advocates the dissemination of a 'noble' or 'necessary lie' in order to convince each class that it has a natural place and should keep to it, namely the myth of the three metals, according to which God put gold in the souls of rulers, silver in the auxiliaries, and iron and copper in farmers and craftsmen.[8] Bourdieu, by contrast, seeks to denounce the illegitimacy of the social order instituted in this way. He argues that once it is misrecognized as a universal criterion of intrinsic merit, this socially determined disposition, the *skholè*, can play its role in reproducing social distinctions by naturalizing material inequalities. This is fundamentally unjust, according to Bourdieu, and the role of sociology is to combat such injustice by revealing the mechanism of misrecognition at its core and by highlighting the arbitrary, socially determined nature of the class divisions that such mechanisms legitimize and reproduce.

However, Rancière's point is that behind this evident polemic between Bourdieu and Plato there lurks a fundamental complicity. After all, Bourdieu joins Plato in his assumption that workers are, by definition, incapable of philosophical reflection, aesthetic contemplation, or even rational political deliberation, for lack of their necessary prerequisite, the *skholè*, the leisurely distance from immediate material necessity. In other words, both Plato and Bourdieu are guilty of a slippage from the empirical observation of material inequality to the assumption of an intrinsic inequality of intellectual capacity. Plato is quite open about his reasons for doing this and about the role of the 'necessary lie', the myth of the three metals, in legitimizing the unequal social order he advocates. Rancière's argument is that the notion of 'misrecognition' plays the same structural role in Bourdieu's sociology as does the myth of the three metals in Plato since it works from the assumption that workers or the 'dominated classes' possess a set of limited intellectual and political capacities that are defined, *a priori*, by the social roles they occupy (Disciplines, 100; PhP132). Indeed, in one sense Bourdieu reinforces this Platonic hierarchy, for where Plato openly admits his hierarchy corresponds to a 'myth' or 'necessary fiction', he insists that this hierarchy is rooted in social reality. As Rancière puts it:

> Thus sociology enters into a polemical complicity with the Platonic ethical project. What it refuses, and what the philosopher declares, is that inequality is an artifice, a story which is imposed. It wants to claim that inequality is an incorporated reality in social behaviour and

misrecognised in the judgements that this behaviour implies. It wants to claim that what science knows is precisely what its objects do not. (Disciplines, 8)

Paradoxically, in the course of protesting against the fact that the dominated classes lack the material means, the *skholè*, necessary to engage in philosophical reflection, disinterested aesthetic contemplation, or rational political deliberation, Bourdieu rehearses the Platonic assumption that such people are, by their nature, not able to engage in such lofty pursuits. In so doing, Bourdieu repeats, even reinforces the Platonic assumption that there are two qualitatively different kinds of knowledge of the social world available to agents, the purely 'practical knowledge' available to those agents whose social identity is defined by their lack of the *skholè* and the objective sociological knowledge available to intellectuals, whose material wealth is the prerequisite for the *skholè* on which objective knowledge depends. On the basis of this opposition between practical and scientific knowledge, he is obliged to elaborate an account of political change that is explicitly Platonic in inspiration.

The distinction between qualitatively different kinds of knowledge, and hence of intellectual and political capacity, plays a central role in Bourdieu's theory of political change. Thus, he distinguishes between a rational consciousness of the social world, an ability to formulate coherent political projects for the future, dependent on a certain level of material wealth, and the 'doxic' level of consciousness available to the 'dominated classes'. He argues that this 'doxic' level of consciousness implies a 'practical sense' of the social world, which is 'closer to a "class unconscious" than to a "class consciousness" in the Marxist sense', since 'the essential part of experience of the social world it implies takes place in practice, without reaching the level of explicit representation and verbal representation'.[9] It therefore falls to intellectuals to bring this 'practical sense' to the level of 'explicit representation and verbal expression'. Only intellectuals possess the critical distance on the social world necessary to bring the practical, implicit principles inherent to the 'ethos' of the dominated classes and incorporated into their 'habitus' to the level of rational expression. Only intellectuals have the capacity to articulate 'the truth of those who have neither the interest nor the leisure nor the necessary instruments to re-appropriate the objective and subjective truth of what they are and what they do'.[10]

Once again, then, Bourdieu posits 'leisure', Plato's *skholè*, as the absolute prerequisite to rational thought and political agency, attributing to intellectuals the exclusive role of transforming into a rational political project the experiences of injustice and mute resistance incorporated, in purely practical state, into the ethos and habitus of the dominated classes. Political subjectivation, in Bourdieu's account, is defined as involving 'the progressive discovery of what is contained, in practical state, within the class habitus. It is the appropriation of oneself by oneself; it is the taking into one's own's hands, by means of its coherent explanation in an adequate language, of everything which, unconscious and uncontrolled, is exposed to mystification and being deliberately misconstrued.'[11] As we have seen, according to Bourdieu only intellectuals can provide this 'coherent explanation'. Hence their intervention, as the mandated delegates of the dominated classes, is essential in order to transform 'the systematicity "in itself" of practices and judgements generated from the unconscious principles of the ethos' into 'the conscious and almost forced systematicity of the political programme or party'.[12]

Bourdieu figures this role of mandated delegate in explicitly Socratic terms, suggesting that intellectuals should play a role analogous to that played by Socrates in Plato's *Meno*, when he engages the young slave in dialogue in order to encourage him to articulate the laws of geometry, which he masters at the practical level but of which he lacks theoretical knowledge. As Bourdieu puts it:

> In order to explain what I have to say in sociology, I could use the parable of Socrates and the little slave: I think that the sociologist is someone who, at the cost of a labour of inquiry and interrogation, using modern means and techniques, helps others to give birth to something they know without knowing it.[13]

Bourdieu's theory of political action is thus profoundly rooted in Platonism and this in two interrelated ways. Firstly, the appeal to the model of Socrates is explicitly Platonic and rests on the assumption that social inequality corresponds to intrinsic intellectual inequality, the same assumption as underlies the Socratic dialogue in the *Meno*. For in the *Meno*, the philosopher knows in advance the truth of laws which the young slave is assumed capable of mastering purely at the practical, unthinking level. Should the young slave offer answers that contradict the philosopher's prior knowledge or the ordinary agent provide an account of the social world that challenges the sociologist's scientific explanation, the first can be dismissed as the expression of the slave's inherent inferiority and the second as proof of the mechanism of misrecognition at work. Hence Rancière echoes Joseph Jacotot in highlighting the falsity of the Socratic dialogue and in insisting that it can only ever reinforce the assumption of inequality which forms its basis (IS29–30).

Bourdieu's theory of political action also rests on a profound philosophical idealism, according to which political subjectivation is a matter of agents and classes realizing their predetermined class identities in a moment of re-appropriation of a shared set of experiences and attributes taken to form the ideal core of that social identity. In the first instance, Bourdieu's definition of class or social identity is positivist: an agent's class identity is defined by their possession of a range of statistically measurable attributes, in the form of the kind and amount of economic, intellectual and cultural capital they possess. However, in a second move, those positive attributes are taken to form an ideal core, a unity and identity of experience and feeling incorporated into a shared ethos and habitus. Progressive politics becomes a matter of the expression and realization of that ideal core, as facilitated by the indispensable intervention of the Socratic intellectual. The possibility that agents might be capable of being anything other than the sum of the material circumstances incorporated into their habitus and ethos appears to be unthinkable within the terms of this problematic. It is this very possibility that Rancière will insist on in the account of political subjectivation he sketches in *Disagreement*, an account which implicitly defines itself in opposition to Bourdieu's.

Towards an Anti-Platonic Theory of Political Subjectivation

As we have seen, Bourdieu defines political subjectivation as that process whereby a class explicitly expresses the values and experiences incorporated into the unspoken assumptions of its socially determined ethos and habitus, transforming 'the practices and judgements generated from the unconscious principles of the ethos' into 'the conscious and almost forced systematicity of the political programme'. It is this kind of account of political subjectivation as the realization and rendering explicit of values contained in a predetermined ethos that Rancière rejects in *Disagreement*. When proletarians prove themselves capable of expressing not simply pain or distress (the *phônè*) but also rational ideas (the *logos*), this involves something quite different from them simply realizing or expressing their pre-existing, socially determined identity:

> 'Proletarian' political subjectivation, as I have tried to show elsewhere, is in no way a form of 'culture' or of collective *ethos* giving voice to itself. It presupposes, on the contrary, a multiplicity of fractures separating the bodies of workers from their ethos and from the voice that is supposed to express the soul of this ethos, a multiplicity of speech events – that is of one-off experiences of the conflict over speech and voice, over the partition of the perceptible. 'Speaking out' is not consciousness and expression of a self asserting what belongs to it. It is the occupation of a space in which the *logos* defines a nature other than the *phônè*. This occupation presupposes that the fates of workers be, in one way or another, diverted . . . (D36–7)

For Rancière, this capacity of a class to deviate from its allotted path reflects the fact that the 'modern political animal is first a literary animal, caught in the circuit of a literarity that undoes the relationships between the order of words and the order of bodies that determined the place of each' (D37). As we have noted, in the *Republic*, Plato seeks to establish the bases of a stable, hierarchical polity by recourse to the 'noble lie', that is to say to a literary or fictional narrative which seeks to legitimize the fixing of different social classes in their supposedly natural places and roles. The very fact, however, that Plato has recourse to a lie, to fiction, to literature to legitimize this social order reveals that there is nothing natural about this at all. In the very act of seeking to naturalize a hierarchical social order, Plato reveals that order's inherent contingency. Moreover, in so doing, he is forced to have recourse to literature or fiction, that is to a medium or force he will elsewhere condemn as fundamentally disruptive of the order it founds. Literature, fiction, writing are, for Plato, fatherless, mobile, an 'orphan letter', whose powers of mimesis disrupts the order of fixed places and roles. In this, literature is unlike 'living speech' whose unchanging, ideal core of meaning Plato takes to be guaranteed by the presence of a speaker, whose authority controls the meaning speech possesses for its intended addressee. The 'noble lie' is thus both the condition of possibility of Plato's stable republic and the condition of the impossibility of that republic ever actually founding itself on a natural, unchangeable order. In the very act of founding his stable republic, Plato unleashes the disruptive, fatherless force of literature, that 'orphan letter' which threatens to undermine the natural order of places and roles it seeks to establish.

For Rancière, Plato's opposition between written language and spoken or 'living' speech is untenable, based on an idealist account of the purity of the spoken word. He argues that any linguistic utterance, spoken or written, is fundamentally fatherless, its meaning open to being deviated from its author's intended path in ways which may produce real political effects. In any society or polity, 'political statements and literary locutions' seek to 'define models of speech or action' appropriate to the classes or groups whose proper role they attempt to fix. However, the nature of language as inherently fatherless and mobile means that in seeking to 'thereby take hold of unspecified groups of people', such statements and locutions also 'widen gaps, open up space for deviations, modify the speeds, the trajectories, the ways in which groups of people adhere to a condition, react to situations, recognize their images' (PA39). It is in this sense that man is at once a political and a literary animal:

Man is a political animal because he is a literary animal who lets himself be diverted from his 'natural' purpose by the power of words. This *literarity* is at once the condition and the effect of the circulation of 'actual' literary locutions. However, these locutions take hold of bodies and divert them from their end or purpose insofar as they are not bodies in the sense of organisms, but quasi-bodies, blocks of speech circulating without a legitimate father to accompany them toward their authorized addressee. Therefore they do not produce collective bodies. Instead, they introduce lines of fracture and disincorporation into imaginary collective bodies.· (PA39)

This account of the way in which political and literary discourses take hold of bodies, attempting, yet necessarily failing, to fix their roles absolutely also reflects Rancière's rejection of a certain form of sociological analysis. For Rancière's conception of discourse challenges those sociological accounts which attempt to define absolutely the significance of linguistic utterances by reference to the social attributes of their enunciators or the historical context of their enunciation. Once again Bourdieu is taken to epitomize such approaches; his attempt, in a book published in French as *Ce que parler veut dire* (1982),[14] to offer a sociological account of linguistic exchange is alluded to on a number of occasions in *Disagreement*. Early on in that text, Rancière identifies two alternative but analogous accounts of linguistic exchange he characterizes as 'two medicines of language, both consisting similarly in teaching us what speaking means [*ce que parler veut dire*]' (Dx-xi; M13). The first of these is identifiable as the work of Jürgen Habermas, which, according to Rancière, seeks to resolve in advance what is in fact at stake in any situation of 'wrong', by prescribing *a priori* the appropriate terms and form of any rational political debate.

If Habermas's theory of communicative action is to be rejected for its attempt to purge linguistic exchange and political dispute, in advance, of their antagonistic force, this is not, Rancière insists, to 'invoke the inexorability of a law of power that somehow always sets its seal in advance on the language of communication and stamps its violence on all rational argument'. This is merely to state 'that this political rationality of argumentation can never be some simple explanation of what speaking means [*ce que parler veut dire*]' (D45; M73). Although he is not mentioned by name, Bourdieu is clearly being alluded to here since it is in his book *Ce que parler veut dire* that he elaborates a theory of linguistic exchange according to which the form and performative force of every utterance is assumed to be determined in advance by the class position occupied by its enunciator. As Judith Butler has pointed out, the problem with Bourdieu's account of linguistic exchange is precisely this assumption that the performative force of any utterance is always dependent upon the prior symbolic authority of its author, that language is 'a static and closed system whose utterances are functionally secured in advance by the "social positions" to which they are mimetically related'.[15]

Here again, we can identify the idealism that lurks beneath Bourdieu's apparently positivist and materialist account of linguistic exchange. For Bourdieu, to speak is necessarily to give expression to an ideal core of meaning determined in advance by one's positive, socially determined attributes – the social position one occupies, one's class identity, and the varying amounts of linguistic capital this is assumed to endow one with. To embrace such a positivist-idealist account of language is, for Rancière, to overlook the inherent 'literarity' of all linguistic utterances, their inevitable failure absolutely to fix meaning or identity and their consequent openness to 'deviation'. At this level, Rancière's concept of 'literarity' is remarkably similar to Judith Butler's account of the 'iterability' of any performative discursive injunction regarding gender or sexuality. This similarity reflects the fact that both accounts are grounded in an anti-Platonism. In Butler's case, this is derived from her appropriation of Jacques Derrida's deconstruction of both the speech-writing opposition in Plato and of the attempts of John Searle to define the meaning of linguistic utterance in positivist or sociological terms. Rancière's theories of language and politics derive from an analogous anti-Platonism and a similar critique of Bourdieu's particular interpretation of speech-act theory. What both thinkers share, therefore, is an insistence on, to use Butler's terminology, the inherent 'iterability' of any discursive injunction and the consequent openness of any such

injunction to 'resignification'. Rancière prefers the term 'deviation' to 'resignification', yet the process his term describes is an
analogous one:

> In the experiences of worker's [sic] emancipation that I have studied,
> one sees how the very forms that structure the community and assign
> individuals their places – work, family, national belonging, forms
> of cultural (or other) identity – are in each case susceptible to being
> deviated and of provoking a reorganization of the whole: national
> belonging becomes an affirmation of republican equality that entails
> a certain idea of the worker's independence, which is itself combined
> with the fraternity of new religions and appropriates the indecisive
> identities of romantic literature. [. . .] The religious phrase that should
> subjugate, the spectacle that should fascinate, the juridical inscription
> that should set things in order – they constantly lend themselves to the
> construction of unforeseen trajectories of looking and speaking, to the
> formation of deviant lines of subjectivation.[16]

Political subjectivation thus has its origins in language's inherent
openness to being 'deviated' from its intended course or meaning.
It is important to stress that this is not a wholly ahistorical account
of politics, that language is not simply being endowed here with
'a form of transcendence', to use Nordmann's phrase. It is true
that the capacity for linguistic utterances to be deviated from their
intended meaning or destination is seen as inherent to language
itself and, as such, this functions as a kind of transcendental condition of possibility of any human society or polity for Rancière.
However, to posit such a condition as transcendental is no more
problematic than assuming that the capacity to produce and
understand language is a transcendental condition of possibility of
any human polity, something that is routinely assumed by other
theories of politics or society. Moreover, if language's openness to
deviation *is* assumed to be invariant, Rancière emphasizes that its
degree of openness is historically variable.

Historicity against Historicism

Put simply, the political and legal texts produced under conditions of formal democracy are more open to deviation than those characteristic of absolute monarchy. Similarly, the art and literature produced under the 'aesthetic regime' is more open to the logic of democratic emancipation than that produced under the 'representational regime'. However, it is only by acknowledging the openness even of the texts of absolutism to deviation that it will be possible to account for the passage from absolutism to democracy, for the event that is a democratic revolution. Failure to acknowledge that inherent openness would be to repeat the error that the *Annales* historian, Lucien Febvre, commits in his study of François Rabelais, according to Rancière (NH178–9). Febvre seeks to show that Rabelais could not have been an atheist because the possibility of atheism was itself excluded by the historical and cultural circumstances of his time. Yet, as Rancière argues, Febvre's assumption that 'what is not possible according to one's time is impossible', rests on 'a sociological organicism', on 'the representation of society as a body governed by the homogeneity of collective attitudes and common beliefs' (D132). Not only does this organicism reveal once more the social sciences' disavowed debt to the problematic of counter-revolutionary thought, it also seeks to deny the literarity inherent to the 'noble lie', the myth or fiction on which any such organicism ultimately relies, as Plato, in the *Republic*, was the first to acknowledge. The historicism of a Lucien Febvre thus ends up unwittingly denying the historicity whose very condition of possibility is the literarity of Plato's 'noble lie' and its numerous historically specific successors.

It is therefore quite wrong to argue, as Alberto Toscano does, that Rancière's thought involves the 'refusal of any social explanation and causality for politics' (Anti-Sociology, 223). As Rancière himself puts it: 'It is clear that a given form of subjectivation does not occur at just any time and, in any case, not with the same force or the same potential for contestation' (TP202). What he does argue, however, is that the 'form of causality' in question is 'completely different from a relation of expression between a situation and the forms of consciousness of that situation' (TP202). What Rancière rejects is not historical explanation per se but rather 'the limitations of those types of explanation which define, on the basis of certain industrial or economic phenomena, the emergence of a sociological class whose situation is allegedly such that it leads inevitably to a *"prise de conscience"*, that is to say the emergence of a situation which produces, as a consequence, the workers' movement' (TP201). The writings of the worker-poets whom Rancière studies in *The Nights of Labor* are intended to prove this very point. For these highlight the limitations of assuming, as various strands of both Marxism and utopian socialism tend to, that the path to workers' emancipation lies in their re-appropriation of their productive force, that is to say in their realizing more fully the identities determined for them by those 'industrial and economic phenomena'.

To refuse to see political subjectivation as involving the expression of a pre-existing, socially determined identity is also to refuse the slippage from registering material inequalities to assuming these must correspond to inequalities of intellectual capacity. Rancière's presupposition of the equality of intelligences flows from this also; it forestalls that slippage from registering material inequalities to assuming intellectual ones. However, it is important to stress that this is indeed a *presupposition*; different actual manifestations of intelligence may prove to be of different value (IS27) and that presupposition will have to be verified in each case (IS138). Furthermore, to presuppose the equality of all intelligences is by no means to deny that the possibilities or opportunities for realizing that capacity can be affected by historical conditions or material circumstances. Nonetheless, Rancière suggests that such a presupposition will prove essential if we are to think the possibility of historical change, of emancipation and equality and if we are to avoid the contradictions and blind spots that characterize the sociological problematic.

Some proof of the validity of this suggestion can be found among those critics who call upon Rancière to pay more attention to the weight of historical conditions or material circumstance. A case in point is Toscano's recent critique of what he terms Rancière's 'anti-sociology'. According to Toscano, in rejecting sociological analysis, Rancière is guilty of 'a now rather out-dated fixation on a dogmatic Marxism that would read off political action from social analysis (hardly a hegemonic position today!)' (Anti-Sociology, 230). The work of the Italian *operaïstes*, Toscano assures us, offers an example of something Rancière refuses to acknowledge, namely the possible 'socialist uses of sociology' (Anti-Sociology, 231).

The first thing to note here is that reading off political action from social analysis is by no means the preserve of a dogmatic Marxism and nor is it particularly out-dated. As we have shown, this is absolutely central to the work of Bourdieu, currently one of the world's most influential sociologists and no Marxist. Further, multiculturalism and identity politics, themselves extremely common features of contemporary political life, rest upon this same tendency to read political action off from social, sexual, or ethnic identity and this explains why Rancière is so sceptical as to their emancipatory potential in *Disagreement* (D123–6). Most significantly, however, the whole Italian workerist enterprise is premised on the assumption that we can read off political action from social analysis. What the workerists seek to do is to identify the new privileged historical actors of the postwar era by tracking changes in the mode of capitalist accumulation, changes assumed to have produced new political subjects, as the 'mass worker' of Fordism is replaced by the 'cognitive worker' of Post-Fordism. The shift from industrial to 'immaterial' forms of labour, it is argued, is necessarily producing the conditions for capitalism's own downfall, which will result from this new 'cognitariat' re-appropriating their intellectual force and the products of their immaterial labour.

As Rancière notes, such accounts remain wedded to the kinds of idealist and teleological interpretation of history he rejects, rehearsing 'the old Marxist thesis according to which capitalism will prove to be its own gravedigger' by forging 'a new, naturally "communist" subject'. 'This thesis', he continues, 'has never been confirmed by the development of capitalism' (MP162–3). Indeed, the study of Italian workerism Toscano enjoins us to read for evidence of the 'socialist uses of sociology' turns out to be, as much as anything else, an account of Italian workers' persistent failure to correspond to the concepts the workerists have forged

to define them.[17] The different workers in question are thus
defined by 'their common incapacity to respond to the demands
of their concept', to use the phrase Rancière employs to describe
the French bourgeoisie's and proletariat's stubborn refusal, at the
time of Louis-Napoleon's *coup d'état*, to perform the political roles
Marx's social theory had reserved for them (PhP99). As Rancière
shows, Marx is forced to draft in the notion of 'misrecognition'
to explain this refusal, before arguing that it falls to the science
of Marxism to break the spell of misrecognition by revealing the
proletariat's identity to itself on the model of Socratic anamne-
sis or 'reminiscence' (PhP114). To assume that we can correct
Rancière's alleged idealism simply by appealing to established
methods of sociological or historical enquiry would thus indeed
seem to lead us inexorably back into the dead-end of Platonism.

3

Emancipation versus Domination

Geneviève Fraisse

Versus

The point of view of emancipation or the point of view of domination: in this century, the hour of dialectic has passed. And for Jacques Rancière there has never been any question of dialectic. The choice is between understanding the trajectory of emancipatory subjectivation versus the need to analyse mechanisms of domination – everything depends on whether the position is that of the agent, the acting subject or the reader, or rather the learned critic, as Rancière might hasten to add. Now, this small word 'versus', placed between the terms emancipation and domination, has nothing to do with an 'either . . . or . . .', nothing to do with the alternative. We know that Rancière's decision from the outset has been to follow the proletarian, the student, the artist, the spectator, the subject, the one who works in its collective singularity towards its dream of emancipation by escaping from those who would supply it with . . . what? Precisely, an analysis that prevents emancipation. By escaping from those who create separation and who prevent the sharing of the sensible as much as the community of dispute. But where does domination, which, in any event,

stands opposite emancipation, play out? This is my question,
my problem. My point here, then, will be to clarify, outside the
dialectic, outside the alternative, the necessary link between emancipation and domination in the political tension of contemporary
history. It is a link that both prevails in that which preoccupies me,
namely feminism, a space devoted to the emancipation of women,
and one which set me on the path to a meeting with Rancière in
the autumn of 1973.

Rancière has clearly stated Althusser's lesson: domination can
take the figure of science and close on its analyst like a trap. The
science of domination does not create emancipation; on the contrary, it is continuously recycled in the service of domination. This
is what Rancière calls the 'inversion of thoughts of subversion to
the advantage of order'.[1] Yes, the dialectic came undone; we must
also undo the dialectic of revolution.

That is why the image of recto–verso, of the 'versus', shapes the
problematic of reflection proposed here. The movement is, in fact,
twofold and undoes me: the science of domination that should
enlighten me traps me and, as a result, subversive thought, which
ought to liberate me, is not always reliable. Contradictions abound
. . . reversals are everywhere. There is one marker: during emancipation, subversion takes place and is embodied. We shall return to
the question of the body.

In his recent preface to the new French edition of *La Leçon
d'Althusser* [Althusser's Lesson], Rancière speaks of a 'confrontation' between emancipation and domination.[2] Now, at the very
moment of founding the journal *Les Révoltes Logiques*, a high
point in the aftermath of May '68 and the MLF [Mouvement de
Libération des Femmes], when tackling the question of women's
emancipation I quickly understood that many of my interlocutors doubted the reality of masculine domination. This manifested
itself in general and continues to do so, in two complementary
ways: there are people of both sexes, who, convinced that we
already have equality between the sexes, claim that a few correc-
tive measures in the real will suffice and others who state, more
speciously, that they do not 'see' masculine domination at work.
As a result, when it comes to the feminist question people cannot
have been stifled by the science of domination and its traps. Quite

the contrary! So, from the point of view of my task, it is necessary to convince people about the reality of domination, to localize it, to visualize it, to make it visible. Masculine domination is a reality that evades 'science', whereas it happens in Rancière's work that social domination is referred to as 'dominant thinking', or the 'discourse of domination'.³ This is undeniable. That, then, is where the gap [*écart*] lies between our respective trajectories, as common as they are different. For me it is necessary to make domination visible, since when we are talking about 'masculine' domination it takes forms that are far from obvious; however, for Rancière domination is self-evident but reduplicated in science, from which science he has been in violent flight, having instead opted for a lengthy and determined thinking through of emancipation against science, against the 'empire of the sociologist', for example.⁴

For the philosopher, more acceptable than 'domination' seems to be the Foucauldian expression 'forms of power' and more poetic the proposal 'to cease to live in the world of the enemy',⁵ as a recent newspaper article was titled. Things are not so straightforward, however, for in the 'confrontation' with 'forms of power' something gets exchanged, since the bodies and heads of speaking subjects necessarily disrupt domination. Lastly, what is the status of domination itself? We can be unaware of it, see it, mistreat it, cause it to malfunction. In any case, it is certain that the emancipation of women has an effect on masculine domination, even though as I said a moment ago such domination does not exist in everyone's eyes.

Oppression

It can accordingly be understood why the person who commissioned this chapter changed the title upon receiving it, replacing, as if inadvertently, the word 'domination' with 'oppression'.⁶ I saw this as an interpretation of sorts: precisely, it was necessary to agree with Rancière that the word 'domination' is misplaced in discussion of his work, whereas the word oppression refers more subtly to the subject that suffers or stands up to domination and, as a result, to the

possible subject of emancipation. The editor thought, then, that I
wanted to set out what is meant by emancipation, by the process
of subjectivation understood as a tension between 'being subjected
to' and 'subverting' [*entre subir et subvertir*] – whether from the perspective of proletarians or women, of the Saint-Simonian dreamer
or the feminist of 1848, of the spectator or the female author, of
the rich or the poor, that is to say, from the perspective of anyone
at all. Rancière, we know, posits a system of equivalences of places
between beings, between all beings, which is entirely formidable
and truly fascinating. Twentieth-century cinema afforded him the
exceptional opportunity to discard entirely all hierarchies of place
between individuals. And this is why I chanced the duo rich/poor,
which flowed from my pen almost without my thinking about it,
in a recent introduction, but which is only the exaggerated image
of the remarkable radicality of the system of equivalences of the
philosophy here under consideration.[7]

This possibly already provides us with enough to form a
problem, a subject for discussion. Emancipation versus oppression:
pitting the system of equivalences against the quality of oppression of this or that group might perhaps have obliged one to make
unavoidable distinctions and establish unexpected and cumbersome hierarchies. This line of research is currently very popular.
What about the articulation of forms of exploitation, oppression
and struggle (class, race and sex)? This question was all the rage
at the start of the 1970s and is alive today under the name of
'intersectionality'.

For example, why not recall that in the Marxist saga the
proletarian's wife was even more oppressed than he was? In this
case, the question would then be: how can we treat the diversity
of speaking subjects within the great movements of various emancipations? But an answer had already been given to this question.
At the start of the journal *Les Révoltes Logiques* and the founding of
the Centre de Recherche sur les Idéologies de la Révolte (1974),
what did we make of the categories of the worker, the Catalan, the
woman? Everything and nothing, precisely. The category as such
was not our concern . . . But using categories did make it easy to
identify what was distinctive about the threefold position of revolt.
The Catalan was the nomad, in exile, someone who abandons

one language to learn another, someone whose identity would always be, for better or for worse, betrayed. *La Raison nomade* is the title of a posthumous collection by Jean Borreil.[8] The preface-writer of this volume, Rancière himself, reminds us both about the impossibility of returning to the 'intimacy of the natal' and about the needlessness of waiting for some community to come, since the 'past of oppression and colonization' would necessarily be forgotten. Borreil, having quit his mother tongue, Catalan, had only his reason with which to enter the school of the French Republic, his reason that was, simply, 'nomadic'.

Women, for their part, are constantly in superposition with themselves: on the one hand, in the impossible position of not being able to flee their supposedly natural origin; and on the other, in a state of avidness for science, which they have been denied for so long. This is why I wrote *Reason's Muse,* a book about the improbable tenth muse that a male poet (Joseph Chénier) dreamt up during the French Revolution to refer to a subversive poetess (Constance de Salm), the dream figure of a new reason.[9] There is no definitive exile this time, yet the lie is given to the origin (or supposed origin, a 'mother nature'), the transgression is repeated and the barrier leapt over to gather flowers, as the French translator of Darwin, Clémence Royer, would later say . . . Appropriate the reason of the dominant only so as to transform it, she would say . . .

The author of *Proletarian Nights,* on an equal footing in school and therefore in the legitimate exercise of his reason, just like all his predecessors for over a century, those Marxist and anarchist thinkers of the Revolution, not being proletarian himself was better placed to view science from a distance, the science of emancipation, of domination, of oppression. Jacques Rancière simply sought, then, to mark the distance [*l'écart*] between the best of dreams and the worst of science; since the thinkable is the possible, this approach was used to plot the line along which the path of revolt was to be followed, a path that had no origin to categorize or utopia to invent. As Rancière says, he has a right to this dream [*rêve*], which he has pinched from the word *g-rêve* (strike). This is why he was subsequently able to vigorously affirm the possibility of an 'ignorant schoolmaster', as well as of an 'emancipated spectator' and here we are all agreed that 'an individual is only ever learned by the knowledge he gives himself'.[10] As for the worker, or proletarian, the term can by no means be said to form a category, since it is occasioned only by the dispute forged in the incessant movement of the part of those without part, the verifying of equality, or the figure of politics.

In the midst of emancipatory struggle these three kinds of 'reason' do not require any theoretical structuration to organize them in relation to each other. Between the nomadic reason of the immigrant forced into forgetting, the reason of women repeating transgression and the reason of 'universal' emancipation, we move terribly far from the categories of 'class, race and sex' that people have been trying to impose on us as essential epistemology for two centuries, roughly speaking ever since Kantian anthropology. For, it is always worth underlining the fact that it is modern anthropology, much more than radical politics, that has demanded the intersectionality of sex (or gender), colour (or race) and social category (or class).

But no, the organization of these categories, their logical articulation, was pointless. By contrast, their contiguity was desired, for the universal has no categories.[11] 'Domination' was most certainly what I wrote. 'Oppression' presented no problem, raised no question with regard to the word 'emancipation'.

So I would have to explain myself. The watchword of my problematic, at any rate, was 'reason'. The reason to revolt, there are always reasons to revolt – or, as the slogan of '68 had it, one is always right to revolt [*on a toujours raison de se révolter*], to organize the subjectivation of emancipation, on one hand; but one is also right to think, on the other, in terms of science, of a giving account [*rendre raison*] of the domination that stands in the way of emancipation, this giving account which riles Rancière.

Seeing Domination

Granted, Rancière's essential concern is to expose the mechanism of emancipation. Nevertheless, he knows that not every attempt to think through domination is the enemy of subversion.

Such attempts can simply miss their target, as in the case of the thought of Guy Debord and the Situationists, or else they can come undone, as in the case – and this is closer to my speculative interest – of the Frankfurt School's *Dialectic of Enlightenment* . . . Too much melancholy, Rancière says. The 'dialectic in the dialectic', a self-critique of Western rationality, in its modern and ancient figures, forges an ambiguity that is the enemy of politics . . . The Frankfurt School, he says, lacks 'a *political* conception of emancipation' (CC27). Its analysis of the fissure in the dialectic of the Enlightenment, he tells us, is banal and it can also, and here I agree, be folded back onto its Heideggerian lineage. But in reading Rancière's chronicles, we see that sexuation in the story of Ulysses and the sirens is left by the wayside.[12] Now, it is precisely at this wayside that I stop. For it is precisely here that I have discovered the contradiction between emancipations, one of which Jacques Rancière is unaware.

I recall that my task is to make masculine domination visible, not in order to strengthen it obligingly but simply to say that it exists. Today, much research is devoted to deconstructing 'gender stereotypes', in the manner of the science-supposed-to-liberate against which Rancière, the philosopher, has risen up in revolt. My concern is different, as I underscored at the outset; it is to name and thereby to foil the denial of masculine domination. For this denial paralyses strategies of emancipation.

Let us take, as an example, Rancière's criticisms of the authors of Volume 4 of *A History of Women in the West* (the nineteenth century), namely Michelle Perrot and myself, and more specifically of their joint introduction (its being joint made the criticism slightly easier to bear) and of some of the texts in the volume that illustrate it.[13] He rightly reproached us for insisting on a long, motionless history, on a history of representations (today, one would speak of 'norms'!), in a way which was itself crushing for the women of a century which marked a break, yes a break, since it was the century following the French Revolution, the century which opened onto the democratic era and practices of emancipation. Rancière wrote: 'The analysis of representations takes the place, then, of a thinking of subjectivation. [. . .] We can call this history, critique, semiology, or sociology of the image. But the

only true name for this operation is the one Mallarmé settled once
and for all: "universal reporting".'[14] From this quotation I have
cut a passage which shows how the image forms a screen without
giving an interpretation – no disagreement there.

In publishing *Reason's Muse* the previous year, which provided
an analysis of 'exclusive democracy' as regards women – 'exclusive'
and not 'excluding' – I foregrounded not the excessive visibility of
domination but rather its lack of visibility, and in demonstrating
this I inscribed resistance to exclusion within the same movement.
This jigsaw puzzle, that of the 'exclusive democracy' established in
1800, was a clever ellipsis that left the fragments of its exclusion of
women dispersed and in this very way rendered domination itself
incomprehensible. Such was my argument in that book and it is
one I continue to defend today: domination resides not so much
in the multiplicity of its 'forms of power' (Michel Foucault) and
therefore of its representations, as it does in its fragmentation. It
is accordingly well worth reconstituting the overall design of the
jigsaw puzzle precisely because this design is not made to be seen.
Why reconstitute the overall design of masculine domination? Not
in order to create, as Pierre Bourdieu did, a theory of domination
that leaves emancipation aside as a mechanical practice external
to domination, but to show the extent to which these 'forms of
power' are scattered fragments (nature, school, public life, citizenship, the female author, etc.) and are therefore illegible.

I did not take undue offence at Rancière's critique. But I did
remark one thing, which is that the piece I had contributed to that
volume of *A History of Women*, one that undertook a reading of
philosophers from Kant to Freud, entitled 'From Destination to
Destiny' – i.e. from the globality of a feminine fate to the singularity of possible pathways for women (this time authorized and not
subversive) – was neither audible within, nor able to be integrated
into, his critique.[15] This is because the article concerned the transition from a global marking of women, a destination, to a singular
tracing, 'a destiny'. In both cases, the question of domination
and its fissures demonstrated what I referred to as the 'lucidity'
of philosophers faced with the advent of women's emancipation.
That Kierkegaard can have imagined going to mourn in the town
square at the idea of women's emancipation, that the dominant

saw clearly this emancipation coming, justifies our pausing for a moment on the thinking of domination and its adequation to the history which is playing itself out . . . I shall be a bit evocative and repeat the titles of this reading from Kant to Freud: 'The family, the subject and the sexuated division of the world'; 'Love, conflict and the metaphysics of sex'; 'Autonomy, emancipation and justice'; and 'The individual, the history of the family and feminine evil.' Each of these titles bespeaks the confrontation between a possible subjectivation and the forms of power that thinkers of the nineteenth century strived to attach to their philosophy. It was therefore possible to reveal domination in its relation to the dynamics of an emancipation to come. This is indeed something I found to be necessary. I also thought that it would have been too easy a choice to write an article on currently emerging feminisms for that volume, as Michelle Perrot had indeed proposed. By doing so, I would obviously have remained, far from the 'appearances' of images devoid of depth and in continuity with the singular 'apparitions' saluted by the philosopher. In this way, it seemed necessary to me to have this harsh confrontation between worlds over equality between the sexes. Yet Rancière seemed to have sidestepped the confrontation between emancipation and domination.

Indeed, we are situated at an important point of his demonstration, which is certainly also a moment of disagreement. In a text following his critique of *A History of Women*, deemed too beholden to the concept of representation ('a jumble of images'), he starts by linking the following three terms: 'the history of a type of domination, resistance to it, and a contestatory subjectivation'.[16] But he then goes on to explain that the analysis of images tends towards a liquefaction that causes the question of 'proscription' to disappear. As Rancière writes: 'Then there is only ignorance, oppression that produces ignorance, and ignorance that reproduces oppression.' The crushing effect of a history of representations can, he says, be replaced with 'the relation between proscription [*l'interdit*] and possibles'. By virtue of this, by virtue of these possibles – 'series of acts' – the path of subjectivation and emancipation then opens up. Let us underline the word 'proscription', which replaces both the concept of domination, which Rancière recognizes in the importance of its history, and the word representation, which he

denounces in the falsity of its science. I must say that the word
'proscription' surprises me, as if emancipation were above all a
matter of transgression, far more than a contestation of domination. And yet both the words 'conflict' [*conflit*] and 'dispute' [*litige*]
have been conceptualized by Rancière. Ought I to understand that
initiating a dispute occurs without any critique and that confrontation does not require any formulating?

However, the emphasis here is laid on introducing the 'possible', and therefore on designating the cause of the obstacle ('the
proscription') – this or that barrier – in order to turn towards the
possible, towards subjectivation and emancipation. At this point
my discussion becomes more heated. For domination has become
mere proscription and impossibility. The desire to oppose sexual
equality, the idea of confrontation, has disappeared. There is no
trace of struggle. There are many forms of power, faceless enemies,
granted. Why not? Masculine domination has no face, no design.
Rancière talks about 'blurring' [*brouillage*] in a good many texts.[17]
For my part, I maintain the importance not only of pointing to
this blurring as it exists but also of reading its historical dynamic
('exclusive democracy').

Seeking to understand why a famous feminist insisted on the
'contretemps' of the French Revolution, I had to find out why
the Revolution seemed to promise equality between the sexes and
then hampered the possibility of it. Julie-Victoire Daubié concluded: 'it was better before'.[18] And nevertheless the revolutionary
rupture had indeed taken place. This paradox, this contradiction,
compels us to consider not the pitfalls of the dialectic, as we said,
not confrontation, which is locatable, but rather the contradiction
between the emancipation of (male) citizens and that of (female)
citizens. This goes back to the double origin of our Western
history, that of the encounter between Ulysses and the sirens, or to
the more political one between Sylvain Maréchal, co-author with
Babeuf of the *Manifesto of Equals* and an 'extreme left-wing' revolutionary resolutely opposed to equality between the sexes, and his
two opponents, two women authors . . .[19]

There is, then, a contradiction of emancipations between the
sexes. Rancière often cites Article 10 of the *Declaration of the Rights
of the Woman and the Citizen* (1791), by Olympe de Gouges, for its

equating of the right to mount the scaffold with the right to take to the political platform, insofar as the former logically leads to the latter, thus underlining that the scaffold (or 'bare life', to speak like Walter Benjamin or Giorgio Agamben) forms the condition of the political subject.[20] This is to show the way in which women really are included in politics. This complicated [*savant*] equilibrium between exclusion and inclusion is founded on a logical play of equivalences. Granted. If I understand 'exclusive democracy' as a tension between implicit exclusion and possible inclusion, it is because I have come up against the contradiction between emancipations. Who closed the women's clubs in 1793 (and again in June 1848)? Rancière may retort that to respond is to fall into the trap of categories. So, right alongside the text of Olympe de Gouges, I will place the text of the non-equivalence of the scaffold and the platform, the text of domination, and yet it is a text that is just as productive of possible inclusion, namely Article 7 of the Civil Code: 'a citizen is any person enjoying all of his civil rights'. Let it be noted: women did not enjoy all of their civil rights, so they were not citizens. But, and I insist on this 'but', nowhere is it said that they are not citizens, and so the struggle can begin – ONE of many other struggles for emancipation during that century. Feminists of the nineteenth century would take advantage of that fissure in domination. That, then, is a statement of equivalence that issued from power. To be continued . . .

This excluding without saying so amounts to making possible the inclusion to come. For, as I am not specifically excluded by name, I will be able, using this or that strategy, to have myself included. But why present Olympe de Gouges *and* the Civil Code?

There are several reasons for this: because Olympe de Gouges attests to the contradiction of emancipations and because her Declaration of the Rights of Women signals that these very rights do not go without saying, that, precisely, women will mount the scaffold more often than they take the platform. Furthermore, relating this article of the Civil Code to Olympe de Gouges's Declaration is interesting since, as I mentioned above, it shows one among many strategies of inclusion, and thus points to domination not as proscription but to domination in its invisibility.

Rancière denounces the motionless history of representations and images; philosophers of the nineteenth century dreaded from on high, from their position of dominance, the arrival of women's emancipation. A feminist from the nineteenth century declared that history out of time and I accept the analysis of the Frankfurt School telling me about the contrariety between Ulysses and the sirens, while post-revolutionary feminists observed the contradiction between types of emancipation. From this brief shortcut into an issue of historicity I want only to conclude that, to give strength to my own work on feminist thought, and therefore on emancipation, I need domination to be recognized.

Equalities

Let us once again follow Rancière's text as it addresses the feminist strategy of equality between the sexes (the sexuation of equality) and that of the relation between the private and the public (the family and the city).[21]

We learn that, in matters of emancipatory strategy, feminists played on their 'being women', 'educating mothers', and 'domestic servants of the state', in order 'to prove their aptitude for citizenship. The women of 1848 were a flagrant example of this'. Some historians, such as Joan Scott, have observed paradoxes here.[22] My reading, less concerned with debates on the universal and identity and more interested in the construction of strategies, refers to the diverse paths of inclusion followed in response to mechanisms of exclusion (legal or illegal, individual or collective, intellectual or pragmatic, etc). For his part, however, Rancière has opted to theorize the impossible distribution between the category 'woman' and this or that contingent status, that is, the uselessness of reflections on the part and the whole of the universal, to which he prefers a constant search for equivalence; thus little matter whether it is the mother or the woman who declares her emancipation. The universal defies categories; here we are in agreement.

The story from 1849, involving the feminist Jeanne Deroin and Proudhon, is well known: the day after 1848, Deroin transgressed the 'proscription' (neither was she a voter nor, less so still, eligible for office!) and stood in the elections. Proudhon: 'I can no more imagine a woman deputy than I can a male wet-nurse' (or, more to be precise, 'a female legislator than a male wet-nurse'). To which Deroin responded: 'Show me the organ of legislation; where is it?' The question raised in relation to the division of roles, says Rancière, is that of the monopoly of power by one sex. And he adds: 'to whom does that which is asexual belong'?[23] Is equality asexual? His answer is 'yes', equality is asexual and the answer to the second question, writes the philosopher, is 'yes, the asexual belongs to men, belongs only to men'. Admittedly, it is not a joyous 'yes'! He adds that this is the limit of self-emancipation.

This discourse, Rancière concludes in his essay, is about a beyond of complementarity; its limit is that of identification. No, I do not find this conclusion satisfactory. It is restricted to a matter of sexuation, of the indefinition of equality, of masculine power over the neutral.

However, the question of the sexes is not that of the precariousness of identities, whether they are complementary or not, but rather that of a relation of domination and of the contradiction between emancipations. If Jeanne Deroin ran for office in 1849 it was because 'universal' suffrage had been granted to the masculine sex; if Proudhon opposed this, it was because the equivalence he formed between deputy and wet-nurse was negative. Why does the philosopher who conceives equivalences neglect to comment on this negative equivalence? For it is a mirror image of Olympe de Gouges's own equivalence: eliminate life (scaffold) or give life (breast-feeding) in opposition to the political platform, or deputation. Neither the implicit biopower in this, nor the asexuation of power (universal?) seem sufficient to merit commentary.

So, by way of example, we should read this passage from *Disagreement*: 'The household got turned into a political site not by the simple fact that relations of power were exercised in it, but because it became a subject in a dispute over the capacity of women in the community' (D32–3 [TM]). This sentence deserves all our attention. First of all, 'the simple fact' of domination: 'simple fact'? Does the 'simple fact' provide a sign of the existence of domination? What this essentially gives rise to is the notion that there is nothing to look for or to be thought through in this regard.

Overcoming the proscription, seeking the possible, absolutely;
but opposite this, domination is given as a simple fact; or even
. . . I have often heard the argument that in matters of inequality
between the sexes, there is nothing to be thought, we must act, do
. . . Let's add, as I have said since the start of this chapter, that as
soon as domination is thought, it is, for Rancière, 'badly' thought.
A second, essential remark: the household is the site of the dispute
about what lies outside the household and therefore about the
political capacity of women (wet-nurse or deputy). True, but
let us continue on with Proudhon and the question of the sex of
equality. Proudhon sees in the household not the site of a dispute
on the possible belonging of women to the political community
but the site of the proper justice for both sexes. It is because justice
is embodied in the family that equality can be thought elsewhere.
Now, the just and the equal are not the same thing. Thus, at
issue is by no means the redistribution of roles between men and
women, or even the expression of a complementarity, at issue is
separating the household from the workshop, or the family from
the city (see Rousseau), without equivalence, whether negative or
positive. The household is the site of justice, for the couple is the
organ of justice.

The just is not the equal and thus, for example, men can domi-
nate women. This was Proudhon's thinking, who went on to fuel
the anti-feminism of the French workers' movement. It is for this
reason that his adage 'courtesan or housewife' is always quoted but
in truncated form, since there is a third term, which reads: 'and
not servant'. Some justness is required in the family; the housewife
is to be treated well, not like a domestic. There can be no public
woman prostitute and, as a result, of course, no public woman
citizen. But the important thing is above all to do what is just,
which is not what is equal. From whence comes a sort of masculine
domination that is full of good conscience and therefore lacking in
political visibility.

You understand, then, why I put the word equality in the
plural. First of all, it is in order to recall Rancière's magnificent
analyses, according to which equality is neither a given, nor an
essence, nor a goal, nor a principle. Simply, it is a presupposition.
Secondly, it is to point to the double equality of remote Antiquity,

which still applies fairly well to discussions about equality between the sexes. We just saw it at work in the nineteenth-century distinction between the just and the equal, the geometrical and the arithmetic; and present-day English-language debates sometimes show a predilection for it as well. Equality, in the vacuity of its being put into dispute [*litige*], says the philosopher, is only visible through its repetition, in the very act of dispute.

Geometrical equality, arithmetic equality, equality as condition, equality as rule, equality as entry into the political. As far as I am concerned, equality is a prerequisite for reading the genealogy of democracy; an operator of thought, or more simply a revelation of that thought.

Bodies

For some time I have been observing, as though in passing, the diversity of expressions, of 'speaking subjects', 'speaking bodies' and 'speaking beings'. When it comes to bodies, I sometimes simply ask myself, just like that, whether or not they are sexed, taking the matter no further. Let us acknowledge that from the point of view of a possible subjectivation, sexuation can be more or less significant. However, the issue can become serious when it comes to the contradiction between emancipations. After the above detour via the nineteenth century, here is a simple and contemporary example, namely the headscarf and school, the headscarf and the passing of a bill to ban wearing headscarves at school, in France. This is not a political dispute, was Rancière's immediate response, but rather a 'police' matter with no basis in politics, 'a supposed combat of universalism against particularism' (TP199) for republicans with imaginations fixated on the struggle between secularism and religion. It is not a dispute, not even a political conflict, since, as he puts it, 'there is no singularization of a universal, or constitution of a polemical case of universalization'. During a radio programme in the same period, Rancière developed a long argument about the diverse universalisms put into play in that 'police' matter (MP146). Confronting the differences, communities or inequalities that negatively problematized wearing the headscarf, universalisms of various sorts fell over each other trying to explain the soundness of denouncing it. Now, at the start of the 1990s, that is to say ever since the socialists have been exasperating themselves in a debate on religion and secularism, what is more at the highest ministerial levels, I saw myself embark on an entirely different line of questioning. The real debate was not about religion, since this masked the issue of girls' emancipation, which interested no one at the time. Twenty years on, however, the question has returned and the argument about the freedom of girls has seemed to take centre stage. And so people have reproached political parties (notably on the right) for 'instrumentalizing' female emancipation for political gain in the name of an anti-Muslim crusade. Now, this polemic (religion tied to emancipation) is, in my view, more sterile than archaic or manipulative. When it comes down to it, the contradiction between universalism and communitarianism seems to me devoid of particular interest.

From the outset, in fact, I had suggested that the question be situated elsewhere, at the point where emancipation passes through the body. Since, at school, the very site of reason and the appropriation of knowledge, disputes about the emancipation of girls also happen to pass through the body. Indeed, wearing the headscarf has the effect of eliminating girls' access to sport. A trivial matter, some commentators respond. Now, here is precisely where it gets interesting. To do without sport ('to be excused' from it, as one says in French) supposedly has no importance; that decision is supposedly one the girls can make by themselves, in the same way that one might choose this or that course at school. I think exactly the opposite is true. Sport is not negligible as a means of emancipation in the school environment. Sporting activity is a counterpoint to intellectual exercise that by the same token doubles the sites of possible emancipation. Success at school can also come through sport.

To Rancière, then, I address two questions: where, in this matter, is the 'simple fact' of domination? If the headscarf is a police matter and not a political one, if we leave aside the question of religion and universalisms, the question remains as to what is of the order of domination and thus, since there is conflict, what pertains to the implementation of a dispute and what is not of the order of domination. I detect here the implicit establishment of a divide between good and bad domination.

In this example my interest is focused on this act by which girls are deprived of a space of emancipation (of a possible appropriation of knowledge and a means of access to greater equality). Yes, speaking subjects are speaking bodies, and 'veiled women speak', as it was so nicely put during the polemic that denounced one sort of feminism for only ever seeing victims everywhere. For subjects have bodies and bodies are socially sexed. This is why, as I mentioned above, emancipation comes up against the question of sexuation. Or is equality between the sexes itself without sex?

Or sexed bodies are a site of dispute just as much as of emancipation and sport counts just as much as mathematics as a stake in that conquest . . .

Conclusion

Today, the headscarf, the veil and the niqab are clearly no longer a police matter, as the world in its entirety is my witness. Running for elections in a Mediterranean country, or going to the Olympic Games in religiously connoted clothing, is set in equivalence with all other forms of women's public involvement. It is not bare life that leads to the scaffold that is referred to here, nor the household of the wet-nurse that either creates or not an equivalence with the female citizen, but instead the 'high-calibre' Muslim (sportswoman or deputy). This is a powerful postcolonial response, a politically powerful one. But it is only one political response among others; let's make no mistake about that.

Since I am concluding, I shall say one final word about the confrontation between emancipation and domination: no religion and above all none of the three monotheisms conceives or affirms equality between the sexes. It is therefore difficult for me to accept that in every way and every case, the religious question should be excluded from dispute and the political. Or, put differently, in returning to the question raised here, the question of domination, masculine in this case, remains very present in this domain.

So, it is necessary to pull together the above lines of questioning: how is it possible to conceive of emancipation without confronting the materiality of domination, the recognition of its fact, which is not as simple as all that, or without confronting the multiplicity of sites to be identified where it operates, the forces of its cunning, and so on? In a column devoted to Michel Foucault, Rancière speaks of the 'grain of sand that jams the machine', far removed from a 'central position in the encounter between knowledge and power' (CT126–7). I draw these two parts of sentences together, though they are barely distant from one another in the text, to underline *in fine* the work involved in destabilizing a domination that certainly has a face, an image.

I know full well, for I have read *The Emancipated Spectator*, that 'the question has never been for the dominated to become aware of the mechanisms of domination but to create for themselves a body destined for something other than domination' (SE69).[24] I have no doubt come back to the point of departure, but in order to put it differently: domination is not a matter of 'truth' or 'knowledge'; but a 'consciousness' of it is necessary ('to bear in mind a specific object of thought', according to the dictionary). Yes, at least for the object of my concern, the emancipation of women, I plead for a 'consciousness' of masculine domination. My proposal resides in this simple word. Yes, 'feminism thinks', as I titled the introduction to my recent essay collection, *La Fabrique du féminisme*, and precisely, in full 'consciousness' of the facts.

In the act of emancipation, indetermination wins out over finality, says the philosopher. And this is indeed why there is no utopia. The grain of sand that is introduced into the machine brings me close to what I call the 'unsettling of representations'; indeed, for unsettling domination is certainly not a dream but rather involves the idea of introducing disorder into that which does not always have the courage to declare itself as such: masculine domination. Causing disorder, from my point of view, amounts to creating new links.

Aside from the need to point out domination – since it is not obvious as a reality, since in the eyes of many it is hardly a 'simple fact' – my second concern bears on the contradiction, the site of the contradiction. Already in the founding text of *Les Révoltes*

Logiques, the point was well put that the question of contradiction unites us but emerges more strongly in feminism. Having 'consciousness of' domination means accepting contradiction with those nearest.

Translated by Steven Corcoran

II

History, Reading, Writing

4

Reading Rancière

Carolyn Steedman

Prologue: A Midlands Night Out

This is a story about reading Rancière. It is about historians reading Rancière, reading Rancière in English, the reading history of *Nights of Labor* (*La Nuit des prolétaires*) in the UK, and the innumerable early nineteenth-century acts of reading out of which Rancière wrote.[1] The story attempts to account for the neglect of *Nights of Labor* by practitioners of 'people's history' and 'history from below' in Britain, by consideration of the working-class reading (and writing) subjects who make up so much of the evidence base of *Nights of Labor* and *The Ignorant Schoolmaster*. It begins in Oxford, on a winter Sunday afternoon in 1979.

In the 1970s, if you wanted to undermine the intellectual elitism and social dominance of England's ancient universities, you could talk about Oxford as 'a small South Midlands car town', evoking its second material base of existence, the Morris Motors factory out at Cowley and all the workers and their families who inhabited the city. Historians involved in the History Workshop (HW) movement dreamed that those workers would not only question academic history in the manner of Brecht's 'Worker Who Reads', but also write their own. In a perfect encapsulation of its pedagogic and political project of allowing the workers (past and present) to find their own answers and agency, three early issues of *History Workshop Journal* carried the autobiographical writings of Oxford car worker Arthur Exell, who 'loved and wrote poetry, and [. . .] recognized the importance of his own experiences'.[2] Cars are still made at Cowley; but Oxford is no longer – by reputation – the Motor City it was in the twentieth century. The raucous, street brawling, drunken end of the working week experienced in every English county town since the end of the seventeenth century now involves new social actors and new ways of going out on the Randan.[3] The newspapers often capitalize it as a Saturday Night Out, or even a Saturday Nite Out, in shorthand evocation of the 1980s neon-signed Nite Spots and Nite Clubs lining the roads and alleys behind the High Streets of some provincial town or other.

But this was not an Oxford Saturday night. It was late Sunday afternoon, 2 December 1979, the last day of HW13, 'People's History and Socialist Theory', held at Ruskin College.[4] The final session of the Workshop – the graveyard shift – was to be devoted to 'Socialist history, past, present and future'. A Workshop prospectus announced '2.30–4.00: Critique of French Labour History. Jacques Ranciere (Paris) Alain Cottereau (Paris)'.[5] Rancière's typescript, headed 'Jacques Ranciere on French Labour History', is preserved in the archives. Pencilled annotations and corrections suggest that it was used by HW editors in compiling the book of the conference, which appeared in 1981. The published version of Rancière's talk incorporates all these editorial corrections.[6] There had been the usual difficulties in getting position papers and typescripts out of contributors ahead of time: 'Alain (Cottereau) is writing but not yet finished, Jacques had not read your note for contributors, and has promised to produce a text during the short All Saints school holidays which begin on Wednesday', reported Andrew Lincoln from Paris at the end of October. On one undated 'Sunday midnight', the news was that he 'was just about to go to the Hotel des Postes to post you mine and Jacques texts – do check them, especially for English mistakes as production is going on under some pressure here'.[7]

I remember the December gloom outside, the cruel fluorescent

light of the Ruskin seminar room, and two Frenchmen (one quite
a bit taller than the other) walking to the front to speak. I have the
impression that something or someone was late – not the speakers
– History Workshop was not noted for its time-keeping. I longed
to get away, go home. I did stay until the end of the session, but
have no memory of what Rancière and Cottereau said, and in
Cottereau's case, no essay written up for the book *People's History
and Socialist Theory* to prompt memory later on. Perhaps many in
that shabby, airless room wanted to get away, for we had all had a
long and traumatic Saturday night, indeed a Saturday Nite of epic
verbal violence, not in the pubs and alleys of Oxford town, but a
historian's version of the Randan, in an abandoned church close
by Ruskin College. There, on a battleground named History,
the 1980s Theory Wars were announced. The scene has often
been described: darkness made visible by giant spotlights trained
on a narrow stage where an altar once stood, crowds hanging
from the scaffolding propping up the church roof, like the fallen
angels in Doré's engraving of Milton's Hell. It was a plenary
Workshop session, planned to discuss E. P. Thompson's assault
on Althusserian Marxism in *The Poverty of Theory* (1978). It was
so discussed, by four speakers including Thompson himself, who
rose to dizzying heights of vitriolic polemic. The philistines – the
Althusserians, Continental Theorists – were at that very moment
'massing on the frontiers of history itself'.[8] Wild accusations of
'vulgar Marxism' were flung between the speakers.[9] The scene was
enacted in 'a theatre of arrogance' said some, and the performance
of such intemperate discourtesy had visibly upset many in the
audience (the term 'distressed' was not yet in use).[10] A year later, I
had found a formula for expressing my own responses to that dark
night. Editing the collected papers that emerged from HW14, I
wrote (with my fellow editors, though this paragraph was mine)
that 'HW 13 . . . the last . . . to be held in Oxford, was a dividing
place for more than the Workshop itself. It brought a tradition of
people's history and workers' writing into direct confrontation
with new sources of socialism in Europe, and there was a dramatic
enactment of this confrontation in the darkness of a deconsecrated
church in Walton Street, where titanic figures of the left boomed
the struggle in imperious male voices; and the only woman on the

platform stood up to say, that excluded from the form and rhetoric of the debate, she could only stay silent.'[11] We also described how the theme of HW14, 'Language and History', had been conceived as 'healing device', 'language' signalling a set of problems that all historians would recognize; that it might 'unite the disparate forces that revealed themselves in . . . 1979'. (We could not yet know about the bitter language wars that were to rage throughout the 1980s.)[12]

These reflections are made by the *trahison de l'écriture*, so I am no more likely to know what I meant than anyone else. My paragraph was not a case of 'how to write politics' or 'what is properly political in writing', or 'a certain way of writing history', nor yet writing as constitutive act – 'a way of configuring and dividing the shared domain of the sensible' – though it certainly was a politic and polite way of putting things.[13] Reading at a distance of thirty years, I am interested to note that I thought (or appeared to think) that the danger announced by Thompson was not Theory, but something going by the name of Socialism, that would undermine the common practices of socialist, labour and people's history. Thompson had already alerted us to the fate of the workers' agency under a regime of structuralist Marxism in general, and Althusser's notion of interpellation in particular, as an 'Orrerey of Errors', in *The Poverty of Theory*.[14] And I had had a year to absorb reports of worker-students' reactions to the weekend of 30 November to 2 December 1979. After the event, one journalist had spoken to 'the splendidly named Tom Mole . . . a Rotherham bus driver in his second year at Ruskin'. '"Last year [at HW12], we students made the soup and all the editorial people waltzed in and out", he said. "This year we wanted to give papers, but we're still making the soup and they're still giving the papers."'[15] *This* was the fault-line uncovered that night: not between British social history and 'the theoreticists' (Thompson's phrase) massed on the other side of the Channel, but between the workers and those who wrote their history. It was a fissure to which Jacques Rancière spoke, twenty-four hours later.

This was the last HW held at Ruskin. After 1979 it became peripatetic. A decade later Raphael Samuel named what had happened that weekend as 'an implosion', to be 'speculatively . . .

explained by the fact that it opened up so many socialist wounds
in relation to the cultural politics of the here-and-now, prefig-
uring those psychodramas which in the following decade were
to paralyse the British left'.[16] This was not so much polite and
evasive, as an expression of impossibility out of which all modern
Western history is written, whether it measures an event of twelve
years past, or two hundred. History-writing *has to* incorporate
Afterwards, however much the historian struggles to abandon the
days, weeks, years, between the 'then' he writes, and the 'now' of
his writing.[17]

   What you write as a historian never is, cannot be, what *was*
there, what *was like that,* Once Upon a Time. 'There is history',
says Rancière, after his long contemplation of Jules Michelet in
The Names of History,

> because there is the past and a specific passion for the past. And there is
> history because there is an absence [. . .]. The status of history depends
> on the treatment of this twofold absence of the 'thing itself' that is *no
> longer there* – that is in the past; and that never was – because it never
> *was such as it was told.* (NaH63)

This is the treachery of writing history, maybe especially of writing
history in the tenses of English; not Annie Ernaux's proclamation,
by way of Jean Genet, that all who write about their own (family,
parents, class) have already betrayed them.[18] Or . . . perhaps
Ernaux's stricture does apply to all those who write about *la place* in
the past: in their deep identification with their historical subjects,
many *engagé* scholarship boy and girl historians of the mid twentieth century contemplated the betrayal involved in writing about
the working-class dead and gone.

   But we cannot write it like it was, for the *was* did not exist.
The lost *past* may well have been, but *history-writing* is now. This
linguistic and philosophical conjecture is much plainer in French
than it is in English: French history writing is conducted for the
main part in *le présent historique*; English-language historians write
in the past tense. (A literacy training *au passé simple* made Foucault,
for example, extraordinarily difficult *to read* in English, in the 1970s
and 1980s; I think we have gotten over our difficulties now.)

The untimeliness of all history-writing is much more apparent in French.[19] The tenses of history-writing was the second topic evoked by Rancière on Sunday afternoon, though such recognition could only come later, after reading all the historical and historiographical writing he published between 1981 and 2007.[20]

Sunday Afternoon

Maybe it seemed at first that he was to tell us about our desires – social historians' desire that our historical subjects be the way we want them to be; or about our disconcerting and shameful nowhere-to-be between Saturday night's intellectuals on the stage and the Ruskin students housekeeping for the audience. Rancière spoke in English, to the text he had sent to London some time in November (rather than reading it aloud) and his topic, according to the session report was 'French social historiography, and the gap between French social history as a product and the working class movement'. In retrospect, and listening now to the tape recordings from that afternoon, he emphasized effacement by Annales school *longue durée* history in general and the 'motionless history' of Le Roy Ladurie's work in particular, of what we had already come (after Thompson's *Making*) to know as the workers' experience. It was 'a comeback to earlier history which is nothing to do with the working class', he said.[21] But he said nothing that was not reproduced in the published version, so it is that which will be quoted here.

He opened with 'the real, deep gap between social history as an intellectual product and the organized working-class movements' in France. The two important questions to be addressed were: 'who needs social history, or working-class history; and who does it?' French workers had not, for the main part, wanted their own history. 'For instance', he said (presumably speaking from archival work for *Nuit de prolétaires*), 'there was an important literary movement among French workers in the mid nineteenth century, but they wrote poetry rather than history . . . (they) wanted to gain their identity through other means than history and memory, and even the history of their own struggles, working-class struggles, did not serve their purpose'. Moreover, in early twentieth-century France, it was not academic historians who wrote the history of trade union and labour struggle, but sociologists and anthropologists producing popular ethnological accounts of the habits and manners of the nineteenth-century working class. Sociologists produced the most twentieth-century French working-class history because sociology was 'the official science of the new radical republic'. After 1870, the science of 'social solidarity and reciprocity' wrote the workers and working-class history from the perspective of class harmony, and 'solidarism'. Histories of the working class had been inaugurated by the French state. Rancière described the 1890s legalization of trade unions and monitoring of the law in action by labour bureaux, and the 'tradition of social investigation created by . . . the radical democratic forces of the republican state, whose aim was to effect a conciliation between the Republic, the state and the working class'. Civil servants writing this state-sanctioned history were often themselves veteran militants of the nineteenth-century working-class movement. 'Dismissed and marginalized by the new forces – socialist, collectivist . . . anarchist', the first books 'representing real research into the history of trades unions and the working class were written by men who had been defeated in their own attempts to reconcile the classes when they were militants in the labour movement . . . [they] wanted to take their revenge as civil servants, as investigators for the state'.[22] Rancière concluded his talk by telling us about the underestimation of working-class history in French universities: 'if you write social history, you are taken to be a militant, interested . . . because of your political involvement'. Raphael Samuel's editorial note to the published talk explained that 'social history' has a double meaning in French, the first much as in English, the second inherited from the nineteenth century as 'social movement' – the popular forces that battled to resolve 'the social question'. 'Social history' was the narrative of that struggle, he explained; 'in other words something much more akin to the [English] term "labour history"'. In Rancière's paper the latter meaning was predominant.[23] But exhausted, stunned, by Saturday night, could we have *heard* what Rancière said?

I will make sincere attempts to stop using the dreadful, enclosing 'we', with its outrageous presumption that I speak for others. I do not know what others listening thought; I do not know what I, listening, thought. I know what I *must have* thought when I read the published version two years later: how lucky the French! How lucky to be a French academic historian: to be an object of suspicion in a university system so clear-eyed about the political purposes of the history you write! How much better be able to align yourself with the workers – the Ruskin students – in the soup kitchen and with their struggle, than to be one of those academics waltzing around with yet another paper about nineteenth-century working-class experience of something-or-other in your hand. 'They order, said I, this matter better in France.'[24]

Self-abasement and suffering-envy were deeply ingrained in the practice of British social history. While attempting to give the lost myriads of the past, all the nameless ones, a voice and a history, social historians sought out the saddest stories ever told, of what the English fiscal-military state, the legal system, industrial capitalism, *did to* people in the past.[25] Historians had, and have, the very great power of making immortal ordinary people whose stories of suffering are a passport to the historical record, in a way that their everyday, ordinary life never would have been.[26] The sympathies and empathies of twentieth-century British social history can be read as part of a long-standing project of modernity (originating in the eighteenth century and given its most elegant exposition by Adam Smith in *The Theory of the Moral Sentiments*) of finding your own soul finer in its ability to apprehend the pain of others. After the eighteenth century empathetic turn, you do not ask: how does, or did, this person feel? Rather you ask: how would I feel if that happened to me? How do I feel, looking at the weight of the world, the suffering of others?[27] Western historical practice is, as Marc Bloch remarked, deeply Christian, eschatological, in its structures of temporality and meaning.[28] Reading what Rancière wrote for the 1979 Workshop, now, after all the turns taken by historical studies these thirty years past, what he said can only be a signal that one day, someone would ask not only about who needs and wants the history of working-class experience that historians write, but about the propriety of writing it in the first place, with all the acts of treachery it involves. Beyond the cultural, linguistic,

subjective, and archival 'turns' in historical studies, beyond historiographical questions asked from the postcolony about the West
as the Subject, or 'I', of historical writing, historians have started to
interrogate their relationship with all their subjects, asking juridical
questions to do with rights, duties, obligation, and ownership.[29]
Who owns history? Who has the right to speak for the dead? For
particular categories of the dead?[30] New protocols of imagining
and writing emerged from Holocaust history and sociology – from
the event that 'resisted . . . long-standing frameworks of historical reasoning, development, and emplotment . . . Who can claim
the moral ground to consider the meaning . . . of the lives and
deaths of others?'[31] In this ethical turn, Rancière's two questions,
asked thirty years ago, have become one and the same. Now, in
Anglophone social history at least, Michelet's dream, that through
their labours, historians might construct 'une cité commune entre
les vivants et les morts', has actually come to pass, at least in the
poetic realm of our imagination (which must be something of
what we're talking about here).[32]

Questions from Historians Who Read

It was pretty difficult to read (literally and materially; to get hold
of) the translated version of *La Nuit des prolétaires* (1981) after its
publication in the United States in 1989. *Nights of Labor* has just
been re-issued by a British press (as *Proletarian Nights*), but up until
the time of writing (April 2012) COPAC (the merged online cata-
logues of university and deposit libraries in the UK), showed there
to be a mere ten loanable copies available across the entire country,
including the one deposited in the British Library. The copy in
my own university library is almost impossible to borrow, always
out on loan. As of yesterday, there were no second-hand copies
for sale in the entire UK (though three available from the US, at
enormous cost). Geoff Eley says that during the publication inter-
regnum (1981–9), the French edition was 'extensively discussed
among English-speaking social historians'; but he must mean US
historians. In 1984 *History Workshop Journal* noted Jonathan Rée's

discussion and a 'translation of the book's preface' in the journal *Radical Philosophy*, but I can trace only one review of *La Nuit* in the UK historical journals before 1989.[33] Rancière's contribution to the US collection *Work in France* (1986) was praised in *HWJ*, and highlighted in another UK-historical journal. But by far the most intense discussion of *La Nuit* took place in the United States, or certainly in US-edited historical journals. (A little bibliographic excursion, which suggests that English social and labour historians did not often read the philosophy journals; I believe this to be a true observation.) By way of contrast, *Nights of Labor* (1989) was extensively discussed, on both sides of the Atlantic. But then, after 1989, it was difficult to read in the other sense: US typesetting conventions (especially double-quotation marks) make all texts appear florid and hyperbolic to the English reading-eye. The *présent historique* cannot be done into English historical prose: it is made to appear irreducibly . . . pretentious and self-regarding to its readers. Moreover, to English-language readers the present-tense voice raises serious doubts about *who is speaking* in Rancière's text: the 1840s worker or the historian?[34] Doubts on this score may have been felt very keenly by those of us schooled in the first (impossible) duty of English social history: to let the dead *speak for themselves.* 'A fine one to talk about Michelet's poetic effusions!' I find myself writing of *The Nights of Labor* in one undated notebook entry from the 1990s. Poor Gabriel Gauny! Poor floor-layer who speaks so much of Rancière's argument, whose voice is so often incorporated in the historian's. Above all, poor Gauny, to have your rather fine 1840s prose translated into cumbersome English, in 1989! It was 'the wisps of umbrage beyond the walls' (NL86) that finally drove me to *La Nuit* itself, to find Gauny looking up from his work and through a window (as so many nineteenth-century workers did) at the vast prison house of the city.[35] In 1989 he sees 'the wisps of umbrage beyond the walls, and the venturesome clouds in the infinite atmosphere', not what he said he saw in 1848, which was 'les touffes d'ombrage au-delà des murailles' (PN97) . . . not a social attitude (slight; condescension) beyond the city walls, but a shadow, more likely to do with trees or bushes than clouds: an area of darkness.[36] They order, said I, this matter better in French.

But Gabriel Gauny – all the worker writers of *La Nuit* – did experience – see – slight and exclusion. A problem for British social historians, far greater than translation-trouble, was the story Rancière told of their struggle, not to ameliorate working conditions and social relations, not (as in some strictly Marxist versions of the tale) organization and struggle for a world turned upside down, but rather to read and write themselves into men worthy of the respect of their betters, to become full citizens of the republic of letters. If you hadn't read Noel Parker's 1982 translation of the Preface in *Radical Philosophy*, you would know this was the story from reading Donald Reid's fine introduction to *Nights*, or from Patrick Joyce's account of Rancière's 'Myth of the Artisan' – working-class militancy arising not from 'pride of [a] trade' but from those trades that were most debased and despised.[37] You would not have had to read the book to know that Rancière 'called into question the projections of proletarian authenticity only recently constructed by social historians around the figure of the radical artisan'.[38] A patiently constructed *artisanal* identity for nineteenth-century men – men and women who took pride in their work and the exercise of their labour – looked as if it were about to be . . . well, deconstructed.[39] '[The] philosopher-historian has questioned the significance of workplace changes, skill loss, trade unionism as response, and more deeply . . . [cast] doubt upon the conceptual verities that have been associated with the word "artisan"'.[40] And you could leave it at that, pausing only to wonder, in a parody of your own doughty empiricism, why no one but you had ever asked exactly *why* the poets and dreamers who joined US Icarian communities in the 1840s, commented so frequently on the impossible pace of work set by all American labourers and immigrants.[41] You wondered how much café life, nights spent writing and money spent on booze, had diminished their resource of labour-power . . .

A Reading Lesson

You wanted to know more about the artisans who wrote poetry and philosophy and edited newspapers, more than their reveries of childhood to which Rancière gave access, more than their written words, more than the contours of their ideas, their intellectual life.[42] You wanted Rancière to exceed what he had inscribed in the figures of *Proletarian Nights*. Social historians worked hard in the 1980s to bestow subjectivity and interior life on their long-dead working-class subjects. By giving them individual psychologies shaped by their own past, we might redistribute the good of a shaping childhood experience formerly reserved for the depiction of elite subjects.[43] Rancière's account of young men and women understanding themselves as made by their own experience, was an important marker of the subjective turn in historical studies. We learned also, perhaps, what Rancière told us only in 2012, that 'we cannot know if their childhood memories, their descriptions of the working day, or the tales of their encounter with writing are authentic', that no narrative 'is a simple recounting of facts', that it is 'a way of constructing – or deconstructing – a world of experience' (PNx). But the social historian always wants more. How, exactly did 'each one . . . [find] his or her own way to penetrate the secret of those blackened white pages'? (PN51)[44] How did they live as readers as well as writers?

Rancière's historical subjects were probably taught to read, in childhood or adolescence, by some form of the syllabic method. Indeed, there is no evidence of any other method of reading instruction being used on either side of the Channel in the later eighteenth century. The English-language life of the 'Ignorant Schoolmaster', Joseph Jacotot, is instructive on this point. His work was well known in 1830s Britain, where his pedagogy was discussed as 'the word method'. Translations of his work were widely advertised in the British press; provincial schools promoted themselves as following his method.[45] Jacotot's name is still evoked in modern histories of literacy, and by modern educationalists contesting methods of reading teaching.[46] In his compendious account of the ways to literacy in England from the sixteenth century onwards, Ian Michael acknowledges Jacotot's influence, but suggests that 'although Jacotot's pupils took words as whole initially they were soon made to divide them into syllables and then into letters'. Jacotot's approach, which he did not claim to be innovative, was in the mainstream of eighteenth-century experimentation with syllabification as literacy instruction.[47] And contemporary British advocates had no trouble understanding Jacotot's method as entirely syllabic: 'the system is an excellent one, and which we are not inclined to think the worse of, that it has frequently occurred to ourselves', said one Scottish correspondent. 'M. Jacotot in French, takes *Telemachus*. He reads the first syllables to an infant – he points out the letters which they contain – he makes the child repeat them – he then goes on to the next syllables – new acquisitions are made – the old ones are continually repeated. The child is taught thus gradually to read. Writing is taught by giving the words acquired to be copied . . .'[48] All of this is *not* designed to point out that Jacotot's historical reputation is rather different from the pedagogical persona inscribed in *The Ignorant Schoolmaster*. It is rather to underline the social historian's desire for more, for more of what is hidden in the spaces of Rancière's footnotes, and in his reading of the workers' writing: for the shaping of the minds that produced it; for a *mentalité*.

In the British Isles the syllabic method of literacy teaching produced certain poetic and rhetorical effects in the worker-writers so instructed – at home, at school, or on the street (as was the acrobat Claude Genoux).[49] It provided learners with a form of linguistic analysis that did not, in fact, reflect the way English is organized at the structural level, but in which English-language worker writers of the early nineteenth century clearly found a profound intellectual resource. A late eighteenth-century English reading lesson proceeded something like this: a child, or young adult learner, was expected to learn the alphabet, that is, get by heart the letter names rather than the sounds the letters represent. Rapidly (and sometimes, if nineteenth-century evidence is anything to go by, in parallel, for you could recite the alphabet on a daily basis for years in an English village school, while doing quite other and sophisticated things with the written word) the learner was introduced to the phonetic qualities (though not so named) of the twenty-six letters by articulating strings of syllables: *ba–ca–da–* (in reading primers these were usually set in rows). The child must then build the syllables up into units that conveyed meaning, as do *bat–cat–fat*. Then he or she must gain further experience of letter sounds (and the variety

of sounds that might be conveyed by the same letter) by combining
syllables (*bat–on; fat–ter*).[50] After this, as might be supposed, the
primers took wildly divergent approaches, for as contemporary
language theorists were at pains to point out, English is not organized at the structural level by syllables, but rather, by stress: by the
irregular emphasis of the human (English) voice in articulation.[51]
But the syllabic method of literacy teaching may have allowed
English-speaking children and other learners access to the rhythmic
structure of English by allowing them to play about with its sound
system. Repeated chanting of strings of syllables was thought to
provide the key to unlock the reading process.[52] All of this method
involved voicing: the runs of syllables (and sometimes, the wild
nonsense of their conjunction) were said out loud, often in chorus
with other children. It has been argued elsewhere that this method
of literacy teaching had discernable effect on the poetic output of
working-class people in the period ca.1740–1840, and may explain
why they chose to write verse rather than prose in the first place.
The aesthetic regime of late eighteenth-century England gave very
high status to blank verse, to language ordered by the principle of
stress; when its splendours were extolled it was usual to remind
readers that it was the form of choice for Shakespeare and Milton;
the iambic pentameter is, as many an eighteenth-century language-
theorist also pointed out, a highly encapsulated item of information
about the way in which English works as a system of sound and
articulation – the 'most natural' to it, in their terms.[53] But one shoemaker poet explained how syllabification, not stress, organized both
his verse and his thinking about it. Robert Bloomfield described
composing *The Farmer's Boy* in this way: 'Nine tenths of it was put
together as I sat at work', he wrote in September 1798, 'where
there were usually six of us.'

> No one in the house has any knowledge of what I have employed
> my thoughts about when I did not talk. I chose to do it in rhime for
> this reason; because I found allways that when I put two or three lines
> together in blank verse, or something that sounded like it, it was a
> great chance if it stood right when it came to be wrote down, for blank
> verse has ten syllables in a line, and this particular I could not adjust nor
> bear in memory as I could rhimes.[54]

Of course, had Bloomfield read Beattie's *Theory of Language* or one of the many other technical guides to English prosody available, he would have known that while the five-stress line of English blank verse *may* have ten syllables, his was not the correct form of analysis. The correct way (of composition *and* analysis) is by stress: five strong stresses make an iambic line, each strong stress preceded by a weak one.[55] But syllabification, however incorrect, drew a different kind of analytic and poetic attention to the English language, not least, one surmises, because it connected with oral culture and a child's experience of early speech development: syllabic methods of literacy instruction may promote play with rhyme and rhythm. And syllables are perceptually salient. The syllabic method underscored the *thinginess,* the real existence of *bat* and *cat* and *mat,* as entities in the world and of language, in a way that learning that "buh" is the sound with which *bat* begins, is not to learn of something perceptually real, in the same way. We might expect the salience of syllables and syllabification – and of these arguments – to be even greater in a strongly syllable-timed language like French. A syllabic reading lesson might give us more access to the worker-writers of *La Nuit,* and to Jacotot's students: to their philosophy of writing as well as their written words.

One of Jacotot's reading lessons is reported in *The Ignorant Schoolmaster.* It is, presumably, a compilation account of many reading lessons conducted over the fifty-year period during which he taught: the subject of the lesson is 'a poor person' being told how once, a former student, a locksmith by trade, had responded to Jacotot's hectoring insistence that *he could do it*, could make sense of the marks on the page. And also present is Rancière, to orchestrate this lesson about reading lessons. He announces the entry of Jacotot, coming 'on stage with his *Télémaque,* a book, a thing'. 'Take it and read it', he says to the poor person, who not unreasonably responds that he doesn't know how. In a pedagogic strategy frequently resented by students who are told about the brilliant successes of their predecessors, Jacotot continues his harangue by asking the man if he can at least 'recognize the O that one of my students, a locksmith by profession, calls "the round," the letter L that he calls "the square"? Tell me the form of each letter as you would describe the form of an object . . . Don't say that you can't' (IS22–3). The materiality of written language was certainly inscribed here: the thinginess of letter-shapes and letter-sounds, *was* Jacotot's revelation to the poor man. To be sure, there is not a whole word, nor yet a syllable in this brief fragment of a much longer lesson. This would have surprised no contemporary English commentator on Jacotot's method, but is not strictly to the point here. For this lesson only exists textually; it is impossible to retrieve as something that took place, once upon a time. Is the dialogue between poor man and pedagogue scripted from Jacotot's memories recorded in the *Enseignement universel* of 1829, or in the *Journal de l'émancipation intellectuelle* of 1835–6, or from both, as Rancière's notes suggest? Who harangues the poor man, scorns his diffidence and self-doubt, across time and space? Is it Jacotot or Rancière who teaches this lesson? But *Proletarian Nights* recounts how the pedagogue, whoever he was or is, may be discarded; that no matter how they were taught to read, by whatever method, some working people took the liberty of writing.

5

The Paradoxical Pedagogy of Creative Writing

Caroline Pelletier and Tim Jarvis

[Literature] has the misfortune to have only the language of written words at its disposal to stage myths of a writing beyond writing, everywhere inscribed in the flesh of things. This misfortune obliges it to the sceptical fortune of words that make believe they are more than words and critique this claim themselves. (MS175)

Jacques Rancière's literary poetics rest on the claim that there is a paradox at the heart of literature. Literary language is, at one and the same time, a language which does not signify, refers to nothing save itself, and a language written on bodies. Literature asserts it points to a 'real' beyond the page and yet is constantly in the process of interrogating and undermining its transitivity. This self-reflexiveness, for Rancière, is key to literature's specific energy.

The pedagogy of the academic discipline of Creative Writing is not generally characterized by reflexivity. As a number of recent publications in the field have argued, Creative Writing lacks theorization.[1] The discipline's emphasis on formalist approaches tends to exclude the historical, sociopolitical, ideological and affective dimensions of literature from the classroom. Yet while this situation has been lamented and solutions proposed, analysis of the factors that have led to it has been limited. Paul Dawson, in his *Creative Writing and the New Humanities*, argues that it arises largely from efforts of earlier Creative Writing pedagogues to establish a disciplinary identity, distinct from the study of literature. This has led to an over-emphasis on craft. For Michelene Wandor, in her *The Author is Not Dead, Merely Somewhere Else*, the situation results from a Romantic figuring of the writer combined with attachment to therapeutic self-expression: the former leads to an overvaluing of the art, the latter of the person. Attempts to reconcile these perspectives, Wandor maintains, have encouraged a focus on process rather than product. In her Creative Writing coursebook, *The Writing Experiment*, Hazel Smith argues that the unreflexive nature of the discipline partly arises from its affiliation to literary realism, which, in an argument indebted to poststructuralist theory, she claims is a mode of writing that perpetuates inegalitarian social hierarchies. She argues that this can be overcome with a focus on radical and destabilizing experimental uses of language. But these, and other explorations of this problem, tend either to rely on a theory/praxis binary which overlooks the specific role of literature in society, or require the decay of literary specificity to the point of incommunicative intransitivity by privileging experimental works that erode signification to the point of non-meaning.

In this chapter we will, by reading the pedagogy of Creative Writing through the work of Rancière, propose another view of this situation: one which draws on Rancière's argument about the specificity of literature, his defence of the novel against avant-gardist critiques and his analysis of what happens to knowledge when it enters the academy. It is our contention that Creative Writing makes stable, ossifies, the volatile, labile aspects of writing, those propensities Rancière terms literarity.

A note on who we are: we are both teachers, one of Education, one of Creative Writing. We are engaging with Rancière's ideas in terms of their implications for both these disciplines and we are interested in bringing his work on these two areas into dialogue. We read Rancière because he speaks to both our practical and our theoretical concerns, or rather because his thought tends towards the dissolution of any such distinction.

Jacotot's Universal Teaching Method and Creative Writing

It might be thought that the pedagogy of Creative Writing would share certain principles with the emancipatory 'universal teaching' method proposed by radical educator Joseph Jacotot, whose story Rancière tells in *The Ignorant Schoolmaster*. After experimenting with traditional teaching methods Jacotot concluded, according to Rancière and contrary to every established precept of pedagogy, that a teacher's knowledge was not necessary to a student's learning. Furthermore, he concluded that the effect of pedagogy was not to bring about learning and intellectual freedom, but to defer these and thereby stultify students. These insights led him to devise his universal teaching, which was based on the principle that '*all men have equal intelligence*' (IS18). Universal teaching takes place through the mediation of 'common', or collective, objects of knowledge: books, paintings, music, or any artefact of culture – the arbitrary example in Jacotot's first experiment being Fénelon's *Télémaque*. These objects make it possible to reconfigure the disposition of will and intelligence in the teaching situation: rather than transfer his intelligence about them, the teacher can instead force the student to manifest his intelligence simply by asking, in relation to the object: what do you see? what do you hear? what do you make of it? how does it relate to what you already know? Universal teaching is emancipatory, in Rancière's narrative, because it makes the student demonstrate her or his equal capacity to produce signs about the world, to interpret and translate it – something that anyone can do and in fact everybody does all the time.

Creative Writing teaching might thus be thought empancipatory because it is freed, arguably to a greater degree than almost any other discipline, from the imperative to convey a particular body of knowledge for assessment and, as a result, from explanation as a teaching methodology. Its existence, as a subject area in higher education, challenges a conception of literature as the product of a uniquely gifted elite, foregrounds literary writing as the expression of a will to write rather than something only those with particular prior knowledge, or innate skills, can accomplish. The tangible products of Creative Writing courses are usually treated as expressions of students' capabilities rather than of teachers' intelligences, a move which effectively frames teachers as ignorant masters in Rancière's sense. Teaching Creative Writing involves using a common, or collective, object of knowledge as a mediator between students and teachers, with students ostensibly developing their own practice in dialogue with their reading of literary works.

However, the pedagogy of Creative Writing, as it is generally practised in the UK, US and Australian higher education, is not, we argue, an example of universal teaching. Exploring why this is so tells us something about the tensions within Creative Writing, as a discipline, and also in more general terms about what happens to knowledge when it enters the academy, a central question in the sociology of knowledge, which has examined this in terms of the exercise of control by particular social groups through the determination of curriculum and discipline.[2] Rancière's *The Ignorant Schoolmaster* enables a different approach to be taken, focusing on the conditions under which knowledge becomes sensible in pedagogic practices. This makes it possible to examine how the teaching of Creative Writing assigns or distributes particular capabilities to readers and writers, teachers and students. Similarly, Rancière's conception of the politics of literature enables an exploration of the ideological dynamic of Creative Writing that moves beyond the theory/praxis binary and which is not confused by the fraught antinomy of conservatism versus avant-gardism.

In interpreting how Creative Writing teaches, therefore, we are trying to bring together Rancière's work on education and his work on literature. This endeavour risks making the mistake of bringing together two disparate bodies of thought. Rancière is careful to frame his writing as a series of interventions rather than the attempt to construct a coherent philosophical system. However, correlations and narrative threads can be traced through his work. Thus the following passage, from *The Ignorant Schoolmaster*, anticipates Rancière's subsequent work on literature:

> The book is the equality of intelligence. This is why [. . .] [t]he Platonic philosopher-king favored the living word to the dead letter of

the book – that [. . .] discourse at once silent and too loquacious, wandering at random among those whose only business is thinking. (IS38)

In addition, in a recent essay, 'The Thinking of Dissensus', Rancière argues that Jacotot's adventure points to the 'poetical' character of experience:

This is the meaning of the 'equality of intelligence' that I borrowed from Jacotot [. . .] it means that the same intelligence makes poetic fictions, political inventions or historical explanations, that the same intelligence makes and understands sentences in general.[3]

It is this idea of 'sameness' which provides the strongest justification for linking Rancière's work on education and his work on literature; sameness is at play in the paradoxes he evokes in both fields. Sameness is an attribute of the distribution of the sensible in 'democracy', which posits the equal capability of all members of a society to perform its various functions. Sameness also results from the collapse of the neo-Aristotelian system of fictional genres, as a consequence of which anything can become the subject of literary writing and the realm of fiction becomes indistinguishable from lived reality. But this sameness is not just equality; it is simultaneously a fearful indifference, the indifference of people and words, to do or become attached to anything, an indifference that engenders a fear of loss, the loss of community, of social bonds between citizens, and between writers/artists and the mass of readers. There accordingly arises the yearning for a mark of difference. Pedagogy and literature are responses to this difficulty of collective life in a 'democratic' society, answers which Rancière's writings variously interrogate and trouble.

In the next part of this chapter we will look more closely at Rancière's argument about the emergence of literature in the aesthetic regime and at literature's tensions or paradoxes. We will then elaborate on the way in which Creative Writing is literary in Rancière's sense, before moving on to an account of the pedagogic principles at work in the teaching of Creative Writing and exploring the effects these have on what counts as literature, reading and writing, including what is thereby discounted.

The Novel's Bastardy

It is with the ascendency of the aesthetic regime in the Western world, at roughly the same time as the emergence of democratic movements issuing from the Enlightenment and the French Revolution, that literature begins to have direct political effects, that it 'intervenes as literature in [the] carving up of space and time, the visible and the invisible, speech and noise', or in what Rancière calls the distribution of the sensible (PoL4). The aesthetic regime overtakes the regime that had previously held sway, the representational regime, which grew out of the neo-Aristotelian elaboration of the principle of *mimesis*, itself a response to Platonic anxieties about writing as wandering, inappropriate, not tied to context as speech is. Aristotelian *mimesis*, as characterized by Rancière, tames and tethers writing by defining a particular relationship between speech and action. The key principles of this relationship are that fictionality is emphasized and confusion between the artwork and reality is avoided; form is always socially appropriate and the emphasis is on oration, as a counter to the mute, errant, written word. The choice of subject matter (*inventio*) accordingly governs both plot (*dispositio*) and style (*elocutio*); all artworks adopt a form suited to their object of representation, the tragic for noble characters and the comic for low. In the representational regime the word is conceived as an act, a spoken performance.

The aesthetic regime overtakes the representational regime. Its principles are that language is foregrounded and *elocutio* privileged; all subjects are treated as equal; style is no longer aligned to subject matter and writing is the substance of poeticism, no longer simply the transcription of speech.

Literature's power, as Rancière sees it, derives from the fact it has a constitutive paradox at its heart. It is, in Hector Kollias's formulation, an 'agonistic literature'.[4] In overturning representational poetics, literature proclaims the indifference of the form with respect to the content and treats poetry as a specific mode of language. The errant word ('literarity', to use Rancière's term) is freed from the rigid hierarchies of the representational regime, from appropriateness of subject and address, because it has the potential, identified during the Romantic period, to refer to itself alone; literary language is autotelic to the point of muteness and refers only to itself: it disincorporates. Yet at the same time, in its egalitarian democratic address, literature calls into being a community, a body of people: it incorporates. As Rancière writes in *Mute Speech*: 'the concept of writing is split in two: It can be orphaned speech lacking a body that might accompany it and attest to it, or, on the contrary, it can be a hieroglyph that bears its idea upon its body' (MS36).

Literature's paradox is that it pulls both towards dissipation in the molecular flows of the disembodied Word and towards fixity in the molar Truth of the Word made flesh. It is from efforts to hold these two poles in tension that it draws its unique energies.

One general tendency, Rancière claims, has thrown up the most interesting attempts to negotiate the paradox at the heart of literature: the novel. The novel's *dispositio*, or structure, reconciles the mute errant word and the community it calls forth by 'accompanying the representative molar scheme, its procedures of identification and its narrative sequences, by the molecular power of emancipated expressive details' (FW151). The flood of freed atoms produces flux, an endless shifting between fleeting configurations, which Rancière, in *The Politics of Literature*, after Gilles Deleuze, terms *heccéités* or haecceities (PoL62). According to Deleuze, in *A Thousand Plateaus*, haecceities 'consist entirely of relations of movement and rest between molecules or particles, capacities to affect and be affected.'[5] As these elements are, though possessed of expressive power, unstable, meaningless, Rancière argues that they require insertion into a mimetic system derived from the representational regime, in order that their potency is harnessed, does not simply dissipate. This is the literary compromise. It endures because tensions between the two regimes give the novel added dynamism, making it:

> [T]he place where the contradiction between the old poetics and the new is aggravated by the contradiction internal to the new. But this is part of what makes it the essential genre of literature, the genre that draws life from the banging together of its principles. (MS109)

Rancière examines other attempts to solve the paradox, foremost among them the fable, or tale. In his essay on Jorge Luis Borges, 'Borges and the French Disease' (PoL128–46), Rancière engages with Borges's attack on the French realist tradition and critiques the Argentine writer's particular solution to the paradox of literature. Rancière's claim in this essay is that the tale yokes the power of literature to a communitarian principle derived from myth, sets a universal fabulation, a collective dream, and an imaginary society of the past, in tension with the utopian community literarity calls forth. This, he argues, is less powerful than the novel's solution to the literary paradox, in which a 'real', present society grounds literarity's communitarian impulse. This privileging of 'the novel's bastardy,' over the unities of the fable, of literarity being held in tension with the mimetic, and not the mythic, can be related to Rancière's claim that: 'The "fictions" of art and politics are [. . .] heterotopias rather than utopias' (MS108, PA41). In the essay 'Of Other Spaces', Foucault describes heterotopic sites, in contrast to imaginary utopias, as real spaces, counter-sites that are 'a kind of effectively enacted utopia in which the real sites, all the other real sites that can be found within the culture, are simultaneously represented, contested, and inverted.'[6] The fable or tale, a literature linked to an imaginary community, is utopian, unreal, and as such has no power to disrupt culture's orders, because utopias figure other kinds of orders, other orthodoxies. The novel, in which literature is linked to a 'real' social order drawn from *mimesis*, is heterotopic and has the power to contest and invert, because it is disordered and allows for allodoxy. This helps explain why Rancière also critiques Deleuze for seeking, in his poetics, 'to reduce the confusion of novelistic plots to the magical formulas and mythical figures of folktales,' for reading texts through the filter of fable, and for privileging those experimental modern tales which are particularly suited to such a reading (MS108). Rancière claims Deleuze's analyses of literary texts unravel the literary compromise and move towards an extreme point, which art is only able to reach 'at the expense of annulling itself.'[7] Rancière's critique of Deleuze's poetics and, by implication, the avant-gardist literary tradition it exemplifies, allows us to recuperate the Creative Writing setting: to read its privileging of novelistic realism as constitutive compromise, rather than loss of nerve, or a conservative impulse.

The Pedagogy of Creative Writing

Creative Writing would appear, at first glance, to be a discipline ideally suited to the practice of an 'emancipatory pedagogy'. In his article, 'The Radical Pedagogies of François Bon and Jacques Rancière', Oliver Davis applies a Rancierian perspective to one particular Creative Writing pedagogic setting, that of François Bon's radical *ateliers d'écriture* (writing workshops) and concludes that they do indeed function in accordance with Jacotot's model of universal teaching. However, while Bon's teaching echoes principles described in *The Ignorant Schoolmaster*, his *ateliers* fail to enact the compromise integral to the regime of literature. They do not have a novelistic logic but instead derive their poetics from the kinds of experimental modern tales Deleuze privileges in his poetics (indeed, Davis describes Bon's aesthetic preference for such fictions, which he uses in his classes as stimulus texts), tales in which the mute word wanders into the desert of non-meaning (lists and other iterations are key to Bon's pedagogic method) and is not grounded in any molar structures (in the sense of social life; Bon aims, at least in the early workshops, to cut writers free from their reliance on personal memories). The writer in Bon's setting is encouraged to develop her or his 'own singular voice', which places the emphasis on a unique oration, not on a democratic, communitarian written word.[8]

Creative Writing classes in higher education institutions in the UK, US and Australia – the three countries where the discipline is most well established – operate very differently from Bon's *ateliers*. Bon's ethos is radical in terms of both pedagogy and aesthetics, but conventional Creative Writing teaching involves compromise in the negotiation of pedagogic and poetic tensions. The distinctiveness of the discipline of Creative Writing is articulated through its pedagogic principles. The key pedagogical injunctions upon which Creative Writing, as a discipline in the UK, US and Australian higher education systems, is commonly based are: 'read as a writer', 'find your voice', 'write what you know', and 'show don't tell'.[9] Taking each in turn, we will explore them from a Rancierian perspective.

The demand to 'read as a writer' advocates a specific kind of reading practice which bears some similarities to Jacotot's experiment with *Télémaque*: in each case the book is treated as the single, common, object of knowledge, which requires no explanation from any pedagogue, and to which any intelligence may be applied. However, while in the universal teaching system the student learns something contained in the book, or other artefact with which they engage their intelligences, something they did not previously know (in the case of the experiment with *Télémaque*, the French language), the pedagogical injunction to 'read as a writer' demands that the student assume a particular consciousness, which is not that of a reader. In other words, the injunction turns reading into a specific mode of thought characteristic of a specific group of people – writers – rather than something anyone can do. The pedagogy incorporates, or brings into being, a collective called 'writers', defined in opposition to readers, or people who read as readers only. This incorporating move parallels the distinction, critiqued in *The Ignorant Schoolmaster*, between translation and understanding, or passivity and activity, a distinction which assigns capability to teachers and incapability to learners. Such a distribution is effected, in the Creative Writing classroom, in the practice of interpreting 'read as a writer' as an invitation to judge the gap between the actuality and the ideal, the ideal of creative writing. But if this ideal does not come from an actual book, or instance of writing, which it cannot if reading means interrogating a text to identify the ways in which it is lacking, then it must be derived from something else: either from explication or from some *a priori* knowledge, possessed by the reader, of what 'creative writing' is. The function of the pedagogue is thereby re-introduced; the teacher is required to distinguish between reading (or writing) 'as a writer', and reading (or writing) as anyone reads.

'Reading as a writer' is, in essence, a formalist approach, one that teaches students how to embed literarity's molecular expressive elements in molar structures of language that are derived from a particular literary canon. The technique encourages students to betray the purity of the literary rupture, for it risks turning resolving the literary paradox into a formalist game involving the recombination of tropes and figures drawn from other writers' works. This produces rote works and closes down the novel's mutability.

The injunction to 'find your voice' frames voice as something which is verified by its speaker, rather than something which is transferred from one who already speaks to one who doesn't, who only emits noise. The teacher wills the students to find their voice but does nothing to give it to them. However, one of the injunction's implications is that the students should find their own unique mode of utterance, implying an ethics of self-identity and self-realization whereby a voice has already been given and needs simply to be 'found'. Voice and body are aligned here; the body is incorporated voice, a framing which marginalizes the possibility of voices being borrowed or imitated. At the same time, 'find your voice' can be taken as an instruction to ventriloquize, to take on the voices of the voiceless; it may be read, for instance, as a call to aspiring writers to find, or borrow, the idiom most suited to particular characters, narratives, or sets of concerns. These two contradictory interpretations of the same injunction replicate the tension that characterizes Rancière's analysis of the representational regime; for Rancière, however, voice is grounded in appropriate bodies, those bodies are divided between real and fictional realms. But although 'find your voice' privileges *elocutio* (style) in the production of creative writing, as the aesthetic regime does, at the same time this injunction makes *elocutio* subordinate to *inventio* and *dispositio*: it is a matter of finding the best style in which to express the subject matter or narrative structure previously settled upon. Style, or language, is matched by appropriateness to content. Yet the emphasis on style, on finding a voice, also lends voice a mute and errant autonomy. The injunction to 'find your voice' thus points to the simultaneous desire to ground voice in bodies and to foreground its circulation, its creative wanderings, which are both essential to the production of writing and yet which must be halted if voice is to speak from a particular place or body. This contradiction of the individual and the social is a tension Rancière identifies, in *Mute Speech*, as one of the founding forces of literary poetics, an unresolved conflict in Romantic discourse which the novel attempts to settle: 'Literature as an expression of individual genius and literature as an expression of society are the two versions of a single text' (MS 70).

'Write what you know' turns creative writing into an expression of knowledge rather than a sign of the gap between the teacher's and the student's experience. The explicator's function here is redundant; the precept is emancipatory. But what does the creative writer know? What they write. Creative Writing thereby becomes the expression of incorporated experience; indeed, whatever one writes is then framed as being about one's own experience. Writing becomes a form of sociology in which voice becomes the expression of a particular social history. The emphasis, in practice, tends to be to pay homage to victimhood by developing further the cultural stasis, or violation, implied by the preceding injunction to 'find your voice': poor people write celebratory resistance writing, rich people write the meaning of their guilt and colonial pretensions. The effect of 'write what you know' is therefore to treat writing as speech from a determined sociological place and historical time, spoken from that assigned space and nowhere else. Writing is then the expression of the incapacity to be anywhere and anyone. Creative Writing is treated, as a consequence of this injunction, both as intensely personal and also as the expression of a social history, which is reminiscent of Rancière's claim, quoted above, that one of the founding contradictions of the novel is the idea that, at one and the same time, literature is an expression of individual genius and an expression of society. The injunction also delimits the proper subject of writing, that which the writer knows, a move which implies a contextual appropriateness antagonistic to the free circulation of writing.

Like 'write what you know', 'show, don't tell' privileges the realist mode. As Dawson notes, 'The appeal to convincing and authentic depiction of sensory experience which this advice relies upon can work to perpetuate implicit favouring of the genre of realism and the mimetic philosophy behind it' (Dawson 2005, p.103). The idea that writers should be expressing meaning, character motivations and so forth, by grounding them in the details of ordinary life, mirrors Rancière's description of the novel as freed expressive details reinserted into molar structures. But there is one crucial difference: whereas the elements and their meanings, in Rancière's analyses, bear no necessary interrelationship, here students are advised to find the details that best express the affective intensities they wish to ground. The realism of Creative Writing is not that of a 'proliferation of being and things' but one which suppresses the pullulation of details by insisting on their 'rightness' (PoL39).

In addition to the pedagogic principles, the discipline of Creative Writing is characterized by an emphasis on a particular arrangement for teaching: the workshop. The workshop, in its standard form, consists of the critiquing of students' work in progress by their peers, under the guidance of a workshop leader, generally a published, and, therefore, 'experienced' writer. Like the pedagogic principles, it holds together different ideas about the nature of writing. On the one hand, the workshop is founded upon the premise of an equal capacity to write and is structured to verify this premise. On the other, the workshop turns students' writing into a sign of lack, incomplete until others in the workshop setting (one of whom, significantly, will be the 'experienced', 'knowledgeable' writer who facilitates the discussion) remedy its deficiencies. Writing is visible, in the workshop, as a product, but one to be rewritten following critique. Since the process of writing is effectively excluded from the setting, scrutiny falls either on the individual writer, leading to a psychological or psychotherapeutic inflection, or on the product and its aesthetic merit, which leads to a focus on talent or ability, and on the writer as the possessor of these attributes. The workshop format therefore treats the success or failure of a work in terms of either the life experiences of a writer or their 'genius'. But these are not so much alternatives as equivalent, indistinguishable. The Creative Writing workshop is thus both a pedagogic setting marked by a tension between emancipation and stultification, and a place for literary production structured by that tension between literature as an expression of individual genius and literature as an expression of society, which, in Rancière's aesthetic history, gives rise to the novel.

Conclusion – A Note Both Melancholy and Hopeful

One conclusion to be drawn from our analysis of Creative Writing pedagogy is that its paradoxes are intimately related to its pedagogic aim of producing literary writing; it is a pedagogy that produces works riven by literature's contradiction, a pedagogy built upon a paradox akin to that which structures literature in the aesthetic regime.

In fact, it could be claimed that pedagogy, in general, by nature, has at its core this paradox. This may be why *The Ignorant Schoolmaster* ends on a note both melancholy and hopeful: 'The Founder had predicted it all: universal teaching wouldn't take. He had also added that it would not perish' (IS139). Rancière's work makes visible the paradox of seeking to emancipate, to foster political subjectivation, through pedagogy. This paradox is what constitutes pedagogy; in this article we have been exploring its particular implications in the instance of Creative Writing. In order to negotiate this paradox, to hold in tension its contradictions, it is necessary to compromise. Pedagogy under the aesthetic regime holds in tension universalism and explication, emancipation and stultification: the dynamic of the regime is precisely about such tensions. But, where literature dramatizes the structuring contradiction by seeking its resolution, pedagogy seeks to disguise it: it turns it into a temporal problem, what Rancière refers to as the structure of delay in education.[10] We hope this analysis has drawn out the implications of the aesthetic paradox for pedagogy, how it operates by reinserting the disincorporating tendencies of an emancipatory assumption of the equal capability of all learners into an incorporating structure of explication. That pedagogy is riven by a paradox in this way does not mean it cannot be emancipatory, but the manner in which pedagogy refuses to acknowledge the compromise on which it is founded, feeds, and feeds on, the passion for inequality in education. One role Creative Writing could have in the academy is that of dramatizing the agonism of pedagogy, of participating in making it visible. Less optimistically, though, it could be claimed that the rise of Creative Writing, as a discipline, is shifting the balance of the aesthetic regime by providing a permanent and detrimental resolution to the agonism that gives literature its vitality. The rise of Creative Writing, as a discipline in the academy, has contributed to a situation in which an expressive poetics, that of the novel, has begun to collapse back into a representational, normative, poetics. The focus of Creative Writing pedagogy is on the *how* of producing textual effects; its emphasis on form restores an unhelpful opposition between form and content which is characteristic of the representational regime. So Creative Writing may be the site where the holding in tension of disincorporation and incorporation through strategies derived from the representational regime fails, the place where the representational regime begins to reassert itself against the aesthetic.

The pedagogy of Creative Writing in the academy privileges a realist, novelistic, aesthetic, especially with dicta like 'write what you know' and 'show don't tell'. But the realism of Creative Writing is arguably not the same realism Rancière privileges in his discussions, a realism which 'marks the ruin of all that was in harmony with the stability of the social body' (PoL39). Creative Writing's realism is based not on excess but concision, on the excision of redundant detail; this is what really lies behind the injunction 'show don't tell', which demands that only certain carefully chosen elements be included, so as to create balance and leave something to the reader's imagination. Harmony is restored by the edict of the right detail in the right place and the mute power of words is subsumed by the imagination of the reader who fills in the gaps to make a whole from fragments. Instead of proceeding towards dissensus, ruin and fragmentation, the new literary realist paradigm makes wholes, unities, out of fragments. In fact, there appears to be a drift away from style and towards story, that is, away from intransitive language, the mute orphaned word, and towards language as a signifying system.

Indeed it could be argued that Creative Writing, as an academic discipline, has begun to turn the novel into an ossified genre. Creative Writing enshrines the necessary betrayal of the purity of rupture, the literary compromise, in a pedagogy. It inclines the novel towards a narrative poetics of causes and effects and away from an expressive poetics of language, reducing its effectiveness as a solution to the literary paradox. Writers should come to the paradox in their own unique way, should agonize over it, because those throes are what produces literature's vitality. Creative Writing pedagogy makes accepting the compromise easy, naturalizes it, and thereby suppresses literature's agonistic quality.

This could be part of a general trend. In *The Politics of Aesthetics* Rancière writes:

> Postmodernism [. . .] became the grand threnody of the unrepresentable/ intractable/irredeemable, denouncing the modern madness of the idea of a self-emancipation of mankind's humanity and its inevitable and interminable culmination in the death camps. (PA29)

While Rancière does not see postmodernism as representing a distinct rupture, he discerns in it a reining in of some of the more extreme tendencies implicit in the aesthetic regime. And the agonism of the aesthetic regime, the necessary betrayal of the purity of rupture, *can* end in illness, and absolute dissolution:

> But Virginia Woolf can no longer play the role of the healthy schizophrenic. She knows only too well what schizophrenia entails. She knows what is covered up by the beautiful dream of the free association of splotches of colour, plumes of dust and drops of water: the reality of dissociation. (PoL70)

Perhaps the rise of Creative Writing in the academy is one means by which the contemporary moment attempts to resist the aesthetic regime's ineluctable movement towards ruin. Yet fear of ruin must not be allowed to close down agonism, as this would lead to stagnation and stasis. What we hope to have shown in this chapter is that Creative Writing can, by reading its practices through the work of Rancière, instigate a vivifying process of self-interrogation, can begin to open up a gap and situate the constitutive paradoxes of pedagogy and the literary at its heart. The implications of this, for pedagogy and literature alike, are profound.

6

The Sharing of Uncertainty

Sabine Prokhoris

How is one to be a reader – in this case a woman reader – of the works of Jacques Rancière? These works are organized with impressive systematicity, giving the feeling of a 'homogeneous and complete' edifice, to reprise Mauclair's expression, which Rancière quotes apropos of Art Nouveau, the formula of which is exemplarily encapsulated, he maintains, in Mallarmé's commentary on the dance of Loïe Fuller (A133). This is a remarkably unified construction, the explicit kernel of which is the political and philosophical question – admittedly, essential to think through – of equality. The matter of equality, then, the linchpin of Rancière's reflections as a whole, also structures, indeed is central to, the section of works devoted to what he calls the 'aesthetic regime of art', that is to say, a specific and recent distribution of the sensible – barely two centuries old, he explains – on the basis of which is defined both what will work as 'art' and what will come to be construed as 'aesthetic' perception in the community of citizens.

This 'aesthetic regime' of art, Rancière tells us, breaks with the representational regime of art and the hierarchies it prescribes to plot the forms of a community of equals. As he writes, 'the representational order works according to a model of clear distribution of roles and the hierarchical dividing up of parts (it privileges action and the narrative over life and the descriptive, separates out and hierarchizes regimes of expression, etc.)', whereas 'the aesthetic regime of art works according to an egalitarian principle' (TP389). Elsewhere he refers to it as an 'aesthetic revolution', claiming that it is consubstantial with an 'aesthetic unconscious', itself defined by a specific 'relationship between thought and non-thought', which, on his analysis, was decisively constituted by Romanticism and then consolidated by post-Kantian idealism (AU3). 'The aesthetic unconscious', says Rancière, 'has redefined the subject matter of art as specific modes of union between the thought that thinks and the thought that does not think' (AU45). 'The thought that does not think': this is a paradoxical formulation. Put differently, this is what Rancière also designates elsewhere as 'silent speech', or as that 'pathos' which both contrasts and identifies with the 'logos'. 'Logos' is also a Freudian term – but in what sense? In *The Future of an Illusion*, a strange text that is simultaneously disenchanted and paradoxically confident in the capacity of any intelligence not 'atrophied' by religious illusion, Freud speaks of 'our god, Logos', probably a disappointing god, 'perhaps not really all-powerful', but one whose *critical demand* it is important not to disclaim.[1] This demand is what is really at stake here: a demand that is initially present in anyone at all and not especially in scholars or philosophers. 'Think of the depressing contrast between the radiant intelligence of a healthy child and the feeble intellectual powers of the average adult. Can we be quite certain that it is not precisely religious education that bears a large share of the blame for this relative atrophy?', he wonders, perhaps not without a hint of provocation.[2] He is taking aim here at 'religious education' insofar as it claims to provide the conviction of a *Weltanschauung* (worldview), one that was constantly challenged by a thinker that Foucault would define as a 'founder of discursivity', that is, a figure who has fundamentally changed our ways of thinking.[3] Freud, then; for a little later it will be a case of Rancière's Freud. It seems to me, to offer a first impression for the time being, that because of the distance from which he is apprehended, this real Freud is one which Rancière's account misses. Extraordinarily fixed and wooden, probably not without reason, is the Freud of this philosopher's very self-assured discourse.

To return to aesthetics and its specific 'unconscious', Rancière adds: 'Aesthetics for me does not designate the science and the discipline that deals with art. Aesthetics designates a mode of thought that is deployed about the things of art and strives to say how they are things of thought. More fundamentally, it is a specific historical regime of thinking about art and an idea according to which the things of art are things of thought' (AU4–5 [TM]). Basing himself on this new *epistemè*, to use a Foucauldian category here – indeed Rancière himself explicitly acknowledges his proximity to Foucault on this point: 'I would say that my approach resembles Foucault's somewhat. It retains from the Kantian transcendental the principle of substituting conditions of possibility for a dogmatism of the truth' (TP501) – he makes Freudianism the object of certain evaluations, without it ever being very clear exactly why there is a need for him to delve, in a way that is at the very least rapid and fairly assertoric, into this question. It is even tempting, in view of the somewhat rhetorical conclusion to the opuscule that Rancière devotes to giving, very brilliantly it must be admitted, his opinion on the relationship between the 'aesthetic unconscious' and the 'Freudian unconscious', to parody in Rancière's case the – certainly rather unfair – verdict that Pascal delivers on Descartes: 'Descartes, useless and uncertain'.[4] However, let me add that the usual Pascalian reversal from 'for to against' may perhaps apply here. For Pascal also wrote that it is eminently sensible to 'work for the uncertain',[5] and indeed that this is how those who really understand the world proceed; which is to say not those he calls the 'demi-habiles' but rather 'the people', with their 'sane opinions'.

So, it is a temptation tinged with ambivalence. It is accordingly appropriate to try to understand why it arises, in order perhaps to draw usefully upon the perception of Rancière's philosophical discourse that it translates – a discourse that, it might be underscored in passing, constitutes quite an authority, at least in the French intellectual landscape, and on many topics, in any case when it comes to thinking about art and politics. In this regard, irrespective of Rancière's intentions – and indeed these matter little – the fact is that at no point does he frustrate, by way of the style of address that is his, the expectations by which he has been assigned the eminent *place* of the intellectual, and moreover of the philosopher – a sovereign figure, then – liable to bestow enlightened, never hesitant [*tâtonnante*], discourse on that of which he speaks. It is a discourse, on the other hand, in which one is unable to identify any single *position,* be it one that is mobile, or unstable, and which thereby threatens to make its own foundation tremble. This is a specific feature of Rancière's work, which differentiates him from Sartre and even more so from Foucault.

To return to our initial question: how are we to be readers of Rancière? That is to say, how do we grasp – understand – what he is saying to us, but also how are we to take hold of this for ourselves – in order to do something with it and reopen reflection on the questions it tackles. It seems to me, in the end, that though his work constantly – this is undeniable and has an obvious force – seeks to formulate, via the objects it encounters, the problematic of equality, as far as those objects themselves are concerned – in this instance art and psychoanalysis – it is only by a kind of optical illusion that they will appear to have been actually encountered. It is as if the discourse on aesthetics – one of the pillars of Rancière's edifice – and that on Freudianism – a sort of bolt that works to tighten the joints of his discourse, with the added bonus of a pretty poor critique of what it passes off as established Freudian positions – work to obstruct both a meditation on the *dynamics* of art – of which its effects in the common world are part – and an informed word – which also means a critical one – on psychoanalysis and its contemporary challenges. It is not that Rancière shows a lack, in any case not when it comes to the field of art, of encyclopedic knowledge of the subject matter, since he is extraordinarily learned within a certain area of operation, and no doubt remarkably perceptive in his reading of specific works – if not all those he discusses then first and foremost those of Mallarmé, who seems to be an object of particular dilection. However, he never says so in such terms.

The difficulty involved in elaborating a movement of reading Rancière that finds some hold on its object – but perhaps this is due to an entirely personal inability, even to a sort of professional deformation linked to the practice of psychoanalysis and to the taste it attests for a mode of thought akin instead to the work of

Penelope, to that which does not cease to do, undo, and redo differently the cloth of things and thoughts – the difficulty involved, therefore, in confronting Rancière's intimidating constructions, resides in something that could be summed up as follows: this system of thought, itself an edifice rather than a more or less complicated and entangled complex of pathways, seems to offer (indeed perhaps I am not alone in perceiving his oeuvre in this way), on the large number of questions it tackles, something like a cavalier perspective [*une vue cavalière*] – if I may be excused for speaking in images rather than having direct recourse to the concept. A cavalier perspective in the precise meaning of the term: a representation of a three-dimensional object without a vanishing point, and *a fortiori* without any vanishing lines. This perspective was adopted in the design of military fortifications, indeed in French it is known as *une vue cavalière* because *cavalier* was the term used for an artificial mound erected behind the fortifications to enable a view over them. So it is a high vantage point, which, though it permits an extensive and, in a certain way, complete view – as it is in three dimensions – of the things one wants to represent, it crushes their spatial relations and, as a result, can even become a source of error concerning the objects thus figured. It can therefore be useful in providing a quick idea of things but not of relations, which, if one examines them in this way, also get treated as things and not as the space of possible movements.

Let there be no mistake: for me it is not a matter here of some restorative nostalgia for the hierarchies instituted by classical perspective, hierarchies intended to prescribe what there is to be seen and to fix the place from which one ought to look. Such hierarchies, though, are likely to come undone when, from the pen of Diderot for example, an unexpected description arises of a painted canvas – in this case of a landscape painting – which, by fictionalizing a leap into the painting, then a promenade through the pictorial matter that passes from one point of view to the next, sets the gaze in movement. So much so that 'the overall point of view' and the stability of places it presupposes is subverted by surprise, since it gets ceaselessly displaced, and therefore 'dislocated', as Daniel Arasse has very well shown.[6] Such events of the gaze cannot be said to be inscribed in the initial proposition of classical perspective, but they are nevertheless rendered possible by it, indeed suggested, by the temptation inherent in the vanishing point(s) and the vanishing lines and what they can lead to by way of disruption to the the balance between fixed points. This is because the wandering of the gaze that disorders the painting, and that does so through the intervention of its spectator – which is untimely even when it lets itself be guided by the painting – opens a space of possibles and allows for an open multiplicity of interpretations. It is probably in this that the fecundity of a work resides, whether it be artistic or, to come back to Rancière, philosophical; which is to say that such a work can be transported infinitely beyond itself.

A cavalier perspective leads to nothing of the sort. At most, all one can do, by returning in a more precise fashion to the objects with which it presents us, that is, by exiting the perspective by which it governs our perception, is to question its accuracy.

Is there any interest in doing this or not? I am not entirely sure. Unless, that is, it is to mark a very real perplexity concerning Rancière's endeavour and method, the feeling of a sort of unresolved contradiction – but perhaps their value resides in this very tension – between his apparent political preoccupation with the democratic dissolution of hierarchies – to start with, the one instituted through the position of the Master – and a manner of constructing his intention that – for the objects treated as well as for the readers of/listeners to his works – is fairly crushing. In fact, regardless of what Rancière says about it – he maintains he has 'always sought to undo globalizing ways of thinking' – and notwithstanding his oft-repeated refusal to take a seat 'on the throne of explanation', it remains the case that many of his statements, to say nothing of his positions of enunciation, explicitly belie this declared concern (TP587). How, for example, are we to understand that he can write something like the following: 'You cannot understand people like Malevich, Mondrian or Schönberg if you do not bear in mind that their "pure" art is bound up with problems of synaesthesia, of constructing the individual or collective setting of life, of utopias of community, of new forms of spirituality, and so on' (TP348).[7] Differently put, you cannot understand anything here if you are, let's say the word, ignorant, if you do not have a broad *knowledge* at your disposal of what Rancière a little earlier in this interview calls 'the context'. We will return below to what seems to me to be the deadlock which this 'context' imposes on the perception of works – or indeed of every past or present reality that we come to encounter.

Perhaps, then, we can content ourselves with what Rancière invariably claims about his concern for equality and with his constant contesting of all positions of mastery – and very often I can but concur with the content of his analyses – without delving into the way in which he approaches all this. The trouble is that, on a certain number of points – and we will delve more specifically into his reading of Freudianism, as well as into some of his examples from the domain of aesthetics, since the two are connected in his own analyses – his developments are hedged, even warped, by the cavalier perspective according to which he constructs them for his readers. As a result, not only are the objects he treats considerably impoverished, but, more seriously, there is something like a concealment of those critical perspectives – in the most fertile sense of the term – by which his position on the question of equality might be queried, exemplarily signalled in the way that, it might be said, he adopts Mallarmé's reading of the dance of Loïe Fuller. The dancer, who Rancière reminds us is 'static' – and this point, to which he repeatedly returns, seems to me central to his remarks – the dancer, we may recall, is according to Mallarmé 'not a woman dancing', 'but a metaphor summing up one of the elementary aspects of our form: knife, goblet, flower, etc.', words that Rancière cites several times. She thus exists, in the 'aesthetic regime of art', as a series of equivalent graphical, and in some sense neutral, signs, which, inhabiting a pure surface freed of any perspectival mirage, on which therefore any point equals any other, are able to be indefinitely substituted for one another. Here, in 'the pure place of an ideality' (M12, 51), a representation of equality is signalled which for Rancière also articulates the essential nature of the 'type' by which industrial design – in this case Peter Behrens is the subject of analysis, an analysis that Rancière, like a Loïe Fuller of philosophy, unfolds before us in a virtuoso performance – democratically rejoins the Mallarmean symbolist poet (FI91–7). And in support of this we could also cite Lacan – in this an heir to Mallarmé – whose politics of the signifier, which we know can prove so pointedly double-edged [*à double fond*] – we must *and* we must not be duped by it, as he never tired of warning us – who states that 'a signifier is that which represents a signifier for another signifier'.

This representation of equality is one – in view of which, as Rancière sees it, a critique forms of the representational order and the inequality of places and 'parts' it engenders – that we might call formal, abstract, and above all static. It does not take into account either the tension between relations of force, or the critical stakes of the *very movement* of modification: namely that which plays out, in a perfectly uncertain and unassignable way, *in the transition* from one (supposedly) 'essential' form – one 'type' – to another. Now, taking this dynamic dimension into account would perhaps delineate another, yet to be realized, figure of an equality that is continually in tension and subject to rearrangement, one that struggles against that which aims to fix and assign for all time the forms of the true and the corresponding places it purports to pre-scribe. This would be a figure of instability that is ever renewed and that undoes the empire and influence of every prescriptively global view, just as it contemplates the diversity of figures that take shape – however refined and 'complete' – not so much as 'types', which, according to Rancière, 'plot the figure of the specific sensible community' (FI95 [TM]) thus unified, but in line with a logic of fragmentation. The potential of this logic would reside in the power of ellipsis to which it gives rise – ellipsis, the gap [*l'écart*] between two moments, between two forms, as a condition of unforeseeable flowering of interpretation – rather than in the indication, emerging through the punctuation of the fragment, that something 'essential' is to be seen, as Rancière suggests in par-ticular in his reading of Bressonian fragmentation (FI6).

Now, with such a fate reserved for fragments, the filmmaker is afforded a position of authority over the value of what is given to be seen. It might be more accurate, however, to consider that the elliptical character of the image – a simple 'sign-post',[8] to use Wittgenstein's expression – is here a way to leave space open for the free, but not erratic, circulation of the spectator's gaze. To leave it open, not just in any old way, of course, but so as to 'draw the contours of objects, which *also* means to draw the contours of the void *between* these objects', to quote Cézanne as Claude Simon does.[9] It is precisely this 'space between' [*espace entre*], clearly signified but not saturated, that it seems Rancière neglects to take into account, focusing as he does on this or that form, purified exemplification of a 'type' or 'essential' ideality, however fleeting. But might we not more fruitfully shift attention onto the promise borne by this 'space between' – which, moreover, is eminently egalitarian since it is up to each individual to imagine how to realize a version of it? This 'space between' is not only a *principle,* unifying as such, of the democratic space comprising the community of spectators or readers evoked by Rancière in *The Emancipated Spectator,* but is, perhaps paradoxically, the material and mobile *reality* of a void that leads us towards an open and non-homogeneous multiplicity of paths to plot.

All the more so as – to pause a moment longer on this question of fragmentation, which, according to Rancière, breaks, in Flaubert as well as in Proust or Bresson, with 'the representational regime of art', and connects with the Mallarmean wager that he deciphers as the advent of the 'aesthetic regime of art' – can it really be said that the fragment, whether in Bresson, Proust, Faulkner, Maguy Marin or others, has as its design and proper consistency 'the reduction to its essence' of an action or of any other figured element of the real, as a result purifying it of all other representations? Or rather is this regime of the fragment, which we could call 'pedagogical' – in the most traditional sense of the term: 'look closely, *like this, this* is what you must see' – not belied by an inverse perception, relating back to what Bresson names 'expression through compression'?[10] Compression into an image, into a fragment, into an impure multiplicity of other images, situations, figures. This is a type of compression, then, that is close, in its partly chance-ridden internal articulation, to the movement of condensation that Freud makes, together with displacement, into one of the processes by which dream images are formed, which are on no account purified of the jumble that mingles in them, are not 'symbols' or 'types', but instead multiply signifying knots, whose interpretation, indeterminate due to their very indefinite overdetermination, is never closed or certain. This is how I would rather tend to see things: to rely instead on the mere sensation afforded by the fragment in Bresson's work, since Rancière mentions him, and in that of others – sensation of which anyone at all is capable if he or she happens to be exposed to that fragment. But this obviously presupposes that you allow the impression that the fragment affords, the effect of contact with its specific density, to act without interposing between this sensation and our thought the famous 'context' so dear to Rancière. Now, this is indeed a *method*. It is an eminently Freudian one and is shared by many others, from the above-mentioned Diderot to Daniel Arasse or Michel Foucault, including many that I cannot mention here. It is a method that can be shared both by the anonymous reader/spectator/citizen who articulates his thought in a specific way, including even theoretical thought, should he happen upon a certain way of attending to the *very subject matter* of things and thoughts. It is in keeping with the decision to let oneself, we might say, be worked upon by the impact of a perception, an impact that is in part always *heterogeneous* to our knowledge and our prejudices, and is indeed likely to disrupt them. And in this we are all, notwithstanding differences of 'cultural capital', equal. Equal, that is, on the condition of creating within ourselves the necessary space of availability [*disponibilité*], a vacancy that requires no prior knowledge, simply because it appertains – but this democratic simplicity is sometimes difficult to defend – to a position freed from the trappings of the knower. This effort is impossible if one stands squarely on the mound, or *cavalier*, erected for the proper conception of theoretical fortifications; if the distance remains fixed it will be a source of disdain, the distance of the high vantage point and not that which proceeds from this incessant movement of adapting to objects, coupled with a movement of gaining distance from all that one regards as self-evident. As far as the above-mentioned sensation is concerned, more than any sort of certainty it brings the trouble of its enigma. It is with this enigma that the work begins. The work of anyone at all.

'Anything your reader can do for himself leave to him', Wittgenstein also remarked.[11] Rancière would probably not object. But the conditions under which a reader/spectator/citizen can 'do the work for himself', under which the 'community of storytellers' – evoked on several occasions by Rancière, referring

in his way to Walter Benjamin's text 'The Storyteller' – can exist
and under which equality, construed as 'the sharing of uncertainty', can take shape (to draw here on one of Freud's expressions
at the end of his study of Michelangelo's *Moses*, which we shall
return to shortly), demands, or so it seems to me, that access to
a certain experience of what in a work resists the knowledge, or
theory, claiming to account for it, not be barred by speculative
inflation. As Freud, who liked to cite this expression attributed to
Charcot, recalled: 'Theory is good; but it doesn't prevent things
from existing'.

Exactly, Freud.

Here is what Freud wrote at the end – I alluded to this above –
of his essay on Michelangelo's *Moses*, discussed by Rancière in *The
Aesthetic Unconscious*, disturbing at a stroke all the developments he
had set out in the main text: 'And finally we may be allowed to
point out, in all modesty, that the artist is no less responsible than
his interpreters for the obscurity which surrounds his work.'[12] Such
a movement is not rare in his writings, and is similarly attested
by the ending of his essay on Leonardo da Vinci, qualified by its
author as a 'psychoanalytical novel', but as well by many paragraph
endings, footnotes that fissure the discourse to which they refer,
or even the very frequent literary citations that, contrary to what
Rancière too hastily maintains from his cavalier perspective, do not
serve to support Freud's 'demonstrations' (AU2) – for the good
reason that the way of Freudian theory, as concerned with rationality and explanation as it is, is not *demonstration* but a specific kind
of *dynamic description* that proceeds essentially by images and com-
parisons, which are precisely always in part inadequate, as Freud
himself does not fail to underline calmly many times over and in
diverse ways. Take, as an example, his words on the occasion of
a strange piece of pedagogical oratory intended to explain psychic
'geography' to his listeners: 'let me give you an analogy', he
begins, adding that 'analogies, it is true, decide nothing, but they
can make one feel more at home'. Continuing on from this is an
argumentative development in the form of a geographico-political
comparison that becomes ever more uncertain as to the conclusions that can be drawn from it, and then this ending: 'Indeed,
the picture of the region that you brought with you may on the

whole fit the facts, but you will have to put up with deviations in the details'.[13] For a precise commentary on this page, allow me to refer to my book *La psychanalyse excentrée*.[14] Let me simply note that this clearly shows that Freud's foremost theoretical concern is not exactly demonstration and above all that his method, reflected in the very import of his remarks here, is not to propose an overall systematic view of the landscape he wants to think through or to have thought set out from some high vantage point, but, just like Diderot in the painting, to wend his way through a complexity that changes its face the more one ventures through it. The method, assuredly, is disappointing, and is directly grafted onto the system set to work by the analytic cure, in the course of which, ceaselessly and with no possibility of totalization, the psychic landscape that unfolds therein comes to be reconfigured.

So, there is no demonstration in Freud, but instead successive descriptions that superimpose themselves on one another without really cancelling each other out – in the way that the Freud who introduces the death drive and the second topography does not erase the first topography – increasing in complexity as so many perspectives on psychic reality that will never exhaust its proliferating complication. And in a certain way, but this is a subject for another article, Lacan would put all that into the cord of the Symbolic, along with a celebrated prosopopeia of the Truth for good measure. As a result, nor is there in Freud, as Rancière thinks, any strategy for interpreting art works, literary or otherwise, so as to establish the soundness of psychoanalysis's claims, whether its theoretical statements or its forms of interpretation. Instead, there are surprises and often games of interpretation, the imaginative character and limits of which Freud always marks. I signalled above the very frequent occurrence of literary citations in his work, as Rancière also remarks, and indeed very often of ones from Goethe, in particular from *Faust*. However, they do not at all serve as 'glories of the national literary tradition' (AU2 [TM]) designed to legitimate the intentions of Professor Freud, as Rancière writes, in a way that is scarcely attentive to the *movements*, despite their being bizarre enough to warrant a closer look, of Freud's writing; in a way that is scarcely attentive and, all in all, is fairly disagreeable, if not disdainful (the 'glories of the national literary tradition'), but above all in a way that, for want of simple modesty in interpretation, is stripped of the slightest perspicacity. For these sudden occurrences of literary fragments in the Freudian text rather intervene as zones of perturbation and discord within the theoretical movement underway. They are something like the 'umbilical cords' of theory, similar to those 'dream navels', or, writes Freud, to those 'tangles of dream-thoughts that cannot be unravelled',[15] veritable interpretative vanishing lines, and this goes especially for quotes from *Faust*.[16] As for Kafka – a point that Deleuze and Guattari recall – references to Goethe are to be taken not as academic references or as signs of allegiance to a 'Master', but instead as indications of the lure for the author of the drama of the pact with Mephisto, the figure par excellence of *détournement*.[17] The following sentence from Walter Benjamin could serve to describe the function of the often intempestive appearance of literary citations in Freud's writing: 'Quotations in my work are like wayside robbers who leap out armed and relieve the stroller of his conviction.'[18] As for the Oedipal story, Rancière deems its Freudian interpretation 'univocal' (AU59), as he does that of Jensen's *Gradiva,* which is probably the greatest error one can make regarding absolutely any Freudian interpretation whatsoever. He imagines here that Freudianism is inhabited by a sort of causalist dross of the representational regime, which itself enters into tension in Freud's work with what it supposedly owes to the regime of the 'aesthetic unconscious' – if it is true that a cavalier perspective such as the one Rancière seems to me to deploy can lend weight to this vision of things. Lacan apparently also bears this viewpoint out, insofar as he sees Oedipus as a 'quilting point' in the structure prescribing the sexual order and the good distribution of masculine and feminine positions. Yet, as soon as one delves even a little into the meandering of Freudian thought and, in particular, into the question, a considerably equivocal one in Freud, of the masculine and the feminine, to which the scarcely simple business of Oedipus is closely connected, all that starts to fissure and threatens collapse. All the more so as, by virtue of its strong rooting in Freud's *The Interpretation of Dreams,* the Oedpial narrative stands exposed, despite its centrality in Freudian theory, to the dissolution of its univocity of interpretation: 'the legend of Oedipus

sprang from some primeval dream-material,'[19] notes Freud, who
further adds a point that, though made in relation to *Hamlet,* would
equally apply to Sophocles' *Œdipus* and therefore to the use he
makes of it: 'But just as all neurotic symptoms, and, for that matter,
dreams, are capable of being "over-interpreted" and indeed need
to be, if they are to be fully understood, so all genuinely creative
writings are the product of more than a single motive and more
than a single impulse in the poet's mind, and are open to more than
a single interpretation.'[20]

As a result, to come back to the end of the essay on Michelangelo's
Moses, one understands better the scope of that concluding statement about the claimed sharing of uncertainty, which takes the
form of a vanishing line. For it bears within it the central wager
of a method articulated to a specific regime of interpretation,
around which Freudianism is constituted. But it is constituted in a
manner that is very different from what Rancière, this time with
the appearance of great certainty, has to say about it. This sharing
has as its counterpart a method that consists in being exposed to
the effects of the subject matter, similar to the way one is exposed
to words in the cure, words that, it must be remembered, are *a
priori* not learned, and to which a specific kind of listening worked
to graft Freudian theory – that is, a no less floating attention that
indeed undoes discursive hierarchies, so that by the disorder thus
created a psychic landscape that had been bogged down in whatever constituted it can recompose itself differently. In might be
said, then, that the theory is innately shaky. But from this shakiness
its potential does not cease to grow, a potential irreducible to the
arrangements in which Rancière wants, without our really being
able to discern why, to inscribe it at the cost of approximations
that are at the very least disappointing. Like the one that guides his
reading of the start of Michelango's *Moses,* where Freud presents
the requisite of his method in these terms: 'I may say at once that
I am no connoisseur in art, but simply a layman [. . .] Nevertheless
artworks do exercise a powerful effect on me, especially those of
literature and sculpture, less often of painting. This has occasioned
me, when I have been contemplating such things, to spend a long
time before them trying to apprehend them in my own way, i.e. to
explain to myself what their effect is due to. Wherever I cannot do

this, as for instance with music, I am almost incapable of obtaining any pleasure. Some rationalistic, or perhaps analytic, turn of mind in me rebels against being moved by a thing without knowing why I am thus affected and what it is that affects me.'[21] Following this is Freud's stated refusal to make 'the state of intellectual bewilderment' 'a necessary condition when a work of art is to achieve its greatest effects', or turn it into the support of any discourse (on his part at least) about a work. It is an avowal of a personal limitation faced with specific arts, in which Freud speaks of his own sensation of incapacity, which proves nothing about a work that can be strictly generalized, since some other person would have been able to make something of the musical affect, since it is a matter here of something that Freud, for his part, is unable to do. So much so that he will not get involved in discoursing or theorizing about something that he is incapable of examining directly. But Rancière, instead of taking this remark for what it is – an idiosyncratic inaptitude – attributes it to the primacy of the 'representational regime' infiltrating – discrediting? – Freudian theory as though it was fighting yesterday's battles. However, he does so by omitting to signal the above-cited description that precedes it and opens the essay, that is, Freud's detailing of his confrontation – patient, prolonged, direct – with the *subject matter*. This relation is not that of the learned scholar, or the specialist, but of the 'layperson'; which is to say, of any amateur at all, one both enriched by his own personal baggage – here the 'rationalist or perhaps analytic disposition' – and encumbered by it. It involves a 'long association', then, as Borges put it, speaking of the relationship to reading. That is, an association that cannot do without the support, uncertain, shifting, and unstable in its stratification, taken in the multiple sensations that the work produces. This is why the result is an ever renewed uncertainty of interpretation. And not what Rancière hurls down with authority, as he visibly has not bothered – this is a pity – to read Freud's short essay right to the end if he can write: 'Much more than a circumstantial self-portrait, this *Moses* reproduces a classic scene of the representational age: the triumph of the will and the conscience as embodied either in the tragic stage, in *opera seria*, or in the history paintings by some Roman hero who has regained mastery of himself as well as of the universe: Brutus or

Augustus, Scipion or Titus' (AU67 [TM]). From afar, perhaps, this is not wrong. But only from afar. From a cavalier perspective that is missing the question of uncertainty, and that, through an unforeseen turn, itself becomes (useless?) and uncertain. . . . Unwittingly. Just a word before continuing. Rancière touches on what Freud suggests, more or less in passing, concerning the sharing with the artist of the uncertainty that he supposes is also the active driver of the work's production. This is a vast subject that I shall not develop further here, but on this topic I gladly refer readers to Luigi Pareyson's remarkable and subtle analyses,[22] as he puts both artist and interpreter on a veritably *equal* footing relative to the process of the work, capitalizing on a view of the work's autonomy that can in no way be reduced to the auctorial closure in which Rancière, somewhat arbitrarily, confines all attempts to conceive that autonomy (TP611). It seems to me indispensable, however, to think through this matter of 'context' and to give it its proper place.

So, let's reprise, in order to finish, our line of questioning on the pertinence of the method 'via the context', as Rancière implements it, in blatant contradiction with everything he has also written on the irrelevance of that method in the historical field.[23] As far as the passage via the context is concerned, I am not targeting here an approach like the one Carlo Ginzburg takes up in his *The Enigma of Piero della Francesca*,[24] or even in *The Cheese and the Worms*,[25] in which the very finely detailed and very close study of context has an obverse aim and effect to those in evidence in Rancière. At issue in Ginzburg's work is to make clear how the context in question not only allows us to understand how this or that subject has taken shape – the strange metaphysical discourse of the Friulian miller Menocchio, or some composition by Piero della Francesca – but also and above all how it will have rendered possible a form or bit of speech that disturbs it, fissures it, a form that is also an unforeseeably fugitive figure and remains, precisely, irreducible to the 'context'. Hence the reason, moreover, why this figure can be so intriguing. In Rancière, when it comes to the things of art, everything proceeds entirely differently: not only does the 'context approach' – ultimately careless although unquestionably erudite, careless since, when all is said and done, it evades the cost of making that 'long (and free) association' with the subject matter of works – break down some doors – yes, Nijinsky composed in the same epoch as the symbolists, yes, Rudolf Laban conceived kinetography and composed choral dances in Germany in the 1920s and 1930s – not only is it eminently intimidating for anyone wishing to experience, while being far more ignorant than Rancière of, let's say, Nijinsky's *Faun*, or Rudolf Laban's invented system of writing for movement, but it is also, this time more annoyingly, led, by the effect of saturation and the certainties it conveys, to make statements on these objects that are quite simply erroneous – an effect of the cavalier perspective.

Apropos of Laban, to take this example because Rancière mentions him on several occasions,[26] this context-driven approach will entitle us only to the most hackneyed clichés about his character, since it dispenses with examining what precisely the invention of kinetography consisted in – the translation in some respects of Feuillet's project of *Chorégraphie*, and of the paradox formed by Louis XIV's commissioning of a writing system to permit all and sundry to 'learn all kinds of dances *without a teacher*'. And not one word does it give us on the subject matter, complex in other ways, of this work, which calls out for interpretation – at the cost of a real effort to experience it directly and not through hearsay. Another example: as for Nijinsky's *Faun*, the very learned discourse that Rancière sets forth on this ballet in a long interview for an educational DVD[27] – a stack of knowledge rather than the construction of a critical gaze – is not only, for want of an appreciation of choreography in its continuing strangeness, extremely impoverished despite its abundance of references to the artistic context of the era, but it misses the real force of the ballet, since the obsession with the Mallarmean paradigm leads to a misreading of the significance of its two-dimensional appearance [*aplat*]. This occurs twice: first when Rancière does not see the rather obvious fact, which should interest him, that the roles of the faun and the nymph (or nymphs) obey the *same logic* of writing – so much so that the division that assigns each a place becomes disturbed, and consequently severely challenged (here in the order of sexuation). Instead, Rancière is wont to maintain, as though without *looking at* how the ballet is made, that both faun and nymph(s) remain as it was intended they should, in keeping with the cliché that pre-interprets each of the figures. Second, when he reads the matter of two-dimensionality, fictionalized by Nijinsky through the Egyptian-style postures, as a production of that pure surface of signs that are equivalent yet not similar – again the 'aesthetic regime' of art – and at no moment as that which, according to a logic of the same order as that which Foucault sheds light on in his analysis of Manet's painting *A Bar at the Folies-Bergères*,[28] renders the place of the spectator definitively *unassignable*, dooming him, in his partnership with the work, to the uncertainty of interpretation, which gets re-formed in multiple ways.

Particularly when it comes to Nijinsky's ballet, but also, in another way, to Manet's paintings, this logic comes to be materially inscribed in the structures of the works from the moment they twist, as they do, the question of classical perspective. Diderot, in the *Salons*, as I mentioned above, Winckelmann in his reflections on description, and others, had all prepared the ground, though this effect could only have been stated retroactively. From then on – but this has perhaps also been one of the effects of Freudianism – we can come back to the attempt to think the work, any work at all, from the side of the reader/spectator, as he stands before it. We can return to that task when, in one way or another, some vanishing line, or some anxious irresolution, enable the reader to get at the work and to put himself to work in turn. Besides, Rancière does not fail to uphold, very clearly, this preoccupying activity on the part of the reader/spectator in experiencing art objects, although without really being able to relate this to the exercise of a gaze – his own – that gets disturbed, displaced, by the subject matter of the works. He sometimes manages this and then his remarks become convincing – on Mallarmé for example – until the moment that his reading is once again invaded, and interfered with, by the mass of his knowledge, and by his unshakeable theoretical aim, which – contrary to Freud's ever sinuous one, let us note in passing since Rancière assumes too much about Freud's intentions in claiming that he uses works to demonstrate his theory – never deviates from its initial trajectory.

If the cavalier perspective governs the method, it is indeed impossible to veer off course, if only by the smallest *clinamen*, to use Lucretius' beautiful image. It is a method whose success, but this is also its most serious limitation, lies in its intrinsically static character. In military terms its aim is to build or maintain fortified places: Vauban rather than Clausewitz. It is, indeed, a point of strategy, and much less one of tactics, as for instance with Foucault, with whom thought can be so very bellicose, but by ceaselessly modifying its lines and its trajectories and therefore its positions. And without losing sight of what is at stake, which is always clearly stated. With Rancière, there is no shifting whatsoever, but instead a homogenous series of impeccably deployed figures. The thought of Rancière invariably returns to Loïe Fuller as seen by Mallarmé, the model motionless ballerina sketched above. You will recall that Mallarmé wrote: 'the dancer is not a woman dancing' on the grounds that 'she is not a woman' and that 'she does not dance', since she reduces to the series of metaphors that she lays before our eyes. Rancière takes up this remark in full, it seems, and without any critical distance. But in seeing this or that dance of Pina Bausch, or the Indian dancer in Jean Renoir's *The River*, or the young girl in *Mafrouza*,[29] or indeed any dancer, female or male, at all, and even, why not, but in a different way from Rancière, a reinterpreted dance of Loïe Fuller, it could be said, on the contrary, that the dancer is probably all that (flower, sword, etc.), but that she is *also* – just as for Freud 'a cigar is *also* a cigar' – and beyond all mastery, *a woman who dances. Any woman* (or man, or child) *at all.* This is when *dance* occurs: dance as that volatile state in which 'all would be there, not in substance, not in notions, but in transitions (Is it a better way of knowing?)', as Henri Michaux writes.[30] Dance: in other words, the figuration and pleasure of thought in movement. In this way, the thinker, and even the philosopher, will be simply a person that thinks. This is also to say, a person who searches, wanders, goes back over his tracks, and ventures to imagine different ones.

So, how does one succeed in reading Rancière? Perhaps I have not managed to articulate a satisfying way of answering that question. Perhaps this is simply because I have been unable, within such an accomplished architecture, one in which we recognize such essential issues for us all, to find an area of uncertainty to share?

Translated by Steven Corcoran

III
Literature, Film, Art, Aesthetics

7

Why Julien Sorel Had to Be Killed

Joseph J. Tanke

In this chapter I make a series of critical observations regarding what I take to be some of the limitations of Rancière's conception of the aesthetic in *Aisthesis: Scènes du régime esthétique de l'art*. The book aims to be a 'counter-history of "artistic modernity"', one which enriches our experience of contemporary artistic production, even if the period in question is 1764 to 1941. *Aisthesis* reconstructs the terrain upon which the artistic and political avant-garde once met, allowing for a progressive, egalitarian, picture of aesthetics to emerge. I wish nevertheless to suggest that while *Aisthesis* offers a compelling account of the ways in which 'the people' come to occupy the spaces formerly reserved for kings and queens, the book does little to elucidate the aesthetic as a form of experience. It seems to me that an embodied account of the experiences occasioned by works of art should form part of any aesthetic project, no matter how nominalist in orientation. Perhaps the irony of Rancière's rightly celebrated engagement with actual works of art is that it leaves him with little to say about the nature of the aesthetic as such. Failing to grapple with the inner significance of the aesthetic means that the democratic appropriation of aesthetics can only be partial and perhaps open to surprising reversals.

In what follows, I reconstruct the methodology at work in

Aisthesis, paying particular attention to the notion of the 'scene'. This allows us to see how Rancière joins together different works of art in order to elaborate the aesthetic regime. It is by means of this narrative that Rancière recovers an older and more democratic picture of art. This populist aesthetics, I submit, effaces crucial aspects of the aesthetic experience, namely its minatory and intoxicating effects. Throughout, I contend that the aesthetic is a more ambiguous phenomenon than Rancière allows. It is an anarchical rupture that undoes the world of shared meanings. As such, it supports the democratic experience that Rancière claims for it. On the other hand, it threatens the sovereignty of the subject in such a way that it may be quite useless for political purposes. I attempt to illustrate this oscillation by considering Rancière's reading of Stendhal's *The Red and the Black*.

I

Throughout his work Rancière assigns 'aesthetics' a number of different significations. This chapter considers the sense given in *Aisthesis*, where Rancière describes it as 'the mode of experience according to which [. . .] we perceive very diverse things [. . .] as belonging in common to art' (A10, all translations are my own). *Aisthesis* tells how a new 'fabric of sensible experience' was created, one which gives art a new identity. It tracks the emergence of the regime of perception, sensation and interpretation known as the aesthetic regime. *Aisthesis* is not a theory of reception, but rather a genealogical presentation of the sensible fabric in which we recognize certain objects as art. The aesthetic regime supplies the means by which we assign meaning to our encounters with art. Rancière attempts to clarify this 'logic' by attending to some neglected works of art. He explains that each scene 'presents a singular event [*événement*] and explores [. . .] the interpretive network that gives it its signification' (A11). The most important aspect of this logic is its repudiation of the logic of the representational regime, one that linked artistic causes directly to spectatorial effects. The dispersive logic of the aesthetic regime allows for an unprecedented freedom to emerge in our encounters with art. The aesthetic logic also rejects the border that once separated art from life, thus placing art in an ambiguous relationship with the sphere of political appearances (A11).

In starting with objects, Rancière attempts to analyse a world that is shared. To accomplish this, *Aisthesis* focuses upon works that have proved capable of creating ripples in the network of critical and theoretical texts to which they are joined. These 'events' include theatrical performances, lectures, exhibitions, a historically significant publication, the release of a film, or a visit by an author or critic to a museum or studio (A11). Situating these events in terms of the networks to which they belong is an important methodological decision; it allows Rancière to reconstruct the emerging web of ideas that allows for these events to be recognized as art. Many of Rancière's readers will be familiar with the book's strategy: across its fourteen chapters, Rancière juxtaposes the frequently misunderstood 'paradigm' of art, the aesthetic regime, to notions of modernity and postmodernity (A12–13).

Aisthesis is the most comprehensive presentation of the aesthetic regime to date. It synthesizes much of the research that earlier publications described only schematically. It charts the genesis of the regime in fourteen key 'scenes'. The scene is unique to this work, although one could argue that a version of it guided Rancière's presentation of Schiller's 'Fifteenth Letter' and the writings of Gabriel Gauny. The scene is an important methodological refinement, one which allows for an account of the aesthetic regime that is simultaneously more comprehensive, genealogical and literary. Rancière acknowledges that the scene is derived from Erich Auerbach's *Mimesis*.[1] Like Auerbach, Rancière begins each chapter with a lengthy quotation from a primary source. The chapter then draws out the significance of the passage, first by means of a close reading and then by contextualizing its ideas. The joining together of these scenes provides a loose chronology of the aesthetic regime. In this respect, there is a critical difference between Auerbach and Rancière. Auerbach offers a trans-historical evolutionary account of realism in literature. For him, Western literature is conceived as culminating in the representation of social reality found in nineteenth-century French realism. Auerbach's central idea is that the New Testament, *as a form of writing,* supplied the means by which the stylistic forms of the classical authors was contested. He explains, 'It was the story of Christ, with its ruthless mixture of everyday reality and the highest and most sublime tragedy, which [. . .] conquered the classical rule of styles.'[2] Auerbach thus searches the history of Western letters for the entry of common people into spaces customarily reserved for elevated subjects, treating instances in which the elevated style of the ancients was temporarily thrown off as anticipations of the modern realist novel.

Absent from *Aisthesis* is the idea that the history of art culminates in a single form or style. This is in part because aesthetics dismantles the idea that there is a single form art must take. Rancière's guiding idea is that our concept of 'art' emerged not by means of a uniform developmental process, but was precipitated by a series of historical contingencies that prompted practical and discursive reorderings. The archaeological discoveries of the eighteenth century, the French revolution and the comings and goings of the Napoleonic armies created the context in which it became necessary to rethink art and its relationship to society. With the aesthetic regime, Rancière is not interested in establishing historical continuities; rather, he attempts to describe how different practices transformed the fabric in which we experience art. The priority accorded to the aesthetic regime stems from the fact that it established unprecedented connections with political experience, not that it belongs to a later stage in the development of art.

Rancière's refusal of teleology does not entail a rejection of narrative and we find that, as a counter-history, *Aisthesis* employs these different scenes to construct a narrative about the form of experience in which we now encounter art. Scenes combine different ideas and practices, allowing us to see the legacy of a particular idea of art put to different uses. Taken together, scenes frame aesthetic art like the events in a novel, suggesting affinities and connections, while rejecting the idea that one can impute a single historical cause to each event.

Scenes, Rancière explains, are 'microcosms' in which one can see intersections between specific works of art and the new axioms put in place by aesthetics. The scene is intended to capture the manner in which the aesthetic regime transfigures works of art that, only a few years earlier, had been thought according to different criteria. Its 'logic' consists of joining together disparate practices and discovering affinities amidst apparent differences. Aesthetics is a process of transmutation and the scene allows Rancière to crys-tallize the 'metamorphoses' carried out by the artists and authors of the aesthetic regime (A12). The scene, Rancière explains, is a 'little optical machine that shows us thought busy weaving the connections that unite [*à tisser les liens unissant*] perceptions, affects, names and ideas, in order to constitute the sensible community that these links weave and the intellectual community that renders that weaving thinkable' (A12).

One could liken scenes to images, provided one does not confuse the image with the icon. An icon is an image lifted from the web of relations that define its significance, erroneously pre-senting it as an instance of pure signification. The image, on the other hand, is a function which generates meaning through pro-cesses of connection and disconnection. The scene momentarily freezes that which is dynamic in order to shuttle readers between specific events in the history of art and the discursive-practical network that grants them significance. The scene insists upon this larger context for establishing the meaning of an aesthetic practice.

It is appropriate to describe Rancière's practice in *Aisthesis* as montage. These scenes follow the logic – the aesthetic logic of metamorphosis, association, connection and crystallization, not the representational logic of cause and effect – by which the new form of experience was defined. It is the drawing out of this logic that allows Rancière to narrate the aesthetic regime. It is neces-sary to remind ourselves, however, that while Rancière's story is extremely compelling, the historico-empirical nature of his inves-tigation means there are inevitably other ways to reconstruct the form of experience defined by aesthetics. In my estimation, this is one of the book's virtues. As readers, we sense that we are fol-lowing less an all-encompassing historical narrative than a specific problematic that illuminates a contemporary impasse, notably the failure to draw meaningful connections between art and politics. In *Aisthesis* there are a number of different avenues one can follow, paths that join with other scenes in order to form currents. It is one such current that is reconstructed below. This is done in order to highlight the connection *Aisthesis* establishes between aesthetic art and democratic politics. It also illustrates how the scene distributes its own sensible, defining what can and cannot be seen in works of art. If we are not attentive to the constitutive blindness of the scene, we run the risk of having our democratic hopes dashed by the re-emergence of some of the more disquieting aspects of aesthetic experience.

II

Space prohibits offering an exhuastive summary of *Aisthesis*. I will recapitulate what I take to be its major arc so that readers will understand the points I want to raise regarding the notion of the scene and the concern regarding Rancière's conception of the aesthetic. *Aisthesis* begins with an analysis of Winckelmann's account of the 'Belvedere Torso', treating Winckelmann's description of the Hercules as the seed from which aesthetics grows. Rancière explains that 'The history of the aesthetic regime of art could be thought as the metamorphoses of this mutilated and perfect statue [. . .] obligated [. . .] to proliferate into a multiplicity of new bodies' (A40). As Rancière explains, Winckelmann's main contribution consists of dissociating beauty from perfection and harmony. This is an uncoupling that, I will contend, is of great significance for understanding why any alliance between aesthetic and political experience will always be fraught. As Rancière reads it, Winckelmann's choice of objects is not accidental. By holding up a mutilated sculpture of Hercules as the masterpiece of Greek sculpture, Winckelmann advanced an idea of art incompatible with the representational order. Representation equated beauty with harmonious proportion and the expressiveness of form. Winckelmann undermined these ideas by identifying beauty with the a-conceptual force that 'speaks' through the stone. Challenging the idea that art is a direct and uncomplicated expression of thought, Winckelmann 'opens this age where artists endeavor to unleash the sensible forces [*les puissances sensibles*] hidden in inexpressivity, indifference, or immobility' (A28).

Aisthesis moves from Winckelmann's *The History of Ancient Art*

Among the Greeks (1764) to Hegel's *Lectures on Aesthetics* (1835). Rancière directs readers away from Hegel's well-known theses regarding the development of art to a less-celebrated reading of Murillo's *Beggar Boys Eating Grapes and Melon* (ca. 1650). He adroitly situates Hegel's account of the painting in the debates over the possibility of founding a *républicain* education on images produced under conditions of servitude. The problem faced by the Louvre's early curators was how to demonstrate that freedom could be found in works of religious mystification and images depicting noble lineages. Rancière speculates that Hegel rehabilitated genre painting in order to dissociate the lesson of art – the idea that the freedom of appearance achieved by art is part of the realization of Spirit – from its avowed subject matter (A53). 'The Little Gods of the Street' shows not only how the partitions that once prevented common people from becoming the subject of great art are breaking down, but also how the gaze fashioned by aesthetics circulates freely. The aesthetic regard is one anyone can deploy in order to elevate the ordinary. This same aesthetic regard idealizes the beggar boys, elevating them from street urchins to everyday gods.

From Germany we travel to New England where we are treated to a riveting reading of Emerson's 'The Poet'. With Emerson, Rancière is interested in how nature, considered as a system of signs in need of recovery, becomes joined with democracy. Emerson's poetics are an example of the breakdown of the representational idea according to which only the elevated could become the subject of art, with the spiritualization of nature serving to expand who and what can be incorporated into art's domain. Emerson explains that nature offers herself to its inhabitants as a picture-language, a fabric of significance that democratizes aesthetic contemplation.[3] Emerson:

> Who loves nature? Who does not? Is it only poets and men of leisure and cultivation, who live with her? No; but also hunters, farmers, grooms and butchers, though they express their affection in their choice of life and not in their choice of words.[4]

Already endowed with spiritual significance, nature brings together the community's inhabitants in a common poem. Even if it is the poet who reconstitutes the silent poem in which all participate, his art simply captures an already shared poem.

According to Rancière, Walt Whitman's 'A Song For Occupations' is an instantiation of Emerson's poetic ideal. He explains that 'The interminable display of objects and vulgar activities is the strict application of the spiritualist principle set out [*énoncé*] by Emerson: the symbolic usage of nature abolishes the distinctions between low and high, between the decent [*honnête*] and the vile' (A93). In expressing the spiritual substance of the new continent, 'A Song For Occupations' confirms the ruin of the representational distinction between high and low. Whitman enumerates all the activities that composed a human community in the second half of the nineteenth century – 'Leatherdressing, coachmaking, boilermaking, ropetwisting, distilling, limeburning, coopering, cottonpicking . . .' – in order to place them in a common fabric.[5] This sensible framework draws out the resemblances between these activities, allowing for the vital importance of each occupation to become manifest and therewith the equality of all labour.

The poet of the new world composes the ideal America by redeploying the idyll of German aesthetes, that of a society free from the division of labour. One can see in Whitman's 'Song' the echo of Schiller's idea that 'Everything in the aesthetic State, even the subservient tool, is a free citizen having equal rights with the noblest.'[6] With Emerson, poetry assumes the role of a civil religion, bestowing meaning and harmony upon the human community. Poetry, Rancière explains, is the activity of 'giving to a community the sense and the *jouissance* of its own spiritual and sensible richness' (A88). As Emerson attempts to make clear, the poet does not impose this 'sens' – this sense, meaning and direction – upon the community; rather, he discovers it in its practices, sheltering it in the written word. Here is how Whitman envisaged the relationship between poet and community:

> I bring what you much need, yet always have,
> I bring not money or amours or dress or eating . . . but I bring as good;
> And send no agent or medium . . . and offer no representative of value – but offer the value itself.[7]

As Whitman sees it, the poet demonstrates the dignity of every activity. 'A Song' attempts to correct faulty notions regarding the relative worth of occupations by creating a sensible framework wherein apparent differences resolve themselves. 'A Song' shrouds daily life in a web of significance and Whitman informs citizens that 'All doctrines, all politics and civilization exurge from you.'[8] This means that the poet does not create meaning; he reads it from the practices of democracy. This hermeneutic conception of creation will be familiar to readers of *Mute Speech* and *The Aesthetic Unconscious*. In the latter book Rancière described the aesthetic regime as giving rise to a new type of artist, one who 'travels through the labyrinths and crypts of the social world' to recover the 'hieroglyphs painted in the configuration of obscure or random things' (AU35).

This idea that the sensible word is an obscure yet meaningful system of signs is also central to Rancière's conception of cinema. In *Aisthesis*, Rancière's presentation of Emerson and Whitman anticipates his discussion of Dziga Vertov. Vertov's famed *Man With A Movie Camera* (1929) is, for Rancière, a particularly interesting example of the politics of aesthetic practices. The specific politics of Vertov's film resides in his montage, a practice which, according to Rancière, consists of 'seeing across things'. By means of montage, Vertov discovers equivalences in ostensibly different activities – the practice of medicine, work on the assembly line and even cosmetology (A270). When incorporated into Vertov's montage, oppositions are 'taken up in the universal dance which renders all activities equivalent' (A284). Rancière thus describes the film as 'cinematographic communism' (A284).

Rancière also sees the legacy of Emersonian and Whitmanian poetics in the collaborative work of James Agee and Walker Evans, *Let Us Now Praise Famous Men* (1941). *Let Us Now Praise* is a journalistic, literary and photographic account of the 'Dust Bowl' era in the American South. It follows three families as they eke out a living as tenant farmers. The book is known for its poetic handling of extreme poverty. As Agee summarized this tension, *Let Us Now Praise* was intended as 'an independent enquiry into certain normal predicaments of human divinity'.[9]

Rancière explains that in breaking with the realist poetics

then in vogue, Agee and Evans saw fit to revive the 'unanimist poetics' of Emerson and Whitman.[10] He describes their work as the attempt to render sensible 'the beauty present at the heart of poverty/misery [*la misère*] and the poverty/misery of not being able to perceive this beauty' (A296). This means that rather than attempting to arrive at an 'objective' account of poverty, Agee and Evans sought to allow the sharecroppers' milieu to communicate itself. The work thus gained its political effect from treating a subject already coded with intellectual and emotional responses in an unexpected way. This politics, claims Rancière, owes more to Proust and Flaubert than Karl Marx and yet is no less forceful (A299). *Let Us Now Praise* did not fit easily into a recognizable genre and, as one might suspect, its initial appearance was unheralded. Rancière attributes this to the changing tastes of the American left prior to the Second World War. Of interest is the special issue the *Partisan Review* devoted to 'The Situation in American Writing' in the summer of 1939.[11] The issue contained responses to questions about everything from the professional side of writing to the political responsibilities of writers on the eve of the entry of the United States into the war. One question asked about the relevance of past literary figures: 'Would you say [. . .] that Henry James's work is more relevant to the present and future of American writing than Walt Whitman's?'[12] Rancière sees in the document 'the desire of the Marxist avant-garde to break with this engaged Whitmanian culture' (A304). Indeed, the very next issue contained one of the essays that would define this break and with which the *Partisan Review* will forever be associated, Clement Greenberg's 'Avant-Garde and Kitsch' (1939).

Greenberg steps out of the shadows in the closing pages of *Aisthesis* to draw the curtain on the fabulous destiny of aesthetic art. Readers know that his writings contain the germ of a 'modernatism' that will dissociate the practices of art from the staging of the people.[13] This is Rancière's way of lamenting the decline of the Whitmanian agenda, one which pushed 'painters, photographers and writers to crisscross the poor quarters of the metropolises or country back roads in order to exalt the work of men, gather testimonies of *la misère sociale*, or to photograph the picturesque calendars which ornament peasant houses' (A304).[14] In Rancière's presentation, however, Greenberg is less the villain that he is for many today and more a symptom of the effacement of a populist aesthetics. The final paragraph sums up this dynamic:

> The time has passed for artists and writers to travel amidst the people and 'popular culture', for the art forms which wanted to transcribe the rhythms of industrial society, the exploits of labor and the struggles of the oppressed, for the new forms of urban experience and of its dissemination in all spheres of society. Clement Greenberg and the 'serious' Marxist intellectuals and artists around him want to turn the page on a certain America, the itinerant and engaged American art of the New Deal and, more profoundly, that of the cultural democracy *à la* Whitman. (A306–7)

This paragraph's force stems from its not unjustified melancholy, our sense of what might have been and our knowledge of how the history of art and criticism unfolds. We know that as art lovers we will endure a poverty of our own, the poverty of seeing everywhere only the purity of form and the doubling back of a medium upon itself. Henceforth, what Foucault once referred to as 'gloomy discourses', those that teach us to despise 'the image, the spectacle, resemblance and the false semblance', will reign.[15] The ambiguous form of experience we have been tracking since the beginning of *Aisthesis* will be replaced by an identity of art formed exclusively through art's history. And, with the advent of modernism, the meeting of artistic practice and political experience will be cancelled.

III

I have been recapitulating this trajectory for it well encapsulates Rancière's project vis-à-vis aesthetics. *Aisthesis* will likely be judged an important advance over books such as *Aesthetics and its Discontents*, where Rancière restricted himself to speaking about classical philosophical aesthetics – Kant, Schiller and Hegel – and its reception in twentieth-century French thought. The

counter-history of modernity contained in *Aisthesis* makes it possible for an earlier picture of the modernist project to re-emerge,
one in which art challenges life by changing the meaning of its
sensible configuration.

This joining together of the artistic and political avant-gardes
is sustained by a 'fabric of sensible of experience' whose history
Aisthesis recounts. I wish only to highlight the difficulties of this
union given that the form of experience Rancière appropriates for
the task never occurs in a pure state. The aesthetic contains both
the democratic sensibility Rancière points to *and* the more reactionary theories of sense found in writers such as Nietzsche.

The ambiguous nature of the aesthetic stems from its position within European philosophy. Its hallmark is its opposition to
everyday experience. This heterogeneity has been the source of
art's power, allowing for it to be construed as an ally in projects of
moral and political reform. It also means that any alliances between
art and politics are always provisional, subject to being continually
undone by an essentially ambiguous form of experience. The aesthetic is unruly. It contains elements that trouble the union of art
and politics from the outset.

As is well known, Kant separated the aesthetic from the cognitive and the moral domains of experience. In terms of the
definition of aesthetic experience, this cut was constitutive. Part
of what one tastes in these experiences is the violence by which
a portion of experience has been torn away from the rest of life.
In having been thus set free, it remains to be seen how such an
experience could be made to serve the moral, the cognitive, or
the political in a univocal fashion. The aesthetic thereby becomes
a deeply ambiguous phenomenon, one capable of sustaining the
progressive projects of aesthetic education as well as the thought
of the Dionysian.

Rancière has been particularly adept at elaborating the first half
of this experience. For him, the aesthetic relationship is indiscriminate, a mode of apprehension anyone can adopt in order to escape
the hierarchical structures of everyday life. What he neglects are
the solipsistic and antisocial aspects of aesthetic experience, the fact
that aesthetic pleasure stems from the ruin of our cognitive powers.

If we are to tally the aspects of aesthetics that are part of its constitutive *malaise*, certainly we must include the violence felt by the individual upon encountering works of art or scenes of nature. Aesthetic contemplation places upon the individual the demand that he experience the immediate from a position of remove – from the position of everyone and no one. This is the paradox Kant articulated when he taught us that the universality of the aesthetic judgment could only be purchased with disinterestedness. As Schopenhauer and Nietzsche were quick to make clear, this form of experience entails a dying-away of the empirical subject of everyday experience. Inasmuch as it is founded upon the paradoxical subjectivity of the 'none and all', one could thus view the overman as the direct product of the aesthetic age.

The aesthetic experience thereby vacillates between, on the one hand, the democratic sentiments inherent to certain shared experiences and an aesthetic intoxication which resembles madness. Kant relegated the disquieting aspects of this experience to the sublime where he outfitted it with a narrative about the human being's capacity for morality. In Schiller, however, the sublime bleeds back into the beautiful and later thinkers will have difficulty keeping beauty separate from the minatory dimensions of the sublime. By the time the aesthetic reaches figures like Baudelaire, Huysmans and Lautréamont the beautiful will swap properties with the demonic. The realism that in Hugo and Zola belonged to a moral picture of the world will assume decadent form, instructing readers in the beauty of vice.

The point here is not to raise against Rancière's counter-history of modernity a counter-Pantheon of writers who cut against the grain of his analysis. It is to try to explain how, at the level of its historical *a prioris*, aesthetics is capable of carrying these countervailing tendencies, the one in which the aesthetic is the harbinger of social emancipation and the other in which it is the celebration of amoral experience.

Rancière's notion of the scene compels the aesthetic to speak the language of democracy. The linking together of scenes grants momentary stability to that which is volatile. When viewed from the inside, however, aesthetic experience contains an admixture of palliative and intoxicating sentiments. It causes spectators to waver between judgments regarding the shareability of pleasure *and* leaves them ill disposed towards the human community. As we can read it from the canonical texts, the aesthetic oscillates between the reassuring and redemptive and the delirium of a sensible-intellectual coagulation too unruly to be deemed 'experience'. The scene prevents us from grappling with an amoral and a-cognitive 'experience' severed from life more generally. It may, therefore, undermine the deployment of aesthetics in the contestation of the distribution of the sensible, inasmuch as aesthetics propagates destructive sentiments.

IV

It can be argued that Rancière's prioritization of individual works of art prevents him from analysing the dynamics internal to the aesthetic experience. The place where Rancière comes closest to fulfilling this demand is in his presentation of Stendhal's *The Red and the Black*. One might even argue that it is by means of a reading of that work that Rancière seeks to correct the dominant ways in which aesthetic experience has been interpreted. The value of idleness, or, as *Aisthesis* expresses it, 'the pure happiness of feeling, the mere feeling of existence', seems to me to be Rancière's contribution to the arsenal of aesthetic sentiments (A66). For Rancière, aesthetics is about the simple joy of doing nothing, as well as the potential shareability of these sensations. It is a reminder of the pleasures to be found in meaningless experiences.

Of course the pleasure of doing nothing can only be experienced against the backdrop of a world composed of tasks demanding completion. In this respect, idleness cannot be equated with 'doing nothing'. Idleness, for Rancière, is a *deliberate* doing nothing, one felt in a suspension of the ends and means calculation that dominates many aspects of our lives. In an artistic or literary work, idleness manifests itself as a momentary break with the logic of cause and effect. It is the interruption of the direction [*sens*] supplied by the plot. As departures from the overall direction/sense imparted by the plot, these moments are a-signifying yet significant blocks of sense. They throw off the causal connections supplied by the arrangement of actions, allowing readers and viewers to grasp the pleasure of sensible experience. On this score, one could fruitfully compare Rancière's invocation of idleness in Stendhal with the analyses contained in *Film Fables*. The latter book explained how a large portion of cinematic pleasure is derived from the moments of idleness that disrupt the representational logic of the well-ordered plot. Doing nothing is, paradoxically, the action that allows us to achieve the happiness that exists before our senses.

According to Rancière, Stendhal's *The Red and the Black* contains such a reflection on the conflict between obligation and pleasure. Hypothetical imperatives structure the life of protagonist, Julien Sorel. Born the son of a woodcutter in the provincial town of Verrières, Julien rose from his humble origins to serve as a tutor in the house of M. de Rênal. There he courted a fateful affair with Madame de Rênal, the account of which forms some of the novel's most moving pages. Julien eventually leaves Verrières to assume the position of personal secretary to the Marquis de La Mole.

From the beginning of the tale almost until its end, Julien is described as weighing every word and gesture as though they formed part of a grand strategy, for if he is to increase his station, Julien must adopt the pleasure-sparse *askêsis* of a plebeian struggling against his facticity. Readers have access to Julien's deeds, but also to the inner workings of his heart. They know that Julien undertakes each of his perceived duties – his studies, the instruction of children, the seduction of a woman – with social advancement in mind. Much of the novel's force follows from the tension between Julien's public face and the resentments he harbors. From one scene to the next, one wonders whether Julien will be successful in sublimating his lust for recognition. For the most part, his better self prevails as Julien trades one post for another and eventually wins the heart of Mathilde de La Mole, daughter of the Marquis.

Just as things are falling into place for the young lovers, Madame de Rênal confesses to the affair, warning the Marquis that Julien is completely without scruples, willing to 'seduce the woman whose assets are the greatest'.[16] Without haste, Julien sets off for Verrières, purchases a pair of pistols and shoots Madame de Rênal, just as the Eucharist is being raised in the local church. The disclosure, the journey and the shots all take place within

the space of two pages. This action, completely devoid of all proportion, reverses Julien's rise, leading him to be condemned to
death.

Placed under the shadow of the guillotine, the book's final
scenes are of the most interest to Rancière. For the first time,
the young man who continually put off happiness learns to take
account of the simple pleasures of existence. In full recognition
of his fate, Julien is at peace; it is as if only after his will-to-power
has been denied outlet, that Julien is able to savour the moment.
For Rancière, it is important that we recognize that Julien's happiness occurs by means of a breakdown of the logic that establishes
the sense of every instant. Julien discovers the joy of sensation in
prison precisely because he no longer overlooks the present; there
is no longer any need to calculate and he is thus free to revel in the
pleasures of sensation.

With this very suggestive reading, Rancière claims that *The Red
and the Black* opposes two models according to which the plebeian
might succeed in breaking the shackles of class society. The first
would be for Julien to surpass his superiors in wealth and power.
The second is what we witness in the tender interludes that disrupt
Julien's striving: the playful suspension of the sensibilities associated with social position. Rancière explains: 'The moment when
Julien triumphs is the one in which he ceases to struggle, where
he simply shares [*partage*] [. . .] the pure equality of an emotion'
(A70–1). These moments of shared happiness break the destiny
of class, placing the characters upon an equal footing, in much
the way that Vertov's montage or Whitman's *Song* established the
universal value of all labour.

We see here, *in nuce*, two ideas central to Rancière's vision of
aesthetics. The first has animated his work from the beginning,
namely the idea that the aesthetic is a form of experience capable of
suspending the identities imposed upon bodies by the distribution
of the sensible. Both creation and contemplation are part of the
process by which individuals cast off their positions through the
assumption of new and expanded identities. Central to this experience, as the analysis of *The Red and the Black* indicates, is equality.
Julien escapes determination inasmuch as he, like Madame de
Rênal, is capable of being moved. These shared sentiments are

not only the source of the novel's strongest affects, but of Julien's triumph over the destiny of class.

The second aspect of this analysis that corresponds with Rancière's approach more generally was alluded to above where idleness was compared with the logic of the 'thwart' in *Film Fables*. Rancière refuses the idea that images are pure or immediately significant. They are shaped by a dynamic field of sense/meaning. This is more than the banal point that images – whether discursive or plastic – need to be contextualized; it is the reminder that as readers and spectators we never access scenes in their pure state. We experience them in terms of their differences from the forms that surround them, primarily as functions that redistribute sense. For example, the moments of idleness punctuating *The Red and the Black* are respite from Julien's incessant striving, not moments of happiness savoured directly. Readers weep at Julien learning to live only after they have followed his breathless ascent through the rungs of French society. Our enjoyment of these scenes stems from their heterogeneity vis-à-vis the larger narrative. Not only do the prison walls disrupt Julien's agency, they indicate to readers that the emotional register has changed as well. Time is drawn out and experience dramatized. Readers, like Julien, know that it is no longer possible to trade pleasure for status.

The much-vaunted affect is nothing in itself. It is created through the interplay of context, the events surrounding it and our expectations regarding what is likely to occur. One advantage of the approach employed by Rancière consists of giving up the supposed purity of the image in order to instead reconstitute the means by which certain aesthetic procedures assume their force. This means that despite his reluctance to engage in a first-person account of the aesthetic experience, one can nevertheless be gleaned from his writings, visceral records of the emotions created by certain procedures within specific works of art.

While these scenes behind the prison wall contain many of the values that Rancière would like to find in aesthetics, most notably the sense in which its experiences are equally shareable and thus capable of being opposed to the overriding distribution of capacities and roles, we also see in them the more harrowing aspects of the aesthetic described earlier. These moments of happiness are, quite literally, the other side of annihilation. The promised cessation of Julien's consciousness is that which focuses it on the present. His attainment of happiness is bound to extinction, in much the way that aesthetic happiness is purchased with the dissolution of the subject. In these scenes outstripping the narrative's logic, we experience the heterogeneity of the aesthetic in all its violence, that which has been forcefully withdrawn from the cognitive and the moral.

The danger inherent to aesthetic contemplation is something Stendhal seems to have been sensitive to. Like all finely tuned souls, he was overwrought, quite possibly due to an overconsumption of art. It is not a stretch to say, then, that Stendhal is also drawing for us a picture of the underside of the aesthetic age. What would happen if we were to approach all of life as though it were purposive but without a purpose? What might it mean to think and feel in a state of heightened sensory awareness, without tying those experiences together with the principle of sufficient reason?

In addition to having penned the memorable adage that 'Beauty is only a promise of happiness', Stendhal bequeaths to aesthetics one of the most forceful textual articulations of an adverse, pathological reaction to art. *Rome, Naples and Florence* recounts Stendhal's journey throughout the Italian peninsula in the years 1816–17. It includes a number of moving descriptions of architecture, literature, music, theatre and visual art, including the following account of Stendhal's visit to the Basilica di Santa Croce dated 22 January 1817. As we see, a number of the arts, as well as Stendhal's sensitivity to the historical significance of Florence, conspired to overwhelm him, thereby leading to one of the most unprecedented descriptions of the aesthetic experience. Stendhal writes that,

> There, seated upon the step of a faldstool, with my head thrown back to rest upon the desk, so that I might let my gaze dwell on the ceiling, I underwent, through the medium of Volterrano's *Sybils*, the profoundest experience of ecstasy that, as far as I am aware, I ever encountered through the painter's art. My soul, affected by the very notion of being in Florence, and by the proximity of those great men whose tombs

I had just beheld, was already in a state of trance. Absorbed in the contemplation of *sublime beauty*, I could perceive its very essence close at hand; I could, as it were, feel the stuff of it beneath my fingertips. I had attained to that supreme degree of sensibility where the *divine intimations* of art merge with the impassioned sensuality of emotion. As I emerged from the porch of *Santa Croce*, I was seized with a fierce palpitation of the heart (the same symptom which, in Berlin, is referred to as an *attack of nerves*); the well-spring of life was dried up within me, and I walked in constant fear of falling to the ground.[17]

'Stendhal Syndrome' is a psychosomatic illness characterized by a racing heart, dizziness and mild hallucinations. Such attacks are prompted by great quantity or qualities of art. In Stendhal's case, an overactive imagination also played a role. Just prior to the passage above, he recounts his thrill at arriving in the city of Dante, Michelangelo and Leonardo. The encounter with Volterrano's *Sybils* was nevertheless the trigger. It occasioned the most profound 'experience of ecstasy', precisely because it became, for Stendhal, a visceral experience, something felt beneath his fingertips.

What is remarkable about Stendhal's experience is that it well encapsulates the dynamic of modern artistic culture that I have been opposing to Rancière's presentation of the aesthetic regime. It suggests that aesthetic phenomena oscillate between the life-affirming and the life-inhibiting, between the redemptive and the minatory. It is a 'sublime beauty' that Stendhal contemplates, one that contains not only an admixture of pleasure and pain, but also varying degrees of self-presence. What Stendhal discovered in Florence is that aesthetic absorption borders on the experience of self-disintegration.[18] From the vantage point of everyday consciousness, the aesthetic will be experienced as an onslaught before it can be interpreted as a moral or political remedy. In it, we experience the liquidation of the empirical content of the self and the emergence of a blank subjectivity that belongs to everyone and no one. Ultimately, it is this harrowing loss of self upon which any ideas of emancipation are erected.

Conclusion

Julien Sorel had to be killed not because the time for social climbing had come to a close; in fact, that age was just dawning. The July Revolution dismissed the idea of hereditary sovereignty, creating the conditions in which the son of a woodcutter could mix freely, if not unproblematically, in Parisian society and in which workers might become poets, if only at night. Julien Sorel had to be killed because the aesthetic is a deeply ambiguous phenomenon, one which promises both happiness and destruction and, more problematically, makes the latter the condition of the former.

For millennia the West has attempted to establish an indissociable bond between the beautiful and the good. This was an effort to reassure itself in advance about the potential impact of its artistic practices upon the shape of consciousness and the rhythms of community. It was an effort to restrict the field of possible experience to prevent beautiful things from becoming overwhelming. Undoubtedly the period once known as modernity will one day be recognized as the place where this association was broken. A large portion of the blame should be placed at the door of philosophical aesthetics. It puts in place the ideas that allow for art to be thought and practised beyond good and evil. The beautiful no longer needs to be good and, as a result, it no longer promises only happiness. Any happiness we may glimpse in the aesthetic phenomenon is shot through with the experience of the immense gulf separating this contentment from the rest of the world and the recognition that, exactly as we are coming into possession of it, the pleasure is no longer our own.

8

Savouring the Surface:
Rancière Between Film and Literature

Tom Conley

Followers of Jacques Rancière are beginning to wonder if he writes at a pace faster than the rate at which they can assimilate. Appearing at what seems a logarithmic progression, his books and articles lead us to wonder not only how he does what he does but also if the writing belongs to a tradition of creative criticism, a mode in which the critic, a writer in his own right, melds with his cherished object of study. The mass and force of the recent work attests to a critic who is, as Paul Valéry once said of Victor Hugo, *un créateur par la forme*, a creator driven by the force of form, especially where his readings of cinema bear on those of literature and vice-versa.[1] His readers are compelled to study the architecture of the essays and, at the same time, to heed how, in sensuously open-ended dialogue, he moves towards as he draws away from his objects of study. The paragraphs that follow will seek to discern where the critical writing, blending itself with cinema and litera-ture, pulls the surface-effects of what it studies into its own form. Two recent works, *Les Écarts du cinéma* (2011) and *Aisthesis: Scènes du régime esthéthique de l'art* (also 2011), will serve as points of refer-ence.

First, *Les Écarts du cinéma*: a tricky task befalls whoever tackles a translation of the title. A nascent ideogram that is scattered throughout the work itself, the title becomes a sign of creative tension indicating that the book is a mosaic shaped from circumstance.[2] Pieces written over the last decade are placed in an imposing symmetry of triads in order to suggest that a latent *form of content* will offer a diagram of what the work is about.[3] *Écart*, a hidden or secret place in the tradition of French poetry of the Renaissance (e.g. Ronsard's *escart recelé* in his *Amours*), in contemporary usage can mean distance, space, gap, interval, divergence, discrepancy, disparity, deviation; also, a condition of remaining aloof or breaking away; and even, in a legal sense, misdemeanor. In the final paragraph of the prologue, Rancière offers a schema of 'three types of deviations [*trois types d'écarts*] between cinema and art, cinema and politics, cinema and theory' (EC8). The reader who no sooner looks at the table of contents is at odds about how each of the *écarts* relates to the others. Part 1, titled 'After Liberations', implies that film can both be in pursuit of literature and one of its consequences. Cinema, in strong likelihood in the postwar years that gave birth to the *Nouvelle Vague*, is sensed to be an effect of a liberation that could be aesthetic, belonging to the advent of Romanticism. Part 2, 'The Frontiers of Art', in which borderlines are at issue, suggests that an intimate gap exists between film and visual forms, except that the figure of demarcation is taken up only later, under the final rubric under Part 3, 'Politics of Films', where differences are addressed through what Rancière takes to be the resurgence of theory in recent work on the seventh art. The plan of the book hinges on frontiers of inclusion and exclusion, of direct address and obliquity and, above all, a craft of deviation. It can be said, in line with the geopolitical sense of a border and a *milieu*, that each of the sections is a mobile entity, an arena or a force-field that shifts according to relations established with what moves about and around it.[4]

If the reader is to believe the postscript locating the origins of the chapters (a sort of colophon, like the title, indicative of the form of content), the commanding figure of deviation dates to 2004, in a piece titled 'Les Écarts du cinéma' that had appeared in the journal *Trafic*. Set in place to draw a commanding line of enquiry through what follows, *écart* (as shape and as concept) antedates many of the contributions that range from 2001 to 2010. Rancière reprises a former reflection on cinephilia and film theory to chart an itinerary through studies of Hitchcock, Bresson, Minnelli, Rossellini (studies that reach back to the turn of the century) and a host of contemporary films by Godard, Pedro Costa and others of recent vintage. *Écart* remains a commanding term attending to a mode of organization of circumstantial writings, like characters in search of an author, that seek cohesion. The chapters are inquisitive, open-ended and of a style of enquiry and execution of their own signature. The term appears to be a variation on what he does with *division* and *distribution* in his studies of politics and aesthetics in the post-Revolutionary age.[5] A poetics of contradiction enables him to discern the nature of events which, understood in their strongest aesthetic and historical sense alike – converge and pull away from each other. *Écarts* becomes a 'signifier' or, better, a *milieu* or site of tension in the creative drift of reflection.[6]

And second, *Aisthesis*: in this compendious study he plots a stratigraphy of the aesthetic regime of art with fourteen successive 'scenes', each set upon the other, illustrating how the drama of the seven arts of the last three centuries has transpired from the age of Kant to Vertov and Eisenstein.[7] Each carries a date and a place and in their implied montage from '1. Divided Beauty: Dresden, 1764' (treating of Winckelmann, Rousseau and Schiller) all the way to '14. The Cruel Explosion of What is: Hale Country, 1936 – New York, 1941' (on James Agee, Walker Evans and American culture on the eve of World War Two) they present a riddled and fractured 'history' of the advent and effects of a new aesthetic regime in a work of criticism that remains 'at once finished and incomplete' (A14). Each episode, 'microcosm', or, better, monad, at once follows and stands in strong contrast to the surrounding scenes or events. The plan is modelled on Erich Auerbach's *Mimesis: The Representation of Reality in Western Literature* (first published 1946): a quotation from a novel, a detail from a memoir or other piece of evidence serves as epigraph and point of reference for both close and general analysis of a manifestation of a new aesthetic regime.[8] Unlike Auerbach, who moved from Homer and the Bible to Virginia Woolf, the ambition is circumscribed and the effect one of repetition and variation over a short stretch of time, not a cavalcade of historical shifts taking place over a millennium.

For Rancière the presence of Auerbach might be something of identification by deviation. *Aisthesis* is juxtaposed to *mimesis* so that each 'will acquire another meaning' (A11), each presenting 'a singular event' through study of the 'interpretive network' that gives meaning to the 'emblematic text' in epigraph. Each chapter is constructed to show how a given piece of art is revolutionary when it takes leave of the inherited forms and forces that shape it. Each deviation, because it is symptomatic of an aesthetic paradigm that departs from an order of representation makes clear how *aisthesis* works against *mimesis* in a continuous or 'interminable rupture with' a 'hierarchical model of the body, of history and of action' (A15). Such, too, is the fractured form of the book itself where, via a reading of Rilke, sensation can be commonly felt on the surfaces of things (notably, Rodin's sculpture). Here and there the impression is that Rancière's mode of approaching the emblematic material is cinematic: he reads as he sees and vice-versa and as a consequence, as it happens in *Mute Speech* and other works, extensive experience of film informs both the analyses and the style that conveys them. To see how, it suffices to return to *Les Écarts du cinéma* where he tells of his happy affliction of cinephilia at the time of his early work on political theory at the beginning of the 1960s.[9]

A common and contagious passion of the 1950s and 1960s marked his early affiliation with Parisian movie-houses.[10] Cinephilia was a *brouillage*, a stew of emotion that a generation of spectators distributed among each other in which *places* became confused, but whose order was mapped along a diagonal line drawn (*tracée*) to distinguish the pleasure that bad taste afforded viewers from a cult of high art (perhaps the world of André Malraux) inherited from the earlier years of the twentieth century. Cinephiles shared a gamut of emotions in the darkness of the movie house.[11] The words are telling:

> First of all, a mix of places [*un brouillage des lieux*]: a singular diagonal
> drawn between cinemathèques, which conserved the memory of an
> art, and movie theaters in far-flung *quartiers*, where a contemptible
> Hollywood film was being shown and where cinephiles nonetheless
> gathered to recognize their treasure in the intensity of a galloping

western, a bank holdup or a child's smile. Cinephilia tied the cult of art to the democracy of entertainment and emotions by challenging the criteria that allowed cinema to be admitted into high culture. (EC8)

These words suggest that in one way or another Rancière took part in Truffaut's rejection of the grandiose *cinéma de qualité* and perhaps found himself moving between the left bank, where the heroes (Hawks, Hitchcock, Lang and Welles) of *Cahiers du cinéma* prevailed and the Avenue Mac-Mahon on the right, where its panoply of *auteurs* (Lang, Losey, Preminger and Walsh) were shown in the original. That American hegemony was imposing 'bad taste' on European culture did not matter. Cinephilia was a passion because it could not put a name to its force of inspiration or its defining traits, even when its adherents called 'mise en scène' [staging] the standard of measure in the evaluation of the great directors. At stake was *passion*, 'which amounts to not knowing what we love or why we do' and which frayed the path to 'a certain wisdom' based on a sort of learned ignorance, allowing partisans to discern within industrial cinema 'an imperceptible difference in the manner of putting traditional stories and emotions into images' (EC8).[12] Unbeknown to themselves, cinephiles were performing (or acting out) the history of the shift to the new aesthetic regime that in the domain of literature and the finer arts Rancière would later study in the collapse of hierarchies that came after 1789, with the advent of *littérature* as such (a term Madame de Staël coined in 1802 to designate belles-lettres) and the impact of German Romantic theory. Cinephilia

called into question the categories of artistic modernism, not by deriding great art but by way of a return to a more intimate and more obscure knotting of the traits of art, the emotions of narrative and the splendour that the most ordinary spectacle could take upon an illuminated screen in the milieu of a dark room: a hand that raises a curtain or plays with a doorknob, a head leaning out of a window, a fire or headlights in the night, glasses that tinkle on the zinc of a bistro. It introduced a positive and no longer an ironical or disabused comprehension of the impurity of art. (EC9)

Cinephiles, casual deviants in the arenas of the museum that, as
Godard had shown in *Bande à part*, had become a major commodity in twentieth-century France, were not only dismantling
the aesthetic experience but also fashioning a practice – though
not yet a theory – of events. The event, as elsewhere Rancière
made clear in his work on the realistic effects in the nineteenth-
century novel, became what cinema availed to viewers with
unforeseen immediacy. The words of a story or a poem, like
the images on a screen, 'prehend' the reader or viewer who
equally 'prehends' them.[13] The cinephile's *écart* that withdraws
from sanctioned art and leads into the indiscriminate world of
the movie theatre stands at the crux of an aesthetics he finds
defining the aesthetic regime of literature. Built upon the force
of perception and fantasy, the affective experience drew adepts
of film in the early 1960s away from high, or official, political
positions based on class conflict and uneven economic development. *Events* experienced in the unlikely décor of the movie
house led to an unconscionable and ever-nagging contradiction felt in the complex pleasures that Hollywood cinema was
affording – and, paradoxically, where commodity fetishism
was being championed. Hollywood cinema pulled spectators
away from a productive awareness of alienation in the ambient
world.[14] What relationship could a student discovering Marxism
in the beginning of the 1960s discern between the battle against
social inequality and 'the hero [James Stewart] of *Winchester
73*, in obsessive pursuit of justice, seeking to kill his murder-
ous brother [Steve McNally] or, in *Colorado Territory*, the joined
hands of the outlaw Wes McQueen [Joel McCrea] and the wild
woman Colorado [Virginia Mayo] under the wall of rock where
the forces of law and order had cornered them and shot them
down? What relationship could be found with the struggle of the
new world of labour against the world of exploitation?' (EC9).
Rancière could not resolve or equate in any adequate fashion
the fact of historical materialism by way of these characters and
their fabulous situations. Admitting that he could only offer a
new version of the old Lukácsian argument that praised Balzac
for making clear social contradiction in his novels despite har-
bouring reactionary sentiments, Rancière notes, as if murmuring

Freud's words, *je sais bien, mais quand même*, that nonetheless visual pleasure cued a heightened awareness of alienation.

He avows that film theory intervened when politics could not be reconciled with cinema. If 'cinema does not *justly* exist in the form of a system of irreducible deviations [*écarts*] among things that bear the same name without being members of a same body' (EC11–12), he led himself to ask (à la Bazin), then *what is cinema?* Approaching a tradition of theory rooted in both the 1920s and in nineteenth-century philosophy, he evasively calls it 'a multitude of things' and, by inference, the site of possible *events* – ineffable surges of emotion that we retrieve and rewrite through memory. What he experienced in the 1960s happened to be a series of events: Rancière admits that to write on film is tantamount to embracing what, building on what was then *la politique des auteurs* – the policy and politics of the former cinephile – he now calls *la politique de l'amateur*. At this point in the essay the words accrue uncommon poetic velocity, particularly where he finds democratic urgency in the viewing experience. The amateur holds a position that is *both* theoretical and political,

> which rejects the authority of specialists by re-examining the manner by which the frontiers of their domains are drawn at the crossing of experience and knowledge. The politics of the amateur affirms that cinema belongs to all those who, in one way or another, have travelled inside a system of deviations [*système d'écarts*] that its name bears and that each and every person can be authorized to draw, between one point or another of this topography, a singular journey that adds to cinema as world and to its knowledge. (EC14)

The words are plotted to move between knowledge and the unknown: where shards of film attach to the everyday and often fleeting perceptions we have of the vagaries of life as we live it. The amateur becomes a traveller, a mental cartographer whose imagination and memory draw psycho-geographical maps that coordinate knowledge and the forces of attraction that shape events comprising intimate and common experience. The manner of the words is multiple, *traces* mirroring *écarts*, such that Rancière's line of an open itinerary deviates and splinters as it is drawn. A topography, taken in a strict geographical sense, is understood to be what concerns local areas *without* attention being paid to how or where they belong to a containing whole. Amateurs hardly need to conform to a worldview or claim any proprietary rights to the events that have crossed them. For Rancière an amateur's topography is also an assemblage of *topoi*, of commonplaces that the viewer refashions to create 'singular adventures of thought'. In the historical drift of Rancière's reflection the cinephile of the 1960s turns into the amateur of our time of reason, passion giving way to more discerned and egalitarian distributions of sensation.

In a turn of phrase of his own he asserts that printed literature of the nineteenth century was to replace its pre-Revolutionary antecedents with 'the impersonal deployment of signs written on things or the restitution of the speeds and intensities of the world' (EC17). Which is what cinema was to become: literature made it happen because 'sensitive intensities were inscribed in the double play [*double jeu*] of words that steal from sight the sensory wealth that they cause to shimmer in the mind' (EC18). Rancière does not acknowledge that cinema provides the perceptual condition of possibility of the remark, or that without cinema or cinephilia words heard and seen in their affective sheen would be improbable. What he calls a play of deviations (*jeu d'écarts*, almost a homonym of *jeu de cartes*, that would qualify Rancière to be a species of *écartographe*) entails a process by which cinema seeks to emancipate itself – *s'écarter* – from the narrative models at its origin and where it seeks to be detached from the model of entertainment [*divertissement*] without which it cannot embrace politics in any creative way.

The topography of deviation that Rancière establishes in the prologue recurs in the keystone essay on art and politics of Jean-Marie Straub/Daniele Huillet, Jean-Luc Godard, Pedro Costa and Tariq Teguia and Béla Tarr. At the outset he announces that there exists 'no politics of cinema', only 'tensions' between 'politics' as the topic (or *topos*) of a film and 'politics' as a strategy of artistic decisions that extend or compress the passage of time and space (EC111). Between the one and the other there remains 'une affaire de justice et une pratique de justesse' (EC111) [a matter of justice and a practice of justness]: justice is uncertain and justness a calculated risk. How can a post-Brechtian cinema be shaped in which aesthetics, far from being of dialectical facture, engage everyday events at a time when militant ideologies are inoperative? An answer lies in the art of 'suspending the promises of dialectics in order to reinvent its sensitive force in the gap [*écart*] between acquiescence to injustice [. . .] and the simple declaration of its refusal' (EC120). The filmmaker, assumed to be an inheritor of literature, must throw commonplaces topsy-turvy. He or she must craft them as units in which the intensity of what is seen and heard overrides their place in a composition. Films become topographies of unlikely places in which the contraries of dialectics are left floating or where they seep into what is seen, heard and felt. Politics turns into aesthetics where commonplaces become sites of communal experience of sensation.

Rancière's treatment of Tariq Teguia's *Inland* (2010, shown at Cannes in 2012) recoups and extends the geography of deviation of the prologue. In this feature two characters happen upon each other, one a black woman having escaped the bloodshed of terrorists and the other an Algerian topographer. The latter is hired to chart the path an electrical line will take to serve inhabitants in the south who have no idea of the political turmoil raging along the coast (ostensibly where the 'electricity' is generated). Politics becomes a 'confrontation of spaces' (EC132) owing to the relation of the two protagonists who wander about the inner country. The topographer appears 'to be the metaphor of a cinema devoted to the highly detailed enquiry that rediscovers, over and above the ideological wars that extend about it, the materiality of a territory of the visible: traces [. . .]' of recent bloodshed that remain suspended: blood of former combat seen in an abandoned trailer, destroyed objects of everyday life and detritus in the midst of which grazes a flock of sheep (EC132). The unsettling beauty of what the lens touches is deviated – *écartée* – when the path of their itinerary [*le tracé* (EC133)] meets groups of Black African migrants who are travelling northward, towards Spain, in search of employment. 'The politics of the film becomes identified with the movement by which one manner of crossing space and giving justice to those who inhabit it is intercepted and deviated by another' (EC133). Dialectics, if dialectics they are, become both

somatic and geographical and on the map their vanishing points
are the fault lines themselves. The dilemmas the film espouses
are geopolitical because they concern shifting borderlines drawn
among groups in conflict originating in struggle for power.[15] The
sensory experience of the landscape is opposed to the 'incertitude'
felt when it is wondered if 'signs of justice can be found on the
surface of visible things' (EC135).[16] Rancière calls the movement
oscillating between doubt and attraction a *sagesse de surface* [wisdom
of surface] where matters of justice are set in tension with the
'imperatives of justness' (EC136).

The optical experience of this film is described in the way
Rancière had discerned *events* in literature in the time of Rousseau,
Kant and Schiller. As he shows in *Aisthesis*, the new relation that
critics and artists have established with the seventh art sensitizes us
to what the nineteenth-century novel and prose-poem had been
connoting through the sight and silence of mute words.[17] The style
of analysis indicates how and why. In '4. Le Ciel du plebéien: Paris,
1830' [The Plebeian's Sky: Paris, 1830] a passage taken from the
final pages of *Le Rouge et le noir* (1830) is set in epigraph to show
how uncommon events mark the French canon extending from
Stendhal to Baudelaire, Maupassant and Zola.[18] In prison, in an
inner monologue while awaiting his execution, Julien Sorel avows
that he has come to peace with himself after having committed a
crime worthy of a *fait divers*. '"Il est singulier pourtant que je n'aie
connu l'art de jouir de la vie que depuis que j'en vois le terme si
près de moi"' (A61) [It is unique however that I come to know the
art of taking pleasure in life only now when I see its end so near to
me]. 'Miming' Auerbach, Rancière goes with and against the grain
of the conclusions to the German critic's study of the same novel
and its after-effects. In order, it appears, to bring cinema into the
context Rancière quotes Auerbach: 'Insofar as the serious realism of
modern times cannot represent men otherwise than as embedded
in a total reality, political, social and economic, which is constantly
evolving and social reality in constant evolution – as is the case
today in any novel or film – Stendhal is its founder.'[19] Julien's
pistol shot, the act that would be the logical result of the converg-
ing lines of narrative, is gratuitous. Its deviation from realism leads
the reader to heed the 'little events' (A66) that were held in the

hero's memory, such as the stuffing of mattresses, Madame de Rênal's dropping of a pair of scissors, or a moment when he and she first held hands. Great events that shape the design of the realist novel 'happen to be split' [*écartelés*] (A67) between two forms of logic: that of the aspiring hero taking revenge on those above him, in a recognized scenario of class conflict and another, in the savour of the surface of things, 'the pure happiness of a shared moment of sensation: a hand that gives itself to another in the sweetness of an evening under a linden tree' (A67). An effort to turn social positions topsy-turvy is countermanded by the 'suspension of the very stakes of these positions' (A67). As Rancière puts it in the conclusion, with and against Auerbach, 'the new novel is born *in the gap* between the two [*dans l'écart des deux*], it is born as the history of the gap that the great upheaval of social conditions and the infinitesimal disorder of plebeian reverie have placed at the center of the logics of action' (A77, emphasis added).

It would not be wrong to see these suspensive events in the novel being filtered through the experience of cinema of which Rancière writes (almost autobiographically) in *Les Écarts du cinéma* or more recently, in work on the films of Béla Tarr. Much as in his reading of Stendhal, or elsewhere in his appreciation of the *dandy* Emma in *Madame Bovary*, who always gazes upon the world before her as it was framed in a window in a Norman town, Tarr's typical character is a man at a window who looks at things coming towards him. And to look at them is to let himself be invaded by them, to be subtracted from the normal path 'that for the sake of action converts solicitation from the outside into impulsions'.[20] Nothing could be closer to the 'nexus of prehensions' that constitute the sensory register Rancière shares with the material he finds moving ineffably between cinema and literature.

A poetics of deviation, born of an experience of cinema, informs the mode of analysis. The writing melds with the material in such a way that the *sagesse de surface* Rancière finds in post-political cinemas is manifest in the play of words describing them. The very tension of politics and aesthetics is, as it were, *à même les mots*, on the sheen of Rancière's words themselves, both on the savoury surface of the discourse and in its force of meaning. Whether on cinema or literature, the writing engages movement that draws both towards and away from political and aesthetic intensities under analysis. Here projective conclusions can be essayed: one is that the passion of Rancière *cinéphile* gives way to the measured politics of the amateur. The return to the earlier condition in light of a more critical appreciation shows that in all events Rancière retains faith in levelling forces, common to cinema and literature alike, that move across inherited boundary lines and hierarchies. The second is that the savour he finds in the mix of literature and cinema is taken to be fragile, delicate and always subject to recuperation and commodification. In the final essay of *Écarts*, on Pedro Costa, the surface tension that the director brings forward in his tableaux is related to what he had known when Hollywood directors – Ford, Walsh, Tourneur, cogwheels in the machinery of capital – crafted uncommon films despite their modes of production. From them the cinephile had made something other, indeed a democracy of sensation. The Parisian cinephile looked at them otherwise, as a savour of surface, with shots 'of a mountainside, a horse or a rocking chair' (EC149) without insisting on any visual hierarchy whatsoever among people, landscapes, animals or objects. Even within the system and its apparatus unpredictable events were possible. Today, however, cinemas that are not formatted for the multiplex theatre, downloaded for viewing on miniature screens mounted on the seatbacks of Airbuses, 'streamed' onto iPods or caught on YouTube are relegated to temples of art and film festivals, white-walled mausoleums 'reserved for the exclusive joy of an elite' (EC149), a very different generation of cinephiles.[21] How to deviate from the multiplex and the citadel of high art in order to share the sensation of cinematic and literary forms remains a question that cannot be easily answered. No practical guide or *mode d'emploi* can be given; Rancière's reader begins by seeing where the words of his reflections on dilemmas of politics and aesthetics belong to what he calls a *sagesse de surface*.

9

The Politics of Art:
Aesthetic Contingency and the
Aesthetic Affect

Oliver Davis

I want to ask a philistine question: 'Why art?' Why this deviation, if deviation it is, via the byways and Biennales of the art world for the philosopher of radical equality and political subjectivation? For since the mid-1990s Rancière has focused, in his major published work, almost exclusively on art and the discourse of aesthetics. Even if he has continued to publish shorter interventionary pieces on politics and to speak about politics when invited to do so and even if there is an axiomatic sense in which he has always been concerned with aesthetics, it is nevertheless undeniable that there has been a marked shift in the focus of his attention after his last big book on politics, *Disagreement* [1995]. Did Rancière, as one nonplussed commentator has hastily concluded, simply fall into writing about art 'just because people asked him to'?[1] Even if his work on art and aesthetics was sociable in origin is that really the end, as well as the beginning, of the story? My concern here is not to account for this shift in the balance of Rancière's interests in intellectual-biographical terms. Rather, asking 'Why art?' will involve reviewing systematically the relationship between politics and aesthetics around which so much of his thought has turned. In so doing I shall attempt – not without some measure of interpretive strong-arming – to bend his ongoing work on art back onto the radical politics of *Disagreement* and the other earlier, more evidently political, writings as well to point to parallels and discontinuities with two of his most significant formative philosophical influences in his writing about art, namely Adorno and Lyotard.

My philistine question is born of a certain unease with Rancière's ongoing work on art; that is, with the trajectory and tenor of his project since *Disagreement* [1995]. In attempting to elaborate the politics of Rancière's engagement with art, the remainder of this essay will not only wield the usual and inevitable critical violence of selective and partial reading but will cut against the grain of his own writing. For Rancière's recent work has resisted giving a single, systematic, answer of its own to the familiar central question it repeatedly poses but only ever answers plurally: how is art political? A particular artwork will readily be said to have, or express, 'a politics', by which it will be meant that it implies a particular vision of how the world should be, that it proposes a particular redistribution of the sensible, a new *partage du sensible*, but no single account will be given of the way in which the existence of and encounter with artworks in the aesthetic regime can itself bring about that redistribution. Indeed, at times it seems as though art is construed as a book of sketches for other worlds, which can be taken up, or not, by some other area of human experience distinguished as 'politics': 'The political efficacy of artistic forms is for politics to construct according to its own scenarios' (EC21, my translation). I shall endeavour to show that Rancière's ongoing work in fact allows us to go further towards a single, unified, account of the politics of (aesthetic) art than this rather non-committal statement suggests.

The account of the politics of art in the aesthetic regime which, I shall argue, is implied in and dispersed through Rancière's recent work is centred on the interlocking concepts of 'aesthetic contingency' and its subjective imprint, namely what Rancière, in an echo of Deleuzian terminology, has called 'the aesthetic affect'. Both the enveloping discourse and the particular artworks of the aesthetic regime, regardless of the individual form, content and determinate meaning of those works, always also offer, I shall argue, a political education in the contingency of domination but not one which proceeds by way of explanations and concepts; rather, one which is *felt* in the artwork and the shared 'fabric' which gives that artwork its meaning. Artworks in the aesthetic regime inevitably impress upon the subject, whom I shall argue, contrary to Rancière's own stated position, notably in *The Emancipated Spectator*, is *not* free not to be affected in this way, an education in contingency which is always also political. This 'education' is, in effect, a process of cognitive adjustment in which the subject becomes disposed to recognize contingency in objects and institutions – in human artefacts which are not artworks in the ordinary sense.

This understanding of the politics of art in terms of aesthetic contingency and the aesthetic affect is advanced as a supplement to Rancière's own now popular shorthand, or 'shibboleth' (MEG180), as he recently called it, of *le partage du sensible*, the 'division' and 'distribution' of 'the sensible', the hinge-concept deployed to illustrate the interconnectedness of politics and aesthetics.[2] If that concept showed, with a remarkable but, by the same token, slightly suspect (structuralist) efficiency, how politics is first of all a matter of aesthetics, in the unusual (wide) sense of perception and the sensory, the notion of aesthetic contingency is intended to show how art and aesthetics (in the more usual (narrow) sense of 'discourse about art') are political, by which I mean political in both the ordinary (wide) sense and in Rancière's narrower sense of the term. The concept of aesthetic contingency better captures the general tenor of Rancière's thought in the years after *le partage du sensible* first entered circulation, in the years up to and including the publication of *Aisthesis* (2011), even if it also requires that certain, I shall claim peripheral, elements of his work on art be set aside.

According to the account of the relationship between politics and aesthetics illustrated in the hinge-concept of *le partage du sensible*, the 'division' and 'distribution' of 'the sensible', politics is first of all a question of whether those who are positioned beyond or beneath an existing sociopolitical order, those whom Rancière terms the *sans-part*, those who have no 'share' in that which is common, can be seen and heard as political subjects voicing meaningful grievances when they seek to contest that order of domination.[3] To be dominated, to be wronged by the order of domination, is first of all to be unable to articulate oneself in terms which are recognized as political and to be unseen or unrecognized as a legitimate political subject. The process of political subjectivation, as Rancière theorizes it in *Disagreement*, is the emergence of the *sans-part* through the declaration and the staging of their own equality. When successful this process is world-changing; it reconfigures the order of domination, redrawing the division and distribution of the sensible. As Rancière summarizes: 'The political is therefore first of all the debate over what is given sensibly, on what is seen, on the way what is seen is sayable and over who can see and say it.'[4] However, the aesthetic character of politics is only obvious *first of all*, in this moment of 'first politics', in the 'now' of egalitarian subjectivation; there is nothing obviously aesthetic (in either the wide or the narrow sense of the term) about politics understood in the usual (wide) sense. There was no subterfuge on Rancière's part: he was always careful to be clear that what *le partage du sensible* connects is not politics in the ordinary (wide) sense with aesthetics in the ordinary (narrow) sense of art and discourse about it but politics in his own very particular (narrow) sense with aesthetics in the more unusual (wide) sense of perception and the sensory. Yet that is not how he has always been understood and explained; far from it. Rather than attempting to reformulate *le partage du sensible* here I want to strike out in a different direction.[5] Re-describing Rancière's project in terms of aesthetic contingency and the aesthetic affect will involve looking again at what he says, or more often does not say and occasionally refuses outright to say, about the interiority of the subject, for it is that subject and its gaze which will be formed to recognize contingency by its frequentation of aesthetic art.

What is distinctive about art today (or art in the age of aesthetics, or art in the aesthetic regime of art) is that anything (any material or conceptual entity whatsoever: any object, person, place, process, vibration, idea, etc.) can, in principle, be art. Aesthetics thus delineates an open field of contingency: what counts as art in the aesthetic regime is contingent. Contingent on what? On the aggregation of individual acts of human meaning-making which collectively constitute the evolving critical-interpretive discourse that allows objects to be recognized, understood and explored as art. Artworks in the aesthetic regime are inseparably bound up with – contingent upon – the shared understanding expressed in the discourses of aesthetics and art history which confer meaning upon them and upon which they in turn – contingently – confer meaning. The relationship between artworks and the discourse of aesthetics is characterized by Rancière in terms of the textile metaphor of artworks being woven into and thereby reconfiguring a common 'fabric of sensible experience' (A10). The discourses of aesthetics and art history confer recognition on particular artworks, allowing them to be experienced as art, but artworks will also leave their own traces in that discourse and reshape it in particular ways and to differing degrees. No single individual, or school of thought, owns this discourse, or 'fabric'; not Greenberg, certainly not Rancière, not even Hegel.

Although *Aisthesis* unfolds chronologically and Rancière speaks, in the closing interview in this volume, in terms reminiscent of Husserl's phenomenology of the Lifeworld, of the successive layers of 'sedimentation' from which the aesthetic regime is formed, that regime also has its own peculiarly non-linear temporality. Thus an artist or critic can, by looking again at an earlier artwork, not only alter the shared understanding – the meaning – of that particular work but reconfigure the aesthetic regime in ways which are productive for the elaboration of future works and new ways of looking. Just as everyday objects – Duchamp's urinal, or 'Fountain' (1917), quintessentially – can be figured as art, so too can works of art from the representational regime be refigured, or as Rancière prefers to say 'defigured', drained of their figural meaning and thereby brought within the purview of the aesthetic regime of art (FI79–86). The peculiar non-linear temporality of the aesthetic regime means that both its discourse and its artworks are constitutively contingent.

It follows from this contingency that both the discourse of aesthetics and the artworks and ways of looking which it conditions and which in turn condition it are *collective*, or *common*, property. While of course artworks can be bought and sold on the art market and can be alternatively sequestered or exhibited, to say that they are collective property is to say that while one may be able to own the material object the artwork in the full sense of the term is a common object. What artworks mean and indeed what they are in the fullness of their being is not, in the aesthetic regime, a private matter. In this sense although artworks in the aesthetic regime may appear to be produced and experienced in isolated individual acts of appreciation, in fact the experience of art as art is no less a collective matter than it was in earlier ages.[6]

Artworks are 'common objects' and, Rancière will come close to saying, the only legitimate educators. All artworks thus resemble *Télémaque*, the book which Jacotot used to guarantee that the encounter between student and teacher occurred under conditions of equality. The meaning of artworks in the aesthetic regime is contingent: they remain constitutively open for interpretive reconfiguration by anyone and everyone. The peculiarly open-ended and non-linear temporality of art in the aesthetic regime implies that the meaning and indeed the being of an artwork *as art* is always contingent, metastable, temporary pending future re-evaluation; it can never be set in stone and no individual's, school's, movement's or community's view of it can ever be definitive or sovereign. While there may well be self-appointed experts and institutionally recognized authorities on particular kinds of aesthetic art, people whose voices will, at any given time, be more influential, it follows from the contingency of the aesthetic regime that their authority can only ever be provisional. Not even a 'strong' critic (Greenberg, for instance, with his theorization of artistic modernism as each art-form turning inward to develop the resources of its medium) can expect to prevail enduringly in the constitutively disputatious provisionality of the aesthetic regime. Thus, challenging Greenberg, Rancière will write: 'The "internal necessity" of the abstract canvas is itself only constructed in the device whereby words work the painted surface so as to construct a different plane of intelligibility for it' (FI87). However, it does not follow from the fact that aesthetic art is contingent that artworks can always simply be conjured into existence by isolated acts of individual volition; *sometimes* they can and indeed this is what happens when an artist makes work, or a 'strong' critic redefines a work of the past and fashions a new way of looking, although in neither case is mere volition or individual effort sufficient.

To say that the aesthetic regime of art, as Rancière theorizes it, is contingently the collective product of numerous acts of individual 'making' (including critics' acts of meaning-making) is to say more than merely that aesthetic art is intersubjective. The artworks of the representational and ethical regimes, Rancière's other two regimes of art, are also intersubjective and indeed far more rigorously and tightly so. Indeed, the 'ethical' function of art, seen here in Rancière's recent analysis of Ruskin's conception of decorative art, is to express 'a shared way of inhabiting a world, so to educate individuals according to a common culture' (A178, my translation). In the representational regime, the primary sociopolitical function of the principle of mimesis is to distinguish between the 'fine arts' and other forms of making: the 'mechanical arts', artisanal labour, shoemaking . . . (AD5–8). In the representational regime there is very little room for artists and critics to manoeuvre with respect to the pre-existing intersubjective consensus over the kinds of artefacts which can be appreciated as artworks. This is very different in the aesthetic regime, Rancière insists, even if a certain conception of modernism, which he seeks to undermine, will pretend otherwise. The political point of Rancière's 'counter-history' of artistic modernism – of *Aisthesis*, in other words – as Joseph J. Tanke argues in this volume and Rancière confirms in his closing interview, is to salvage a democratic, Whitmanian, understanding of aesthetic art from a purist conception such as that advanced by Greenberg and his entourage of Marxist artists and intellectuals. That purist conception sought, Rancière claims, to 'render impermeable the boundary separating serious art, concerned with its own materials and procedures, from the ways ordinary people [*le peuple*] entertained themselves and decorated their homes' (A306). In other words it sought to re-establish the kind of social and aesthetic ordering, or partitioning, which the principle of mimesis had performed in the representational regime. By contrast, in Rancière's anti-purist theorization of the aesthetic regime what counts as art is always contingent on an ongoing and open-ended process of intersubjective renegotiation.

The interrelated contingencies of the artwork in the aesthetic regime impress themselves upon the spectator and provide him or her with what I have been calling an 'education' in the contingency of domination. They do so by way of 'the aesthetic affect'.[7] Artworks in the aesthetic regime are directly political insofar as whatever else they may enable us to think and feel they always also convey an experience of their own contingency as art and this experience is, in turn, formative of a subjective disposition and *way of looking*. The aesthetic affect

> is tied to what we might call the impropriety of art. What touches us in contemporary art is always, as far as I am concerned, of the same order, this same straddling of the border between what is art and what is not art. And I would say that the political effect of art is tied to this indetermination as well.[8]

The aesthetic affect, which is the subjective imprint of aesthetic contingency, is an unavoidable because constitutive part of the experience of any and every particular work of art in the aesthetic regime. In fact – and here I deviate from Rancière – this affect will only occasionally enter reflective consciousness, for example in works which meditate on what Arthur Danto called 'the transformation of the commonplace' into art.[9] Or in tabloid headlines at Turner Prize time, in which the aesthetic affect will be explicitly apprehended but connoted negatively in the mock anguish of the exclamation: 'Yes, but is it art?' I would argue, however, that the aesthetic affect more often operates just below the threshold of awareness, subliminally or unconsciously and that it is by way of this direct and repeated encounter with aesthetic contingency that the spectator is not only 'emancipated' in the modest sense of being freed to interpret the artwork in question but, by the same token, is emancipated by the experience of aesthetic art, formed for 'emancipation' in the properly political sense, by being disposed to recognize contingency in other human artefacts that are not artworks in the strict sense. According to this account, there is only one sense in which the spectator is not 'emancipated': s/he is not free to not experience the aesthetic affect. In cognitive terms there are two dimensions to the experience of artworks: seeing something as art – in the aesthetic regime – always means, at some level of awareness, *feeling* its contingency as art in addition to discerning its determinate content.

In addition to whatever they say by virtue of their determinate content, all artworks in the aesthetic regime also say: 'Things could be otherwise.'[10] Above and beyond, or alongside and below, the specific and narrowly aesthetic training which exposure to artworks provides, they also form the spectator in a more generalized and properly political lesson by conditioning him or her to view other artefacts, including the order of domination – its institutions, hierarchies, personalities and practices – as though they were contingent and open to collective renegotiation in the same way that the aesthetic regime and its artworks are open. Thus art in the aesthetic regime, by way of the aesthetic affect, is formative of emancipatory political consciousness and emancipatory political looking and feeling; it is in that sense that it is political. Aesthetic art is an education in contingency; an education, rather than brainwashing, for the order of domination is, in reality, contingent.[11]

I acknowledged that this reconstruction would require some elements of Rancière's thought to be set aside. Foremost among them is the bar on the interiority of the subject and here I am echoing concerns raised by Jackie Clarke and Carolyn Steedman in this volume and reiterating earlier objections of my own. In a 2010 interview Rancière said: 'I am not interested in what people have in their mind; I am interested in what people have in front of their eyes and what they put in front of them, on the page, on the screen or canvas, etc.'[12] In its immediate context this was a fairly orthodox statement of caution with respect to artists' intentions: the meaning of the work of art is independent of the intentions of its originator; the 'emancipation' of the spectator, or reader, depends on the 'death' of the author. Yet Rancière's statement is also an accurate reflection of the rigorous turning away from the interiority of his subjects after *Proletarian Nights*. In the closing interview in this volume he suggests that his lack of interest in interiority can be attributed to the formative influence of Sartre's early essay, *The Transcendence of the Ego* [1936].[13] However, rather than placing a bar on interiority of the kind apparent in Rancière's work after *Proletarian Nights*, Sartre's essay in fact argued that the self, or ego, is directly knowable by others in the same way as it is by the subject; the ego is public, rather than private, property. The account which I have put forward here of the politics of art demands that Rancière's bar on the interiority of the subject be lifted since it requires a subject capable of being formed in the recognition of contingency. I am also proposing that the freedom of the spectator to recreate the work, emphasized by Rancière, not normally be thought to extend to not experiencing the aesthetic affect. In my view these are minor, justifiable and indeed irresistible revisions although I shall not argue this point further here.

This understanding of the aesthetic affect as a constitutive but not always consciously felt or expicitly thematized part of the experience of art draws on an essay of Lyotard's, 'Anima Minima', which Rancière has himself discussed.[14] In that essay Lyotard suggests that the experience of art evokes in the subject a memory of its dependence on the surrounding environment:

> The *anima* exists only as affected. Sensation, whether likeable or detestable, also announces to the *anima* that it would not even be, that it would remain inanimate, had nothing affected it. This soul is but the awakening of an affectability, and this remains disaffected in the absence of a timbre, a color, a fragrance, in the absence of the sensible event that excites it. [. . .] Existing is to be awoken from the nothingness of disaffection by something sensible over there.[15]

The 'anima minima' of Lyotard's title is an affect, '*that* affect born of *this* sensible apparition, blow by blow [*coup par coup*]'.[16] Rancière has argued that Lyotard reduces the experience of art to 'that of the enslaved human mind, the mind enslaved to the sensory' (AD104) and at the same time 'to the law of alterity' (AD94). Politics disappears from Lyotard's account of art, which becomes 'the indefinite re-inscription, in written lines, painted brushstrokes or musical timbres, of subjugation to the law of the Other' (AD105). While what Rancière objects to most obviously in Lyotard's approach is its suppression of politics in favour of 'aesthetic' and indeed ethical 'metapolitics' (AD105) – its 'ethical turn' – Rancière's other concern, which is less clearly spelled out, is with the way in which Lyotard's account makes out that all artworks are saying essentially the same thing. As Lyotard will say in the preceding essay, on writer Pascal Quignard, 'the transcendence [. . .] of the work of art is found right there in the evocation of this precariousness forever enveloped in sensation'.[17] I want to suggest, however, that Lyotard's account can and should be read non-reductively, such that he be understood to be saying that artworks *both* articulate their specific determinate content *and* testify, by way of an 'affect', to something else. For Lyotard, as Rancière notes, this is a primordial ontic and ethical vulnerability. Yet the content or meaning of this affect, the second component, or layer, of aesthetic experience, need not be as Lyotard suggests; rather, according to Rancière's theorization of the aesthetic regime of art this affect will be a formative experience of contingency. In this hybrid of Rancière's and Lyotard's aesthetics what the work of art in the aesthetic regime always conveys, in addition to its determinate content, is a political education in the contingency of domination. Rather than a backward-looking reminder of a universal 'primitive scene' (AD99) of dependence and ethical exposure, the aesthetic affect forms the subject's gaze, indeed forms the subject, to recognize the contingency of all artefacts.

The aesthetic affect, as I have described it, can also be likened to what Adorno terms the 'tremor' [*Erschütterung*], in which the subject, or the ego, is affected by being 'shaken up' and thus reminded of its limitation and finitude.[18] Except that here again the aesthetic affect would be a reminder not only of the limitation and finitude of the self but more particularly of the contingency of the order of domination. In the account of the politics of art which I am extrapolating from Rancière's ongoing work, the tremor of the subject in the encounter with aesthetic art is not merely a subjective psychic affection or affliction (the 'Stendhal Syndrome' discussed by Tanke in this volume) but also conveys cognitive insight into the objective world. If the subject quakes then so too does the order of domination; the experience of aesthetic art points to the contingency of that very order.

What artworks provide is not only an education in contingency by concepts but also by sensuous particularity: artworks in the aesthetic regime convey not only the thought but also the feel of contingency. The 'feel' of equality, or its 'savour', to borrow the term Tom Conley uses in this volume. Equality, because to encounter artworks in the aesthetic regime is to encounter objects which are, by definition and in the sense I have outlined above, *shared* objects which can only be perceived as artworks if one has already adopted the egalitarian presumption inherent in the aesthetic regime, the aesthetic 'disinterest' which Kant theorized in the aftermath of the French Revolution but which also characterized the 'spontaneous' aesthetic appreciation of Rancière's joiner of predilection, Gauny. In Rancière's account, as I have reconstructed it, works of art in the aesthetic regime and that very regime itself are threads of equality woven through a world of domination. Following those threads – whether by encountering artworks in their sensuous particularity or by thinking about the regime in which they inhere and which is elaborated from them – is formative of a disposition, a consciousness or mode of attending, a way of looking and feeling, which cannot then be confined to art objects.

It is in this idea of the feel of contingency that the common purpose of Rancière's work on art and his work on politics is perhaps most apparent, as will be clear from the following two quotations from a remarkable book of new interviews, *La Méthode de l'égalité* (2012). The first is marked by a certain textural opacity, even as it tries to draw clearly the contours of the Rancierian dialectic:

> For me there are really two kinds of work, two kinds of intervention: there are those works which seek to constitute something like a sensible fabric of the possibility of a different world [*qui cherchent à constituer comme un tissu sensible de la possibilité d'un monde autre*] and those interventions which try to re-describe a situation. When it comes down to it there are two sides to this, my work. There is the attempt to smash the commonly held notions [*casser . . . les notions communes*] that more often than not are shared by those who seek to uphold an order and those who believe they are contesting it – whether by the conceptual analysis that is supposed to be theory or by taking aim at and marking off the watchwords of the police order. But these interventions rest on a certain foundation, that of the work which constructs the sensible fabric that enables us to think that those people who speak of emancipation are reasonable and are proposing things which are desirable. (MEG 271–2, my translation)

The second describes a model of intellectual practice strikingly close to the Situationists' practice of the *dérive*:

There is a sensible texture [*une texture sensible*] of experience which we have to rediscover and which can only be rediscovered by entirely eliminating hierarchies of knowledge, of politics, of the social, of the intellectual and of the popular. I would say that these are things which can be felt by wandering somewhat at random [*en traînant un petit peu au hasard*], by reviewing masses of papers, by consulting almanacks and small brochures by mad inventors and from silly little vaudeville theatres. (MEG 63, my translation)

In these two quotations it is the 'fabric' or 'texture' of 'sensible experience' which interests me. For the attempt to describe the 'fabric' or 'texture' of 'sensible experience' proper to the aesthetic regime of art is quite explicitly the mission of *Aisthesis*; Rancière states in the 'Prelude' to that work that his object of study is not the reception of works of art but, rather, 'the fabric of sensible experience in the midst of which they are produced' (A10). What is clear from the first of my quotations, if not always quite so clear from *Aisthesis* itself, is that this work of recovering the sensible fabric of experience is a political task, one which involves *constituting* or *constructing* the possibility of another world. Moreover, this is not merely a historical matter, even if *Aisthesis* stops in 1941, for as the second quotation intimates, politics in the present must also proceed by way of this rediscovery of the sensible texture of experience.

I characterized the account of the politics of art extrapolated here from Rancière's ongoing work as a response to the 'philistine' question 'Why art?' and I indicated that Rancière has generally been careful to avoid the kind of frontal approach to the question of the politics of art which I have attempted here. The word 'philistine' has a curious history in English, having entered the language from German, probably thanks to Thomas Carlyle, before becoming central to Matthew Arnold's defence of high culture against the anti-intellectual bourgeois materialism of the Victorian era.[19] The German *Philister* seems to have originated in town-on-gown violence in Jena in 1689, in the aftermath of which a university preacher admonished the students with a sermon taken from the story of Samson and the 'Philistines' in the *Book of Judges* and was used to mean something like the (British) English 'townie', someone lacking a university education in the liberal arts. In other words while it may be 'philistine' to ask why Rancière has turned to art and 'philistine' to want to wrest from the rich diversity of his writing on art the kind of synthetic account of its politics presented here, the very term 'philistine' is itself born of just the kind of *partage du sensible* which Rancière's work has so clearly brought into focus. While I am not suggesting that Rancière's avoidance of a frontal assault on the question of the politics of art is motivated by a wish not to appear 'philistine', I am indicating that I am aware that my approach to his ongoing work in this chapter has simplified, selected and extrapolated in ways which inevitably do not reproduce all the nuances of that work.

10

Rancière and Deleuze:
Entanglements of Film Theory

Bill Marshall

The publication in 2001 (and English translation in 2006) of *Film Fables* placed Rancière on lists of essential reading for scholars interested in the relationship between cinema and thought and the implications of this interplay for wider cultural and political analysis. Prolonging his writings on cinema published in the journals *Cahiers du cinéma* and *Trafic* in the 1990s and drawing on personal history in the form of a very Parisian cinephilia, Rancière's contribution to film theory or the more recently conceptualized film-philosophy (in which film is not only seen to illustrate concepts but actively embodies and articulates them)[1] is tricky to locate within the debates that have marked the field over the past three to four decades, partly because its wider relevance has to be made apparent by reference to his more general writings on aesthetics and politics. Following a brief exposition of the central claims of *Film Fables*, the pages that follow seek to explore the political resonances of Rancière's cinematic writings through a close analysis of their fundamental argument and also their affinities with those of Gilles Deleuze and thus to demonstrate how they inform contemporary debates in the field. This will be further pursued in an examination of some of Rancière's most recent writings on filmmakers, notably Béla Tarr.

Rancière's now familiar account of the three regimes of art has three consequences for his work on cinema which will recur here: it affords him a 'long view' which allows him to avoid becoming embroiled in arguments over smaller-scale periodizations such as those of Romanticism, modernism and postmodernism; it presupposes that the category of equality be taken seriously; and it privileges the notion of the impure when looking at art in general and cinema in particular.

Film Fables opens with a challenge to a seductive argument and text by the 1920s avant-garde filmmaker Jean Epstein. Epstein saw the art of moving images as the victory of *opsis* (the perceptible effects of spectacle) over *muthos* (the Aristotelian primacy of plot), with cinema's ability to record the tiny detail and palpitations of life and the world and thus to overcome that ancient distrust of images and copies that Plato associated with *mimesis*. Rancière counters Epstein by pointing out the literary and indeed theatrical origin of both his exemplary film text and his avant-garde predilection for *opsis*, thus invoking the 'long view' of the aesthetic regime of art within which the specificity of the cinematic apparatus weighs less in the balance. The aesthetic regime sees all past art at its disposal for re-reading and adaptation; moreover, the camera as recorder of reality is a double-edged sword, fulfilling the avant-garde dream of a 'becoming-passive' that effaces the trace of the artist's will, but precisely because it cannot be anything but passive and therefore open to be manipulated by whatever artistic, political or commercial interest. Small wonder then that at the height of artistic modernism cinema largely worked to restate conventions of genre, mimesis and plot.

For Rancière, however, it is precisely this paradox that is interesting. A dialectic is installed which means that the vocation for *opsis* that cinema contains can be enacted only through its contradiction or 'thwarting', by *passing through* a *muthos*-driven dramaturgy and artistic heritage. 'The cinematic fable is a thwarted [*contrariée*] fable' (FF11). Much of the rest of *Film Fables* consists of readings of individual films or film directors which illustrate these inconsistencies, discrepancies and rifts, or *écarts*. Thus Eisenstein's *The General Line*, his 1929 film about the joys of Soviet collectivization, has its official political agenda thwarted or 'doubled' by its complicity with older patterns of feeling and thought, as for example in the famous Dionysian scene of the ejaculatory mechanical milk separator that so amused, despite themselves, Rancière and his young communist friends in the 1960s, as recounted in the prologue to *Les Écarts du cinéma* (EC10–11). The resolution of Murnau's *Herr Tartüff* (1925) and its status precisely as a cinematic adaptation of theatre, hangs on the supremely aesthetic figuring of Tartuffe as a shadow and then his reinsertion into a style of genre painting associated with the representational regime. In Hollywood, Anthony Mann's 1950s westerns seem to exemplify the dominance of *opsis* by *muthos*, with their heavily codified genre attributes, goal-oriented narratives and redistributions of masculinity, but the characters played by, and the performance of, James Stewart, as well as the way Mann films his perceptions, belie these representational exigencies and suggest a mysterious lack of fit into community and identity.[2]

What is at stake, for wider debates in film and cultural studies, in Rancière's account of cinema as a 'thwarted fable' caught between, or in tension or play with, two regimes of art? One objection is the risk of idealism, in the philosophical sense, in the account of these regimes. Certainly, it is striking to contrast Rancière's central reliance on the *political* revolution of 1789 and its aftermath with the *social and economic* revolution emphasized by Terry Eagleton when, in *The Ideology of the Aesthetic*, he traces the avatars of the aesthetic since the eighteenth century in the negotiation between general and particular, sensual and rational, subject and object, in an analysis which connects the aesthetic to the emergence of bourgeois society and the commodity form (although Rancière's grasp of the latter in its relationship with the visual arts in the contemporary period is apparent in *The Future of the Image*).[3] Moreover, Rancière's association of 'equality' with some of the most, at first sight, hermetic representatives of the artistic avant-garde, including Stéphane Mallarmé, would seem to leave him open to accusations of neglecting real, socially situated individuals in favour of an abstraction, a future promise. This faultline is also present in his polemic with Pierre Bourdieu (most notably in *The Philosopher and his Poor*), a polemic that revolves around the question of how deterministic, rather than merely determining, are Bourdieu's mappings of structures of taste and position across, for example, the distance/participation binary central to the 'aesthetic disposition', as opposed to the Kantian universalism which produces avant-garde audiences and readerships. It is fair to recall, however, that Rancière also resists those social pessimists, equally if not more suspect of idealism, who see audiences as manipulable and manipulated, notably in *The Emancipated Spectator* (2009). Rancière's *longue durée* approach to history and his critique of historicism and over-contextualization may blind him to implications in the analysis of early cinema, as in for example the work of Charles Musser, that rejoin the perspective of *Film Fables*. Much historical scholarship on early cinema is challengingly non-teleological: as it traces the transformation of a fairground attraction into a form of story-telling and entertainment that built on earlier literary and theatrical modes, including those of exhibition, it suggests there was nothing inevitable about the dominant shape taken by the cinematic institution of cinema, and thus its role, according to Rancière, as a thwarter of fables.

In some ways, the recent renaissance of adaptation studies would seem the most obvious meeting point between contemporary film studies and Rancière's work. The journal *Adaptation* (which began in 2008), and influential work in the mid decade by Robert Stam and Alessandra Raengo,[4] has been determined to surpass the deadening discussion in earlier scholarship based on evaluations of faithfulness to the source text. In Rancière's masterly analysis of Robert Bresson's *Mouchette* (1967), the 1937 literary source by Georges Bernanos is seen, as befits a form of art that shares with cinema a place in the aesthetic regime, already to illustrate a certain 'cinematographism', in that writing anticipates and paradoxically reproduces cinematic form. The impurity of both literature and film is the starting point, for Rancière, of a process of adaptation that both takes away and gives, as the 'thwarting' activity of cinema restores the representational paradoxically through a fragmentation of Bernanos's aesthetic halting of narrative, while undoing it through Bresson's extraordinary handling of actors and performance, as blank 'models': 'What comes after literature is not the art or language of pure images. Nor is it the return to the old representational order. Rather, it is a double excess that pulls the literary element both behind and in front of itself' (EC73–4).

However, the impact of Rancière's work on film studies is likely to turn on his insertion or otherwise into an intellectual landscape within the discipline marked by debates on theory and politics alive since the 1970s and 1980s. What is loosely termed as *Screen* theory was characterized by a modernist cultural politics that channelled 'French theory' and continental philosophy into a project that brought semiotics, psychoanalysis and Althusserean Marxism (including the Comolli/Narboni work at *Cahiers du cinéma*) into analyses of film that emphasized the ideological processes that produced subject positions in cinematic spectatorship. The 1990s were characterized by a turn to history in film studies (of a kind too historicist for Rancière, no doubt) and a reaction against those former philosophical and political agendas that saw a prominent film scholar, David Bordwell, creating an explicit 'anti-theoretical' agenda and embracing cognitive psychological approaches. The agendas of *Screen*, positioning themselves against both Stalinist and social-democratic conceptions of realism in favour of a Brechtian avant-gardism, are now distant, but there persists an academy both eager to take French theorists into the shared embrace of a mutually affirming cultural capital, and desperate to find progressive bearings in a crisis-ridden twenty-first century saturated in images. Rancière's central emphasis on equality, for example in his classification of regimes of art, promises much to such readerships, but what precisely are the cultural-political implications of his view of cinema as characterized by 'thwarted fables'?

They are to be found in *le partage du sensible*, the 'partition' or 'distribution' of 'the sensible' which sets the horizons of perception along which a common world can be shared and grasped:

> Politics resembles art in one essential point. Like art, politics also cuts into that great metaphor where words and images are continuously sliding in and out of each other to produce the sensory evidence of a world in order. And, like art, it constructs novel combinations of words and actions, it shows words borne by bodies in movement to make them audible, to produce another articulation of the visible and sayable. (FF152)

Changes to the conventions of meaning have political relevance because they form part of that movement of dissensus which reveals a hitherto excluded and repressed (invisible, inaudible, unsayable) social reality. Dissensus is the form and terrain of politics, to be distinguished from the 'police order' which is the original or given distribution of the sensible with its exclusions and inequalities. As J. M. Bernstein summarizes, 'Works of art are thus material mechanisms through which the mind can/must suspend its own constitutive functions, thereby allowing the sensible object to be emancipated from the implicit police order of the modern age, to potentially allow each and every object to become a full and equal citizen in the world of appearances.'[5] Cinema can be considered a prime exemplum of this process, in its institutional-'democratic' status (EC149) and moreover in the way in which dialectical processes of contrariety and contradiction propel an 'unresolved dialogue of forms'[6] which promotes, in turn, conversation about and interpretation of films and their position with regard to conventions and new distributions of the sensible. Indeed Rancière writes, in 2011: 'an art is never just an art: it is always at the same time the proposal of a world [*proposition de monde*]. And its formal procedures are often the remains of utopias which, more than the spectator's pleasure, aimed for the redistribution of the forms of collective sensible experience' (EC45).

A devil's advocate might at this point however suggest that 'the distribution of the sensible' is a reworked phantom of the Althusserean category of ideology repositioned in a *longue durée* dating back to the founding egalitarian impulse of 1789 rather than the world revolution begun in 1917 (and ended in 1989–91), with cinema and the other arts picking up a standard formalist and even liberal aesthetic of defamiliarizing the habitual world and its categories rather than being invested with the quasi-Brechtian role of uncovering the mask of appearances. To unpack the implications of this historical chronology and also to probe further Rancière's grappling with the relation between cinema, aesthetics and politics in the contemporary age, it will now be fruitful to clarify his relationship with Deleuze, notably but not exclusively the Deleuze of the *Cinema* books of 1983–5.[7] This relationship can be characterized as both polemical and entangled.

Deleuze's influence on film theory takes two forms. On the one hand, the anti-Oedipal ontology of flows and particles that characterized his collaboration with Félix Guattari (including *Kafka: Towards a Minor Literature* of 1975 and *A Thousand Plateaus* of 1980) has inspired analyses of films which deploy vocabularies of 'schizo-analysis', rhizomes, becoming, lines of flight and so forth.[8] On the other, a more strictly philosophical scrutiny has been brought to bear on his cinema books, in which, drawing on Henri Bergson's notions of duration and the splitting of time, he conceptualizes a funda-mental division within cinema between sets of images belonging to either the movement-image or the time-image. The former offers, like Bergson's description of a clock face, a spatialized, indirect representation of time; while the latter offers a direct representation through its relation with duration, the notion of the present moving into the future ('presents passing') but simultaneously falling back into the past ('pasts preserved') to form a virtual archive.

In his chapter on Deleuze in *Film Fables*, Rancière's objection is first a historical one, against both Deleuze's periodization and his treatment of the relation between historical events and aes-thetic change. From the outset, however, it is clear that there is much at stake for Rancière's own project here. For Deleuze's tax-onomy would seem to anticipate aspects of Rancière's own. The movement-image is organized according to a 'logic', that of the 'sensory-motor schema', which is an element in a 'chain' [*enchaîne-ment*] of actions and perceptions that culminate in Hollywood's 'action-image' and which recall the Aristotelian prioritization of narrative and representation. The time-image breaks with this logic by presenting interruption, 'irrational' relations between images and 'pure' optical situations, culminating in the 'crystal-image' in which actual and virtual images become indiscernible. For Rancière, this smacks too much of the non-dialectical and historically limited way in which modernist art tends to conceive itself as the conquest of an autonomy of form which breaks with *mimesis*. Moreover, Deleuze 'explains' this change – inaugurated by Orson Welles and Italian neo-realism in the 1940s (an insight he shares with André Bazin, theorist of the ontology of the photographic image and of the cinematic real) – by reference to historical events, namely the Second World War and its shattered aftermath, putting into crisis former national, ideological and indeed spatial certainties.

Rancière asks how this can be, significantly not because such an assertion would require a more prolonged micro-analysis of the relationship between text and context (as opposed to the broad brush Rancière brings to his own historiography of regimes of art), but because Deleuze is said here to make a category mistake, as his taxonomy of images is based not on human or social history but on natural history. The Bergsonian and Deleuzian concept of the image (most explicitly elaborated in the former's *Matter and Memory* of 1896) is part of a whole philosophical lineage that can be traced from Lucretius and through Spinoza. This perspective favours a dissolution of the subject/object relation and the notion that everything, in fact, is image. Images are simply 'everything that appears' within the vast continuum of the universe. These 'ontological and cosmological' understandings of 'matter-light in movement' (FF109) are disabling rather than enabling, according to Rancière, because they do not explain how Deleuze deals with the paradox of natural phenomena needing human or institutional intervention (on the part of the film director or film school) to produce them, and in turn they lead him to posit a history of 'redemption' in which a lost world of images is restored to modernist purity.

Rancière in fact answers one of his own objections here, when he writes in that sceptical paragraph on 'matter-light' that a human being's face and mind (merely) 'interrupt' the continuum of images. This is exactly the point made by Bergson and Deleuze: from a plane of immanence there indeed emerges a 'centre of indetermination' which gives images certain forms, but it is precisely an interruption of those flows (of which the 'interrupting' entity is a part) rather than a 'centre' such as a human consciousness shining like a miner's lamp on what is outside of it. Moreover, when Rancière quotes Deleuze quoting Dziga Vertov in *The Movement-Image* on 'putting perception back into things', he does so out of context, failing to take on board what is explained on that very page, that Vertov's cine-eye is able to surpass the limitations of the (individual) human eye by its ability to link multiple points of the universe through a plurality of perspectives and techniques and it is this 'non-human' eye which is the eye of the world, the eye of 'things' without man.[9] I shall suggest in a moment that, whether this misunderstanding is wilful or not, it means that Rancière risks missing an affinity with Deleuze's 'cosmological' thought even while he grapples with it for years afterwards. The rest of Rancière's chapter consists of more specific objections to examples used by Deleuze in his cinema books. Thus the films of Robert Bresson are said to be analysed as examples of both the movement-image and time-image. Quite apart from the fact that Deleuze explicitly says that there is in fact no 'purity' here, that both kinds of image can be present in one film and indeed that one is not necessarily to be evaluated more highly than the other[10] (so much for the 'redemption' thesis), a closer look at the sections on Bresson is revealing. In *The Movement-Image*, the analysis is about space, in *The Time-Image* it is about thought. The 'affection-image' is one of the ways in which the movement-image organizes, along with the perception-image and the action-image, that interruption of the universal movement of images alluded to earlier. The 'purity' that Deleuze sees in its workings (that is, the potential affects lurking in light on a murder weapon or a qualitative change in a facial expression) are simply a result of stripping down the components of the sequence, which are therefore about a potentiality that may or not be prolonged into action. Rancière is concerned that the 'any-space-whatever' (the notion of a heterogeneous space bereft of conventional coordinates and mappings) anomalously ends up in both cinema books. But Deleuze's point in *The Movement-Image* about Bresson's *The Trial of Joan of Arc* and *Pickpocket* is that the affects – Joan's stages of resistance, the thief's disposition – are made spatial and tactile by the abstract-lyrical treatment of a space made heterogeneous through fragmentation. The point about any-spaces-whatever in Rossellini or de Sica is that they bring that abstraction into realism, into the real existing streets, shot on location, of Berlin and Rome, and thus inaugurate something new. The section in *The Time-Image* begins where the previous left off, with an emphasis on the blank voices and performances of Bresson's 'models', so that their 'automatism' figures now not a 'choice' that might be prolonged into action, but the abstract movement of thought itself in its process of becoming. An interdiction on seeing the relation between components of the movement-image and time-image is only possible if, as in Rancière's argument here, there is confusion between the movement-image as a whole and its culmination, the action-image ('a logic of association and attraction between images, conceived on the model of action and reaction', FF114), and there is a need, at the end of the chapter, to see the relations between the classes of images as a dialectic (rendered at one point through the really rather Deleuzian image of 'an infinite spiral', FF119).

Rancière also objects to Deleuze's use of Hitchcock at the end of *The Movement-Image* in the role of the director who touches the limits of the movement-image and blends with the first stirrings of the time-image in his creation of mental images or relation-images through an elaborate manipulation of knowledge, point of view and suspense. Far from welcoming this example of impurity and 'thwarting', Rancière objects to the chronology of 'crisis' and to Deleuze's allegorizing of that crisis of the movement-image in the immobilization of his protagonists, notably the James Stewart characters' paralysis in *Rear Window* and fear of heights in *Vertigo*, which nonetheless insert themselves into a perfectly Aristotelian murder mystery. However, it is not so apparent that Deleuze casts Hitchcock so clearly in the role of the defeated here. And Deleuze's point can clearly be justified by the fact that these protagonists are worlds away from most active heroes of the action-image. Did not Rancière make a similar point about the James Stewart character in Anthony Mann's westerns?

There are numerous objections to Deleuze's historiography and choice of corpus, which have been rehearsed by many commentators.[11] What is extraordinary in Rancière's polemic with Deleuze in *Film Fables* is the complete absence of any engagement with the central preoccupation of the *Cinema* books, namely time and its consequences for truth and truth claims. (This is why Rancière's concluding pages on thought and cinema are limited to the dialectical relationship between thought and the un-thought, activity and passivity, the voluntary and the involuntary, which is said to correspond to cinema's twin encapsulation of the representational and aesthetic regimes.) Rancière confuses spatial and temporal terms; light and time and their milieu of 'infinity' is always negatively — and somewhat obsessively — evaluated as 'chaos'. Thus *The Movement-Image* introduces us to 'the chaotic infinity of the metamorphoses of matter-light' (FF113) and *The Time-Image* is seen to save us from that fate, or to redeem us all, by creating a marriage between 'the infinity – chaos – of matter-image and the infinity – the chaos – characteristic of thought-image' (FF113–4). Instead of the dialectical unity of contraries Rancière is trying to build, he charges Deleuze with the sin of Nietzscheanism, as 'Dionysian power' makes thought abdicate 'the attributes of will and lose itself in stone, in color, in language, and equals its active manifestation to the chaos of things' (FF157). But what if we recast those historical objections, engaged with the issue of time and probed Deleuze further on one of the central unresolved dilemmas of his thought, namely the relation between history and memory? We might alight upon some of Rancière's own writings, notably those on Marker and Godard.

The ongoing dialogue with Deleuze is evident in much of Rancière's writing and is sometimes acknowledged, sometimes not. In *Les Écarts du cinéma* he returns in slightly kinder terms to the debates in *Film Fables* about Vertov and *Vertigo* and he is clearly influenced by Deleuze's analysis of musicals, including those of Minnelli. Where Deleuze saw the transition from realist fiction to song and dance as one from realist fiction to a supra-personal 'world movement' [*mouvement du monde*], Rancière sees it as exemplifying the 'rift' between representational fiction and 'pure performance' (EC81). His analysis of *Mouchette* is replete with Deleuzian terminology, including 'line of flight' (which Deleuze and Guattari use explicitly to avoid the vocabulary of dialectics) and 'time-image' (in the literary text), and this terminology seems to inspire him to invent similar taxonomies ('relay-image', 'screen-image').

This entanglement with Deleuze is already there in *Film Fables* and in sections far less explicit than in 'Deleuze and the ages of cinema'. The essay on Godard's *Histoire(s) du cinéma* is revealing in this regard. Godard's ambitious (1988–98) project was to reflect on the relations between film stories, film history and twentieth-century (European) history in general through what Rancière describes as 'fusional montage' (FF174), as film sequences are abstracted from their context, re-arranged and superimposed. Rancière's first point is to assess this operation as one which falls into a familiar modernist aesthetic, in which the representational is (here inappropriately) repressed in favour of a redemptive purification of form. However, what is also clear is that Godard's operation has much to tell us about history and equality. Godard's text draws on the art historian Élie Faure's discussion of Rembrandt, who in turn represents a new art and a new history for his inclusive choice of style and subjects which emphasizes a 'shared life', the 'universal energy of collective life that does and undoes its forms'. Since the work of the nineteenth-century historian Michelet, history is seen as a 'mode of co-presence, a way of thinking and experiencing the co-belonging of experiences and the inter-expressivity of the forms and signs that give them shape' (FF177). These experiences – 'glorious or mundane' – are to be considered under the sign of equality and to be seen as infinitely conjoined: 'History is this mode of experience where all experiences are equivalent and where the signs of any one experience are capable of expressing all the others' (FF178). We are back with the 'progressive universal poetry' of Schlegel, in which the fragments of world literature can endlessly recombine, freed from particular representational 'enchaining' to be able to metamorphose and gather in a great continuum.

In *The Time-Image* Deleuze took as one starting-point the famous inverted cone that for Bergson diagrammatized the operations of time and memory. Here the contracted point of the (inverted) summit is that of the present moment constantly moving forward in time as the presents pass and fall into the *non-chronological archive of the past* as it stretches towards the ever-receding base. That archive consists of layers or regions (Deleuze calls them *nappes*, or 'sheets') which can be raided by memory, or the time-image, across different circuits: 'A zone of recollections, dreams, or thoughts corresponds to a particular aspect of the thing'[12] and 'we have to place ourselves with a leap into the past in general, into these purely virtual images which have been constantly preserved through time'.[13] Thus in one of Deleuze's favourite practitioners of the time-image, Alain Resnais, those raids into the virtual past emerge out of particular circuits that are passed through and produce, for example, personal but also collective-historical images and memories: the atomic bomb and the Occupation of France in *Hiroshima mon amour* (1956), the Algerian War and the Second World War in *Muriel* (1962), the round up of Jewish prisoners at the

Vél' d'Hiv in 1942 and the Chilean coup d'état of 1973 (*Providence*, 1977). Rancière's evocation of Deleuze's 'cosmological' agenda as implying chaos is thus misleading, for the reader and for himself. This is how Rancière writes of Godard's treatment of history in *Histoire(s) du cinéma*:

> every sensible form is a fabric of more or less obscure signs, a presence capable of signifying the power of the collective experience that brings the sensible form into presence. It also means that each one of these signifying forms is open to striking new relationships with all other forms, generating thereby new signifying arrangements. It is a result of this regime of meaning where everything speaks twice – *as pure presence and as the infinity of its virtual connections* – that experiences are communicated and a common world created. (FF178, my emphasis)

Rancière even uses the word 'nappes' in *The Future of the Image* to describe again Godard's fusional montage: 'the homogeneous great layer [*nappe*] of mystery, where all of yesterday's conflicts become expressions of intense co-presence' (FI62). There is more at stake here than the echoes of a Deleuzian vocabulary, expressed unconsciously or otherwise. Arguably, Deleuzian film theory needs a certain injection of history to counteract the ahistoricism of its Bergsonian roots so criticized by Benjamin. Laura U. Marks has argued that the time-image needs Benjamin's notion of ritual, of 'the association of images with history, of individual with community experience', to form part of the 'shock' that peels away the accretions of habit and official memory 'to create a flow of experience'.[14] Nonetheless, in their different appreciations of the virtual archive of the past, both thinkers share, first of all, a notion of absolute equality. For Deleuze, the past is out there, non-chronological, and accessible only by creating circuits which are open to all and can take as many forms as there are memories for any individual in the world. Who can forget the co-presence in *Providence* of not only images of historical catastrophe but of sexual encounters and the random appearances of a lone soccer player? Rancière no doubt understands the importance of historical memory as an issue in the distribution of the sensible and the possible emergence of dissensus, hence his return to Godard's work in *The Future of the Image* and its role there in the development of the important concept of the 'phrase-image' in which heterogeneous elements are linked in an enigmatic and even 'mysterious' way to provide an interpretive grid in which we can look and perceive differently.[15] In his writing in *The Time-Image* on the cinema of decolonization, Deleuze makes clear the creative possibility of the emergence of the new from the 'disagreement' produced by minority or minor positions.[16]

To this common ground can be added an element which Deleuze largely neglects and to which Rancière gives a certain pride of place: the role of documentary. As Nico Baumbach has argued, Deleuze makes little distinction between documentary and fiction because of his lack of interest in the 'real' as such in favour of a history of types of image (thus Flaherty is wheeled on to illustrate the workings of the action-image). When Deleuze does look at documentary in more detail, he concentrates on the examples of Pierre Perrault and Jean Rouch for their emphasis on the productive fabulations encouraged in their subjects. He therefore 'ignores the circulation of *common images* as a possible grounds [sic] for cinema's "will to art"'.[17] In contrast, Rancière takes documentary as one of the great exempla of cinema's 'thwarted fables', in an examination of *The Last Bolshevik*, the 1993 film by Chris Marker – a figure curiously absent from Deleuze's cinema books – devoted to the memory of the Soviet film director Alexander Medvedkin, and also a meditation on the history of the moving image and revolutionary politics in the twentieth century.

Rancière begins by criticizing the proliferation of memories and stories in information societies, arguing that this does nothing to trouble the sense of a perpetual present, and that there is therefore a need to endow memory with the arrangements and connections associated with the Aristotelian *muthos*. Memory, a certain arrangement of knowledge and sensibility, is therefore a work, a labour, of fiction, but not in the sense of lies or falsehood: 'The real difference [with fiction film] isn't that the documentary sides with the real against the inventions of fiction, it's just that documentary instead of treating the real as an effect to be produced, treats it as a fact to be understood' (FF158). Marker's approach is thus to be admired for the way it brings together heterogeneous – often archive – elements that undo the expectations and recognitions fabricated in the social imaginary of most fiction films. But he also embraces that post-Romantic poetics that endows the signs of the film with the powers of expression (one image, say, embodying the meaning of the whole), of metamorphosis (arising out of the combination of signs) and of reflection (the signs are mutually interpreting). Documentary cinema is uniquely placed here because it is freed from the requirement to produce an 'effect of the real' borne out of narrative convention and, intensifying that poetic relation between the passive realm of non-art and the shaping will of the artist, it can

> play around with the consonance and dissonance between narrative voices, or with the series of period images with different provenances and signifying power. It can join the power of the impression, the power of speech born from the meeting of the mutism of the machine and the silence of things, to the power of montage, in the broad, non-technical sense of the term, as that which constructs a story and a meaning by its self-proclaimed right to combine meanings freely, to re-view images, to arrange them differently, and to diminish or increase their capacity for expression and for generating meaning. (FF161)

Rancière is aware, however, of the challenges presented by Marker's 'pedagogical' strategy of voice-over explanation, and this is what motivates him at the end of this essay to pitch Marker in the camp of 'telling', even and especially as his later films take off into more fictional twists on the documentary form, and Godard in that of 'showing', through the 'joyous disorder of words and images (FF170); this was written before Godard's film-essays, *Éloge de l'amour* of 2001 and *Notre musique* of 2004.[18] Nevertheless, he here explores the specific modalities of cinema when it grapples with issues of memory and the past and grounds the need for this exploration in the urgency and specificity of our own present's common world of experience. He therefore suggests what a more self-consciously historical raiding of the virtual archive of the past might look like. It is one instance when a thinking-together of

Deleuze and Rancière yields productive results, and a look at the latter's most recent writings on cinema confirms the possibilities opened up by that dual track.

In both *The Future of the Image* [2003] and *Aesthetics and its Discontents* [2004] Rancière had diagnosed a post-Berlin Wall, post 9/11 world in which the possibilities of a provocative dissensus are dwarfed by a pervasive *consensus*, in which difference and division – of social position and even of peoples – are reduced to one and the ethical encroaches unhelpfully on the political and the aesthetic. There are thus homologies between the resolution of Clint Eastwood's *Mystic River* (2003), in which the non-punishment of the Sean Penn character who kills the wrong man to avenge his daughter's murder speaks to a breakdown in the relationship between justice and community, with the latter re-founded in relation to trauma and not law, and the work of cinema about the Holocaust, out of which consensus emerges by relying on an externalized past catastrophe and guilt in relation to it.[19]

Rancière's discussion of the cinema of the past decade is an attempt to counteract this malaise, but not by hunting nostalgically for places where an older dialectic, capable of either motivating action or denouncing the world of appearances, might have sought refuge. Indeed, in *Les Écarts du cinéma*, he makes explicit the fact that, given cinema's impure status, the relation between politics and cinema needs to be addressed in terms of both *justice* (involving representations of conflict, suffering, injustice) and *justesse* (the precise and subtle calibrations of its arrangements of space and bodies – EC111). Against the procedure of Godard in *Notre Musique* – who ironically prolongs the basic shot/countershot grammar of cinema to juxtapose, for example, native Americans with the ruined library at Sarajevo and the bridge at Mostar, and who for Rancière is unable to get beyond a denunciatory strategy which denies his protagonists their own voice – Rancière prefers one which is characterized by both equality and ambiguity. Inspired by an episode in Straub/ Huillet's *From the Clouds to the Resistance* (1979), which combined the voices of non-professional actors, an unresolved dialectic, an ambiguous gesture of refusal and the quiddity of landscape, fire, moon and body, Rancière carves out an interesting corpus which for him summarizes the way cinema makes meaning both externally (as an opening out on to the world's injustices) and internally (as the transformation of narrative in its surface vibrations): the Portuguese Pedro Costa, the Algerian Tariq Teguia's *Gabbla/Inland* (2009), and especially the Hungarian Béla Tarr, who began his career during the communist period and whose self-proclaimed last film, *The Turin Horse*, appeared in 2011.

In *Béla Tarr, le temps d'après* (2011), the 'aftertime' is not a morose post-Soviet era in which belief (in change) has been extinguished and flattened, nor is it, from a conservative point of view, a return to reason, or a left-wing point of view, a destruction of all hopes and illusions. Rather, it is a time after stories/histories [*histoires*] in which interest is drawn to the 'stuff of life' or, more precisely, the 'fabric of the sensible' (BT70). In Tarr's extraordinary cinematic universe of long, slow, takes and a palette of greys (mud, rain and fog), it is this interpenetration of affects which offers the possibility of breaking with monotony and repetition, rather than the exigencies of the narrative. The portrayal of the loss of illusions tells us little about our world, writes Rancière, whereas the proximity between 'the normal disorder of the "disillusioned" order of things' and 'the extreme of destruction and madness' tells us much more (BT56). It is not difficult to see the attraction for Rancière of this cinema, as it echoes in heightened form readings in *Film Fables* that emphasized the combination of realism and artifice, and cinema's egalitarian capacity, as here in Tarr's characteristic sequence shots in which every element is 'both interdependent and autonomous' and 'endowed with an equal potential to internalize the situation' (BT74).

What is most striking in the book on Tarr is the overwhelmingly Deleuzian vocabulary that is deployed. For in Tarr the 'cosmic' is now 'absolutely realist, absolutely material' (BT11) and the images in his films culminate in a circulation of affects and intensities within duration or time, so that we get 'an assemblage of crystals of time', time-images in which 'what is made manifest is the duration which is the very fabric from which are woven those individualities called situations or protagonists' (BT41). Moreover, the 'idiot' János (Lars Rudolph), in *Werckmeister Harmonies* (2000), is not, needless to say, the hero of an action-image but the seer [*voyant*] of the time-image. Certainly, Rancière is not here adopting wholesale a Deleuzian system, not least because his notion of repetition here does not reproduce Deleuze's fundamental idea that repetition and the production of the new are linked. However, we glimpse again here the entanglement with Deleuze that we noted earlier. If Rancière offers a distinct historical bridge to Deleuze's fundamental cosmology, Deleuze had already offered proposals for readings of films that were political without being based on a modernist politics: 'it is not the cinema that turns away from politics, it becomes completely political, but in another way', with protagonists who 'know how to extract from the event the part that cannot be reduced to what happens: that part of inexhaustible possibility that constitutes the unbearable, the intolerable, the visionary's part'.[20] Rancière knows as well that a contemporary politics of cinema, which he still calls dialectical, involves the creation of 'new redistributions of words and gestures, times and spaces' in order to evaluate how filmmakers tackle 'the fractures of history, upheavals in journeys between territories, new injustices and conflicts' (EC126). In Béla Tarr, Rancière discovers a filmmaker who bestrides the communist and post-communist eras, the real and the artificial, the historical and the cosmic, the pure and the impure, and who therefore injects into the world a belief in change.

11

Rancière and Metaphysics (Continued)[1]

A Dialogue

Jean-Luc Nancy and Jacques Rancière

Jean-Luc Nancy: To Jacques Rancière it is only possible – and necessary – for me to address two questions. Perhaps they are not questions but only the expression of the major gap [*écart*] that separates us even as nothing opposes us. I have already come to express this gap by questioning Rancière's prohibition of metaphysics. The issue now, of course, is the same – 'metaphysics', or whatever one would like to call it – that which, for Rancière, takes the form only of reverie, or a desire for unjustified envelopment and which for me (turning to the term 'metaphysics' only to hasten myself) simply designates the indisputable experience, as tough and it is enlivening, of being exposed to 'meaning'.

To start with, in the book *Aisthesis* – the studies whereof make up a very remarkable aesthetic ensemble, lacking neither in the most informed knowledge, the most astute taste, nor the keenest discernment (as is the case with Rancière's other studies in aesthetics, to which I feel I can only pay homage) – we read the following, on the first page:

> The conditions of this emergence [he is talking about that of art in the West] do not derive from a general concept of art or of beauty, whether founded on a global thought of the human or of the world, of

the subject or of being. Such concepts themselves depend on a mutation in forms of sensible experience, in ways of perceiving and of being
affected. They articulate a mode of intelligibility of these reconfigura-
tions of experience. (A9)

If the 'mutation' and 'reconfiguration' of which these lines speak
have taken place and if this phenomenon has called for a new
intelligibility, what are we to say about the mutation itself? More
precisely, how shall we grasp the fact that it has taken place at all
levels of human experience, or existence, first of all in Europe
then tendentially globally? If democracy, humanism, the death of
God, the extortion of value from producers, to leave it at that, are
inseparable from the mutation of sensible experience, does this not
mean that this 'sensible' is at least one of the manifestations of an
overall disposition of that which one knows not how to name –
culture, civilization, condition, destiny, existence?

Is it not then inevitable that what emerges with the singular
nomination and conceptualization of 'art' opens up new questions
and that, in this regard, what transpires in thought between Kant
and Hegel obeys a certain necessity – and is not at all, as others
would have it, a sort of philosophers' seizure of artists' territory?

But can this movement – which I shall not attempt to summa-
rize and which runs from Baumgarten to Heidegger, Adorno and
us, which is to say, *nolens volens* also to Rancière – be silhouetted
as it is in these lines: 'general concept [. . .] global thought'? I am
clearly aware of the occasionally hyperbolic expressions and spir-
itualizing assumptions about 'art' that one could refer to here. But
this is to ride roughshod over an entirely different question: does
the invention of art, in the singular and taken absolutely, have a
signification with regard to the subordinate place, or absence of
place, reserved for the beaux-arts by a philosophy built entirely
around the motifs of 'being' or 'knowledge'?

Art appeared very precisely in the hollow opened up by a problematic of 'ends', which itself emerged from the fading of given
and fixed finalities. This is to say that it appeared in the absence of
meaning. This does not mean that it took charge of meaning (it
would still be necessary to know what such an expression could
mean) but that the – relative – erasure of other forms of putting

meaning into play, or of staging meaning (religion, politics, science), opened the possibility out of which came the name 'art' and the nexus of questions it indexes. Nothing general or global here – on the contrary, one might say, since what then appears is also an irreducible plurality (that some have tried to reduce to and subsume under 'total art') with which we must henceforth reckon in matters of 'meaning'.

My second question – or non-question – follows directly from the above. Does the *partage du sensible*, the 'sharing', or 'division', of 'the sensible', a formula that Rancière has long used to characterize the milieu in which 'artistic' practices originate and are exercised, really suffice to name what he is aiming at? Why, for starters, does this category of the 'sensible' remain as though isolated from an 'intelligible' about which nothing is said, whereas, for Rancière himself, everything would suggest that the 'fabric of sensible experience' (A10) constitutes a condition of experience *tout court*, of our way of being in the world, of experiencing others, of exchanging and representing. The 'sensible' is probably by no means extrinsic to a supposed 'intelligible' or 'spiritual'.

On the other hand, it is itself divided, by a wholly primitive datum (a transcendental empirical, one might say), into a diversity of sensorial, sensual and sentimental registers, into a plurality that orders, as it were as a matter of principle, the affective sphere to the extent that it cannot strictly be named in the singular. Thus, there are always and necessarily divisions of the 'division of the sensible'. What is named 'art' cannot escape this condition and in this sense its singular nature is always excessive [*abusif*].

Does this consubstantial fragility, or complexity, of the idea of 'art' not have to be referred to the complexity and fragility of what, when all is said and done, must really be named 'meaning' (the meanings of the supposedly single 'meaning' . . .)? And does this have nothing to do with the other conditions of contemporary experience that we have, or try to have, of the 'sharing' as such, that is to say, of our common existence (common by essence, not by accident and also common with other existing things in the world)?

Lastly, can the fact be ignored that this sensible division [*ce partage sensible*], this sensibility qua intrinsic sharing of meaning or experience, has always accompanied the other regimes of artistic practice?

Has there ever been a religious, political or symbolic art that was not also and independently of these functions grappling with regimes of sensibility, with intensities and diversities, for example of colour, tone, rhythm, etc.? In other words, has art in the singular-plural not in fact been at work ever since there have been humans? And is its singular nomination not *at the same time* the feature of a distinct epoch *and,* through it, a way of pointing to questions, or rather to tensions, expectations and drives that have nothing 'general' or 'global' about them, but which, because they are always being remodelled from top to bottom, oblige us ever anew to 'make sense' in a way that is never other than different and shared?

These are not really questions, as I said. Every question structured by an 'is it not . . .?' already points to its answer. However, I point to no other answer than these very questions – or else to the beyond of every question, one which might not be situated anywhere other than in sensible experience insofar as it is very precisely an experience of meaning.

Jacques Rancière: Jean-Luc Nancy has addressed a request to me apropos of art today, as he did apropos of politics yesterday, which is to leave the risk-free position of the archaeologist of systems of rationality, or regimes of sensibility and to venture onto the terrain where the mutations I describe find their meaning, at the risk of confronting the lack of meaning. More particularly, with regard to what I describe as the invention of art in the singular, this means inscribing that invention in the broader perspective of a destinal mutation of European humanity, the manifestations of which can be felt in other domains of human experience, named religion, politics or science. In this request I distinguish several demands to which I feel more or less able or disposed to respond.

There is the request to go a bit further, a bit deeper, to the bottom of things, to break the reassuring surface of words whose self-evidence obscures the problems: mutation, configuration, experience. In a sense, I have always struggled with words of this sort, which say both more and less than they say, which impose their concrete weight (experience, sensible) to cover up the uncertainty of their content or their abstract generality (configuration) when the question is to know which types of phenomena prove them true. I have constantly struggled with them – that is to say, at once against them and yet by using them – if only to challenge and undermine the dominant dramaturgies that combine them.

That is where the question of meaning plays out for me in the first instance – not in the exposure to meaning (I will come back to this notion), but rather in the risk of constructing meaning: the risk of assembling elements whose connection is underwritten neither by *a priori* reasoning nor empirical statistics. One senses that there are things that make sense together: a new way of exhibiting paintings, the fact of seeing beauty in representations of the lives of nobodies, or of finding life expressed by mutilated statues or ruined buildings, a readiness to shed tears, a way of giving an image and a body to the people gathered in assembly, the aptitude of the popular classes to use words differently, the introduction into philosophy of notions likely to conceptualize these changes, etc. This conjunction is exemplified in the words of such and such a great poet or in letters exchanged between two obscure workers, in the problems faced by the director of a national museum, the price of such and such a private sale, the analysis of a painting or a play by a philosopher . . . There is no global concept that would account for that conjunction, nor is there any statistical proof of its extension. One thus constructs – I construct – an assemblage that links together these phenomena into a signifying unity. In one sense the configuration is nothing other than the assemblage thus constructed. In another, the configuration exceeds the assemblage in that it is a possibility to construct and to link together a multiplicity of assemblages that will show the same signifying elements at work. One builds, all in all, a system of conditions of possibility, a system which can be shown to render thinkable the singular mutations that gather in the existence of a sphere of experience called art or of a mode of subjectivation called sentiment or aesthetic judgement.

The problem with this type of construction is indeed that the system of conditions always remains immanent to the conditioned, verified by it. The operation of 'making sense' thus designates three things: first, one constructs a stable signifying link between elements (for example, ways of exhibiting paintings in public galleries and museums, modifications of the gaze, a new attention to the insignificant, new ways of saying what happens on a painted surface, etc.); second, one constructs it in its distance [*écart*] from another system of relations (for example, the aesthetic distance from the hierarchies of subjects and genres that characterized mimetic logic); third, one constructs it as the system of conditions of possibility that defines a certain type of subject experiencing these connections and these ruptures. One constructs it by setting in relation a certain number of figures: Winckelmann's hero at rest, the Rousseauist dreamer, the Wordsworthian walker, the Schillerian spectator/player, Hegel's small god of the street, the worker-poet, the joiner looking out of the window, the visitor to the Louvre, and so on. A certain number of traits, then, come to appear constitutive of a specific subjective mode that can be properly called aesthetic subjectivity: for example, the deposing of the representational privilege of action – both as arrangement of causes and also as the defining quality of a superior type of humanity; conversely, the promotion of a certain number of states of inactivity (reverie, the aesthetic state, aesthetic judgement . . .) that adopt for themselves what had once been the privilege of action, in the strong sense of the word, namely the fact of being an end for nothing other than oneself.

That is what the operation of 'making sense' designates, which is to say it is limited to that. In opposition to this limitation, the 'metaphysical' question then arises, the question of the meaning of this 'making sense'. This question is manifestly twofold. On the one hand, it is a matter of knowing what conditions, as its reason, the system of conditions of possibility thus constructed. Indeed, this system is manifestly confined to the empirico-transcendental circle: the conditions of possibility that here play the role of transcendental remain contingent historical transformations. They tell us how transformed exhibition surfaces or modes of performance produce new discourses and how, contrary to new arrangements of words and reasons, they produce affective and perceptual displacements, without showing us the primary meaning from which these assemblages derive or the unconditioned element from which these conditions arise. The metaphysical request asks that we go to the reason of reasons, the condition of conditions and, in the last instance, to the unconditioned itself. But this is where it splits into two. It does not make do with asking for a reason of reasons

(God, the One, the Good, Being . . .). It wants to link that reason of reasons to the experience of a being, the destiny of which is to sense the meaning of meaning. It wants that being to be not only the subject of a certain type of global experience but also in a certain position vis-à-vis that experience.

A certain type of global experience: the metaphysical demand, as I sense it, involves the idea of a mutation that is felt in all the spheres of experience as a specific turning point in the destination of being. In this way, Jean-Luc Nancy indicates the distributed figures of the turning point to which it would be necessary to refer the birth of aesthetics: the death of God (religion), humanism (ethics), democracy (politics) and the extortion of surplus value (the economy). Since the counter-revolution, the analytical perspective of which has been more or less reasserted by 'liberals' and 'socialists' alike, whether Romantics of the early nineteenth century or deconstructionists at the close of the twentieth, the articulation of these four terms has been held to be an indisputable historico-theoretical given in the face of which each individual is merely free to chose his first cause (death of God, 'sacrifice' of the king, advent of bourgeois exploitation . . .). For my part, I see nothing self-evident about this tale of modernity. It is easy to connect the birth of aesthetics, qua regime of existence of works, with phenomena of works losing their destination (in particular the disconnection of a whole swathe of European painting from its religious function), with a type of gaze (that of the museum visitor) untied from a sovereign point of view, or again with forms of re-appropriation of the pagan heritage (neo-Hellenism, the return and flight of 'the gods'). To me, nothing in any of this justifies connecting this advent with a global drama that could be called the 'death of God', in which, in the shadow of the Nietzschean prophecy, all the following would come meaningfully together: the flight of the pagan gods, the end of monarchy by divine right, forced revolutionary de-Christianization, or the slow sociological de-Christianization of European societies. The possibility of such a connection implies that the concept 'death of God' already includes a specific relation between the instance that gives meaning and the one that takes it away, a relation that itself determines a specific mode of being of the subject for whom the question of meaning makes sense.

That, for me, is the core of the metaphysical request in its modern form: the way in which the ancient question of the 'condition of the condition' has been tied to the designation of a being that is in a position of deficit, lack or distress in its regard: a finite creature, the abandoned and 'thrown' being, the *infans*, etc. Whatever distance Nancy may take from the spiritualist and pathetic figures of this assignation, for me the core of the disagreement remains the way in which he presents the question of meaning here, namely under the form of absence. 'Art appeared', he writes, 'very precisely in the hollow opened up by a problematic of "ends", which itself emerged from the fading of given and fixed finalities. This is to say that it appeared in the absence of meaning.' Now, I understand lack of meaning in two ways. On the one hand, one thus designates a historical loss – the loss of the meaning assigned to things and beings by superior authorities (religion and monarchy). Here we encounter the story of modernity that I contest. On the other, this 'loss of meaning' appears linked to something more essential: a lack where the being is situated for whom meaning makes sense, the one who, according to Nancy's expression, is exposed to meaning. However, there are again two ways of understanding that exposure: there is the metaphysical way that conceives this exposure under the form of lack – lack of meaning or lack of capacity to riposte to its violence; and there is another way for which lack or excess are above all problems of distribution. If one chooses this second path, one will say, for example, that religion is not, according to the Marxist formula, the 'sigh of the oppressed creature', searching for a meaning to a life of meaninglessness in the heavens; but that it is, in the first place, a body of words (stories and rituals) that saturates without difficulty the space of belief (as it did when I came to know it, with things such as biblical history, learning catechisms by heart, and mass in Latin, all things that met no requirement for meaning but that rendered the very request for it superfluous); and that, in addition, it is possible to divert this repertory of phrases and histories. This is what I have tried to think through with the notions of literarity, the excess of words and the revolution of the children of the Book. Meaning, then, is not that which is lacking; on the one hand, it saturates the field of experience but, on the other, it also opens breaches, by undoing the ordered correspondence of things, words and speakers.

This is precisely what is at stake in the representational order and its destruction. The representational order is a saturated order in which the treated subjects define the forms that must be imitated, the language that this or that type of character has to have, etc. That saturation is itself linked to the predetermination of the relation between the means at the artist's disposal and the effects produced on the sensibility of his or her public. This is the sense in which one can speak of a world of 'fixed and given finalities'. Mimesis is the fit between *poiesis*, which employs means for given ends, and *aisthesis*, which precisely verifies that these ends have been achieved. But this world of fixed finalities – and therefore of codification of the proper means to achieve these ends – is also the world of a fixed division between two types of humans: those who have to do with ends and those who live in the universe of means, free humans and 'mechanical' humans. 'Ends', then, do not so much give meaning or reason as divide humans. Action, which is the principle of Aristotelian fiction, is also the privilege of those who live in the domain of ends as such. The 'deficit' that affects ends here signifies the exact opposite of a lack; it marks, by contrast, self-sufficiency. The 'problematic of ends' at stake in the aesthetic revolution, then, is a matter of redistributing this virtue of self-sufficiency. This is what happened both in the inactivity of Winckelmann's Hercules and that of Murillo's young beggars, but also in the Kantian conceptualization of finality without end and the Schillerian play-drive. The experience of that which is not a means for any end exists to the extent that it can be ascribed to anyone at all; this aesthetic revolution of the kingdom of ends, conceptualized by Kant, is anything but the experience of a lack.

It might be said here that I have too conveniently interpreted deficit [*défaut*] as a lack and exposure as the situation of a helpless being and that, moreover, the meaning to which Nancy thinks the subject is exposed is not signification but that which founds and exceeds it. I could respond that I was led to do so by the very formulation of his first question, in which one feels the Heideggerian background that he shares with others, more, that is, than his own approach in which the exposure to sense is not the situation of the impoverished creature before the flight of the gods, the death of God or the infinite debt towards the Other, but instead involves entering into contact with the way in which a common world is offered through a multiplicity of openings. That approach, his own, is more in evidence in his second question, in which the division of the sensible as I understand it is interrogated from the point of view of another division, one by which the subject takes part in a certain primal experience of the world and discovers this world as a shared world. First, let us clear up an ambiguity: in my work the sensible does not stand against an intelligible about which nothing is known. It is always the experience of a relation between sense and sense: between an 'x' that presents itself as given and the sense that one attributes to it, that is to say, the way in which one links it with another given, in which one attributes it a place, a signification. The sensible/intelligible relation is, for me, one of the possible modalities of this relation between sense and sense. Or, if you will, the intelligible is internal to the division of the sensible. It is clear that this relation between sense and sense is distinguished in two ways from the division as Nancy may understand it. First of all, it excludes what seems to me to be the search, in his work, for meaning as something primal existing prior to signification. This is what is at issue when he asks me if 'art' in the singular-plural has not in actual fact been at work ever since there have been humans, if all art − religious, political, symbolic − does not also and independently of these functions, grapple with regimes of sensibility, intensities and diversities, for example of coloration, tone, rhythm, etc. This is a question that for me contains two further questions: it is certain that humans have always used the resources of rhythm, form, volume and colour, regardless of the destination of the assemblages they have made with them, as is the fact that this has always had to do with singular regimes of sensibility. But the conclusion that 'art in the singular-plural' has, in a sense, always existed seems to me not to follow. Rhythms, forms and colours are subject to very diverse associations with significations and functions and the − for us, artistic − effect of these associations can have been calculated for entirely different ends (besides, for us, sensitivity to these associations very largely exceeds the domain of what we call art). Art, for us, designates a certain relation between procedures, forms of sensibility and significations. On this basis, its singular-plural allows us to include, as objects of *our* sensible experience, assemblages that are made for completely different ends. What we cannot do – in any case, what I cannot do – is to presuppose a universality of the form of experience through which *we* feel them as art. For me, this is the impassable lesson of Vico and Hegel – namely, that we see or understand as art that which, for those who produced it, had been something different. It is nonetheless true that neither of them hesitated to announce the meaning that the thing in question would have had for the sacred poets or the builders of pyramids. I find this impossible to do. I have never been able, as others have, to speak about art on the basis of rock paintings, without having the least idea of what their authors did in painting them and what the experience of viewing them was like. I know, on the other hand, that the paintings of the Australian aborigines, which we view with a gaze informed by abstract painting, are for them the vehicle of cosmological and spiritual significations. This shows that there are different types of association between sensations, significations and powers of affection that enter into contact, but I do not see any possibility of referring to the unique basis of a common experience of meaning.

This impossibility of thinking the common of a human experience in general called art refers to the second difference that I evoked above: a difference in the thought of the common and its sharing. What has been at the centre of my work is a certain approach to the common and its sharing. A common for me is always defined in its difference with another common. Politics and art define ways of tying sense and sense together that are opposed to others – those named the police, the ethical regime of images or the representational regime of the arts. Furthermore, a distribution of relations between the visible, the audible and the thinkable is always also a distribution of competencies, a distribution of humans according to the capacities of sensible experience that they are assigned (voice or speech, etc.). The double sense of the partition [*partage*], as participation in a common and as division of that common, defines the particular nexus on the basis of which I have tackled the subjects of aesthetics and politics. If I was led to think the mutation that constitutes the historical emergence of the notion of art, it was not in the context of a reflection on the concept, or the essence, of artistic activity. It was in the wake of a reflection on a totally different mutation: that by which individuals decide to live a life other than the one intended for them. It is on the basis of this sudden change in the distribution of the parts reserved to humans according to their birth or their occupation that I became interested in these other points of change whereby a sphere of experience, or a territory of knowledge or thought, emerges on the map of the perceptible and the thinkable. Of the sensible there is, in actual fact, a multitude of things to be thought and to be said that I have not dealt with. For my part I have concerned myself with this distribution and this redistribution of forms of possible experience because it seemed to me that it had fallen to me to do, that I could say something unique about it. And a dialogue is also the meeting of two paths that set out poles apart and head towards different destinations.

Jean-Luc Nancy: So, in continuing to head towards another destination, I thank Jacques Rancière for his response. I appreciate his precision and the understanding to which it attests. As the time we have to conclude this dialogue is quite strictly limited – to give it a conclusion that is inevitably very provisional but necessary – I will make do with three remarks. (I will not go back over what Rancière has said about the sensible in response to me, in which it seems to me that there is little or no disagreement and only differences.)

The first remark will be to agree that the risk of an ambiguity was indeed contained in my way of formulating the 'deficit of meaning' [*le défaut du sens*]. It could be just as much a case of loss and the ensuing lack – the loss of a plenitude of signification, such as the 'death of God' along with the lamentations of the Nietzschean *Madman* ('We are the ones who killed him' and 'what holy games will we invent?') – as of a transformation in the horizon of signification (supposedly saturated by a 'meaning of life' that is always ultimately religious, which is to say, as Rancière very rightly remarks, that it renders the question of meaning superfluous) into the horizon of the meaning in 'meaning', precisely, of anteriority in relation to all signification. In this second tenor, the 'horizon' is no longer even a horizon, that is to say a circumscription, but an unlimited opening that I have tried to understand as 'exposure' and not as abandonment and dereliction. 'Exposure' means: to go beyond a preoccupation with 'ends'.

Rancière might suspect that this is still a dialecticized or sublimated, or however you want to put it, way of appropriating the kingdom of ends – and is therefore the prerogative of 'free humans'. And that this 'metaphysics' thus remains at once ungraspable in its generality and dependent on a more or less unavowed elitism. I do not say that he forms this suspicion, but instead that it would seem to me logical to do so.

Now this brings me to my second remark: the way of understanding the old division between 'free' and 'mechanical' human beings should be at issue before one is able to know where to place the question of the transition from a kingdom of ends to a going beyond of this kingdom. Is it possible simply to conceive of millennia of humanity in which some enjoyed playing the varied games of figuring their 'ends' while all the others were merely subject to the constraint of survival? Fundamentally, it is this picture that seems to me difficult to maintain. I may have as little knowledge as the next man of the ends to which the paintings in the Chauvet Cave were painted, but it seems to me impossible to think that these paintings – with all their technicity and their taste (for we must indeed use both these terms) – would have been without relation to the common existence of each and everyone within this or that group, which, in addition, would have possessed, in an interconnected manner, its own forms of organization, its roles, its procedures and so on.

To put it differently: the conception, the formulation and the figuration of 'ends' and/or of 'meaning', either in the form of an 'end' or else in the inverse form (not even a superfluity of the question of meaning, but its absence as a 'question') are at once always exercised by some and in the name of certain functions (determined each time by a specific culture) and endowed with circulation through the whole group. What is more, it is this circulation that makes it possible for the group to form a group.

This circulation – this division of sensible intelligibility – would have to be presented in a much finer way, but I don't have the

time to do so here. I only want to say that 'art' designates something that most certainly has nothing general about it but that
under this modern name gathers a moment or a trait that is present
in every culture (one might say the trait of the 'trait' as such, of the
tracing, of the line, colour, rhythm, timbre . . .).

This brings me to my third remark: if there is a point at which
some individuals 'decide to live a life other than the one intended
for them' – a 'pivotal' moment [*ce point de 'bascule'*], or one of
'mutation', that is decisive for Rancière but probably also no less
so for me – then how are we to understand both the fact that this
mutation came about, it having been preceded by so many different and long-lasting configurations, and indeed that it involved by
definition a problematic of 'ends' (and/or a problematization of the
very scheme of ends itself), since it is a matter both of understanding
a 'having-been-destined' and of inventing a 'destining-oneself-to'?

The pivoting [*bascule*] that Rancière emphasizes does not seem
to me to be fundamentally different from the 'death of God', apart
from in its wording, which is not nothing but nor is it the end of
the matter. I might be tempted to say: in one way or another, we
find ourselves in a situation in which it is not possible simply to
take note of a mutation, since this mutation is not comparable to
those that preceded it (such as we can represent them to ourselves),
or to differences between cultures such as they present themselves,
for example, between the Oceanian and Andean worlds, or the
Siberian and Mediterranean ones, etc. It is not comparable in
several regards, perhaps principally by virtue of the fact that in very
little time it has also involved a mutation in the overall configuration of the world and of the difference between cultures within it.

Does that not ask to be understood as (at least) the concomi-
tance of the decision of some to live differently and each and
everyone's decision to create another world? Now 'decision' is
obviously meaningless, at least in the second case (and, even in the
first, the question remains of what gives rise to it). But nor can the
term 'mutation' suffice in cases where we are no longer dealing
with a variation – even one of great amplitude – but with a sort of
throwing wide open of the entire order in which there could be
differences and mutations.

At this point what crops up may have the look of generality

but instead is a genericity: how is a humankind engendered such
that it is present to itself as the question of its own 'sense' ('end'
or 'without end')? How is a kind engendered whose existence
and activity come to envelop the existence and the movement of
everything that exists – 'nature' or 'cultures', 'histories' or 'forms'?

In other terms, it is difficult not to ask both 'what does that
mean?' and 'what lies at the basis of all that?' Questions in which
neither the 'meaning' nor the 'basis' are ideas floating in the metaphysical ether, but approximate terms announcing necessities that
are pretty much essential not only for thought but also for the most
concrete action.

Might the perception of these necessities be simply the partisan
illusion of the metaphysician threatened with losing his or her job?
I would sincerely be ready to admit as much if I did not have to
note that Rancière's own interests cannot simply be explained as
those of the 'archaeologist' to whose name he lays claim: indeed,
archaeology only exists from the moment one is longer content
merely to raze or bury the rubble of the past but needs to refer
to this past, if only to trace its contours. And this means that the
present no longer rests on stable ground, if indeed there is still a
ground. 'Ground' may seem too earthy and conservative a metaphor; however, it is probably inseparable from the idea of sharing.

Translated by Steven Corcoran

12

On Aisthesis

An Interview

Jacques Rancière and Oliver Davis

Oliver Davis: I would like to concentrate in this interview on your major new work, *Aisthesis: Scènes du régime esthétique de l'art* (2011). Why did you choose to organize the book into fourteen 'scenes'?

Jacques Rancière: It is clear that it could have had a different number of scenes. On the other hand, the decision to proceed by scenes was taken at the outset. Indeed, in contrast to books made as collections of essays, this one was conceived as a personal work of writing – somewhat as *Proletarian Nights* or *The Ignorant Schoolmaster*. Now, the scene really is central to my method. Several characteristics can be used to describe it. First of all, the method of the scene consists in choosing a singularity whose conditions of possibility one tries to reconstitute by exploring all the networks of signification that weave around it. Such is the 'Jacotot method': 'learn something and refer everything else back to it', a method that I instinctively applied even before having read Jacotot. It is the method of the 'ignorant', in a sense, as opposed to the method that first takes a set of general determinations that function as causes and then illustrates their effects in a certain number of concrete cases. In the scene, the conditions are immanent to their effectuation. This also means that the scene, as I conceive it, is fundamentally anti-hierarchical. It is the 'object' that teaches us how we can talk about it, how we can treat it. The scene abolishes the difference between the language of the object and the language of its explanation. It defines a poetics of translations and of paraphrases that maintain the equality of the discursive fabric. But the scene is also important for reflections on art which maintain that art is defined only through a specific regime of identification: through ways of perceiving, of phrasing that perception, of constructing its intelligibility. In this instance, I've chosen scenes in which a voice comments on an 'artistic event' or constitutes the event of a new interpretation of what art means: Winckelmann, inventing 'art' such as we know it by inventing 'the history of art'; Hegel, defining a new visibility of painting around two of Murillo's paintings; Banville, showing how the essence of poetry is realized in the performance of acrobatic clowns; but also such and such an obscure critic, setting out to demonstrate a propos of an exhibition or a film the essence of photographic or filmic novelty. On each occasion, there is an event and at the same time there is a text that sets out to define the sensible textures of that event and the reasons why it is an event. In this way it is possible to constitute a topography on the basis of a certain number of singular emergences that link together a certain number of schemas of perception and of interpretation.

Oliver Davis: It is clear from the title that your book differs from Auerbach's 'representational', largely literary-critical, project in *Mimesis* [1946] but what was it about the method, arrangement, or approach, of his book that you found attractive?

Jacques Rancière: I like the method that first shows the thing and asks what constitutes its specificity and what makes that specific-ity possible and thinkable. This is a way of foiling the opposition, which still lingers pretty much everywhere, between the 'close reading' of the 'canonical' text, qua practice of the aesthete, and the politically correct view that privileges the circulation of themes in the multiplicity of works addressed to the multitude. I continue to think that the attentive reading of a page of Balzac – but also of a letter by joiner Gauny – can tell us more about society and the relations of the novel with society than Franco Moretti's maps of the movements of novelistic characters and of the locations of their readers. And for me this method also approaches the method of intellectual emancipation that, between the 'master' and the 'student', institutes a third element that allows the work of verification to be carried out. In the last instance, it is a matter of knowing whether the work that creates meaning is a case of singular intellectual adventure or of the scholarly treatment of statistical data.

Oliver Davis: Why did you choose to stop in 1941, even though in the 'Prélude' you leave open the possibility of future additions? Does the linear chronological arrangement of the book's 'scenes' imply that the aesthetic regime of art has its own (progressive) teleology? Is that part of what you mean by 'the movement proper to the aesthetic regime' (p.13) or should this phrase be understood in another way?

Jacques Rancière: It is clear that my *Aisthesis* book is, as it were, like one detached piece of a project that exceeds it. Constructing the logic of the aesthetic regime through a multiplicity of interlacings and resonances was more important to me than tracing an immanent teleology. The order is chronological because, on the one hand, it leaves more space for these intertwinings and resonances than a deductive or thematic order and, on the other, sedimented experience is central both to the actors in these scenes and to the reader called on to appropriate them. Winckelmann's formulation of the theoretical invention of motionless movement, Hegel's declaring the 'canonization' of street children, Emerson's explaining the idea of new poetry and Whitman's reprise of it, and so on, are all givens that constitute the sedimented compost on which other figures of the aesthetic regime can be built: motionless theatre, a poetics of seizing the instant, the cinematographic montage of actions, and so on. At the same time, this sequence does not define a schema of evolution. But it does define a polemical attitude regarding such schemas, notably regarding the one known by the name of modernism. The idea of a counter-history of 'modernity' is a central element of the project. And from this point of view, it makes sense to show how that which became the dominant modernist paradigm (the Greenbergian theorization of the avant-garde) is in fact a liquidation of the dominant tendency of the aesthetic regime, which is to abolish the boundaries between 'mediums', between high art and popular art, and ultimately between art and life. This is something that occurred rather dramatically to me as I was simply attempting to see if the book by Agee and Evans, published in 1941, could supply a scene for *Aisthesis*. All of a sudden, I was stopped short by Agee's very violent response to a survey from *Partisan Review* on trends in American literature. Now, it appeared very clearly that this survey was the American Marxist intelligentsia's attempt to settle scores with the Whitmanian tradition and that this was the context in which the meaning of Greenberg's intervention had to be understood: to be done with that tradition of mixing that had in fact constituted the essential axis of the modernist dream, from Emerson and Whitman to Meyerhold and Vertov. Greenberg does not only say that we must do away with this model. He says, roughly speaking: the death of culture and of high art happens when the sons and daughters of peasants take up leisure activities and want culture. In fact he dismisses the entire perceptible logic of redistribution underpinning the aesthetic regime: not only Whitman but also Flaubert. And Agee's text itself is an extraordinary example of a sort of Flauberto-Whitmanism. The clash, then, looked convincing enough so that this particular book could end with this confrontation between one sort of modernism and another. Even if it is not said in *Aisthesis*, Greenberg's text is the second killing of Emma Bovary, that which wants to break the knot that tied Flaubert to Emma, in spite of everything.

Oliver Davis: Will the aesthetic regime of art have been the last regime of art?

Jacques Rancière: I have no means of knowing. That is a question you would have to ask God the Father.

Oliver Davis: You make clear that *Aisthesis* is not intended simply as a reception study: 'At issue is not the "reception" of art works. At issue is the fabric of sensible experience within which they are produced' (A10). Is this because reception theory, in your view, underestimates the power of singular artworks to work upon their audiences and transform the categories of intelligibility and sensibility through which art, in future as well as in the past, is apprehended as art? Is standard-issue reception theory too timid, or too narrow in its scope, or limited in some other way?

Jacques Rancière: My clarification implied no polemic against reception theories or analyses. It is true that such theories tend to oscillate between sociological analyses about the dissemination of works and abstract hermeneutic theories, which limits their interest from my point of view. But my objective was not to challenge reception theories. My remark only anticipated the objection that consists in reducing one regime of the identification of art to a case of reception of art works, and therefore to renewing the opposition between art properly speaking and the thought of art. For me, at issue was to recall that art 'properly speaking' only exists through the regime of identification that carves out its territory.

Oliver Davis: In a ground-breaking article for *Les Révoltes Logiques* you focused on one particular site of cultural interchange: the drinking dens and 'performance spaces' (to use an anachronistic term) lying just beyond the *barrières* of the tax cordon encircling Paris. I see that article as among the most 'sociological' of your works in its attention to a specific zone of social interaction, even if, to the extent that it is concerned with people acting 'out of role', it is the antithesis of 'sociology' as you have sometimes understood that discipline. Does your concern with specific sites and forms of exchange in that article and some of your earlier work contrast with *Aisthesis*? For I take it that the aesthetic regime of art mutates through interconnecting series of 'democratic' exchanges: the errant poet and metrical theorist Banville, for example, happens upon the Hanlon-Lees brothers and is, we might have said some decades ago, 'influenced', even 'inspired'; not just influenced in the production of his own work but in his way of thinking, which will then be transmitted to others in conversations, in *salons*, in literary reviews and other fora. This seems to be a question of influence in the broad sense, about interconnecting circles or circuits of influence along which ideas in general and one idea in particular (namely, that of 'the aesthetic regime of art' itself) is gradually re-formulated and transmitted; or, more straightforwardly and borrowing a notion of J. M. Bernstein's in his recent piece on your work on cinema, we are talking about a series of interlocking 'democratic conversations'. In *Aisthesis* you deftly capture a selection of relatively prominent individuals' singular, sometimes conflicted, invariably passionate, encounters with particular artworks and performances. But what of the networks of influence and transmission along which those reactions are subsequently 'processed', along which they are worked into the fabric of the aesthetic regime? How do they operate? Where and how do these democratic conversations which reshape the aesthetic regime take place? I ask because, in the 'Prélude', you present your project in almost Hegelian terms as one that will show, in fourteen scenes, 'thought taken up with forging the links that unite perceptions, affects, names and ideas, with constituting the sensible community that these links forge and the intellectual community that makes the weaving possible' (A12).

Jacques Rancière: I have not become an idealist in my old age. The analyses of texts presented in *Aisthesis* in 2011 and the work of going through archives upon which the article in *Révoltes Logiques* in 1978 was based on one and the same methodological principle: one that refuses to separate 'sociological reality' from its 'representations'. The 1978 article did not recount what happened in the *guinguettes* [small restaurants with music and dancing] situated on the other side of the *barrières*. The reason for this is simple: what we are able to read about this topic is generally informed by preconceived stereotypes. Thus, on the one hand, the article discussed working class amusements such as they were understood by cabaret artists or policemen, militant workers or bourgeois philanthropists. On the other, it displaced the topic, by discussing the *barrières* not as sites of pleasure but as the symbolic barrier separating 'popular culture' from its other. The article set out to mark this barrier as a form of 'division' [*partage*] in the double meaning of the word: participation and separation. The polemical character of this analysis must not be forgotten. On the one hand, it criticized the models of ideological inculcation (Althusser) and of disciplinary confinement (Foucault) by substituting them with a topography organized around a line of division that was both polemical and subject to transgression. On the other, it criticized identitarian understandings of popular culture. The analysis of Banville's text on the Hanlon-Lees operates in the same way. It does not describe what might have been said between Banville and his buddies when talking about their evenings at the theatre. But it points, in the text of a 'canonical' author who is still classified as an aesthete of the art for art's sake variety, to the fact that 'art for art's sake', properly understood, is working-class or popular entertainment. Put differently, it points to a system of identifications and of exchanges that are perfectly incompatible with identitarian discourses on 'high culture' and 'popular culture'. It points to this just where we can point at it, in texts in which the inspired 'poet' turns into the chronicler of urban entertainments. It is the form of exchange that matters to me here, the traces of which we can follow from the theatrical reporting in newspapers of the 1830s to the productions of Meyerhold and his successors. This is also 'thought taken up with forging links'. It is not the concept engendering itself and engendering reality. It is thought that does not say 'I think' but which actually assembles the elements of a perceptible and shared world: the thought of the entertainment reporter who must turn in his copy as well as that of the police commissioner who has to produce his report. They both create a shared world with what they see on the stage, what they feel of the relation between the stage and the audience, the associations that they weave around it, and so on. Of course, one can devote one's life to studying the ways in which these montages of words, images and ideas circulate in a defined area at a given time (e.g. Parisian press articles on theatre shows between 1875 and 1885). The problem is that by proceeding in this way you become a specialist of literature on entertainment shows for that chronological period and you lose sight of what is at stake. In order not to lose sight of this, I know of no other method than that which proceeds by identifying systematic knots and studying their displacements: for example, the question of theatrical action such as it can be constructed by linking Aristotle's *Poetics* with the Hanlon-Lees's stunts, Maeterlinck's 'motionless' drama, Meyerhold's biomechanical productions, and so on. What interests me is the transformation of these knots, the redistribution of the relations between the visible, movement, action, and so on. Again, this involves the application of the Jacotist principle: learn something and refer everything else back to it. This method will always stand in contrast to the one that requires you to set out from the good point of departure and follow all the stages in good order.

Oliver Davis: Would it be accurate to liken the artwork in the aesthetic regime to a *point de capiton*, a quilting point? (I mean an upholsterer's, rather than a Lacanian's already figurative quilting point.) Would it also be correct to say that the baseline definition of an artwork in that regime is any act, practice, thing, or discourse (including, for example, a piece of de-figurative writing such as Proust's on Chardin) that *works upon*, or reconfigures, already existing elements available to the regime? Do artworks and 'strong' (non-trivial) discursive (art-critical) interventions perform the same or a similar structural function in the aesthetic regime?

Jacques Rancière: I'm not sure I know exactly what a quilting point is – outside the manufacture of mattresses. But it seems to me that it is a privileged point of articulation between two fabrics or two systems. I do not see any such function within the aesthetic regime of arts, to the extent that a regime of identification is a constant intertwining between practices and their modes of interpretation. Simply it seems to me that there are works or texts that more particularly exemplify, or make explicit, the modes of composition and the regimes of perception and interpretation that characterize the aesthetic regime of art. This is the case with the Goncourt brothers' texts that I analysed in *The Future of the Image*: they constituted a new gaze on works of the past, a displaced gaze of the subject of painting towards pictorial materiality. This is also the case, in *Aisthesis,* with the knot constituted between the sculptural work-in-pieces (the fragments of Rodin's *The Gates of Hell*) and an entire regime of interpretation that undoes the traditional articulation between the art of sculpture and the organic model. In this way, there are a certain number of works and interpretative schemas that forge the fabric of the aesthetic regime. It is on the basis of them that I have been able to construct my 'scenes'. And then there are works or interpretative schemas that find their place in this regime in accordance with the mutation of paradigms to which the former have made a significant contribution.

Oliver Davis: Can you expand on the political significance of aesthetic distance (or 'separation', or 'withdrawal', or 'indifference', or 'non-determination')? You show how Winckelmann, in his encounter with the torso of Hercules, which for you is an inaugural moment in the history of the aesthetic regime of art, is among the first to formulate a new understanding of the artwork in this new regime as that which suspends the opposition between activity and passivity. In the 'Prélude' to *Aisthesis* you refer back to your work on the Saint-Simonians and their (theoretically) egalitarian cult of work and highlight the paradox, which you imply has a political meaning, or consequence, that the seductive beauty of this utopian ideal of industriousness brought the hand of one new worker-recruit to a standstill (A16–17). This seems to be reverie disrupting instrumental reason's smooth progress from aims through means to ends; a suspension, in the workplace, of the representational regime's Aristotelian logic of action. At a seminar in London (March 2012), you responded to a question by saying that 'There are different ways of understanding [I understood: politically] what "passivity" is.' One of them, you suggested, is the sudden, inert, 'passive', or static, presence of the emergent *sans-part* in the field of politics at a moment of popular insurrection: 'we, the people, are here'. In what ways is this more than an *analogy* with aesthetic experience?

Jacques Rancière: The necessary point of departure is what one could call the hierarchical square, which is defined by two traditional oppositions: there is the opposition between active people (those who are able to define and pursue ends) and passive people (those who are confined to the universe of means); and there is the opposition that sets the people of leisure (free people living in a time subtracted from necessity) against working people (people living in the mere alternation of activity and rest). In the hierarchical square, 'passive people' manifest their passive condition by their very activity – the activity of production of means of existence – whereas active people are also recognized by their way of not doing anything, by their monopoly of leisure. The hierarchical square structures representational logic just as it structures social domination. There are two ways to conceive a break with it: there is the way that the Saint-Simonians epitomise, that is, the 'rehabilitation' of work – its definition as activity *par excellence*. But this rehabilitation is also a reformulation of the hierarchical logic: Saint-Simonian 'priests' go about recruiting 'strong workers' for the industrial army of workers, an army whose generals are engineers who know which works have to be done and how. And there is the way embodied by the workers who come to listen to their sermons or take part in their celebrations. This way passes via the exploration of a mediation that is apt to redistribute the relations between the terms of the square: *inactivity* becomes a way of not doing what one is supposed to do, but also of changing the meaning of 'not doing', of transforming the worker's rest into the leisure activity of the free individual. Inactivity hollows out 'passivity' in diverse ways: it may be the gaze of the joiner suspending the activity of his arms; the daydream of the tailor dreaming of the beauties of pictorial materiality; or reading, writing or meeting up after the work day. This is also one of the dimensions of striking, that which would come to be summarized in the idea of the general strike: the strike where stopping one's arms is no longer the instrument of a particular negotiation but a global secession with respect to one sensible order. The structure of the general strike is also close to that of the barricade, which starts by transforming the instruments of circulation (carts at the time) into elements for building a roadblock and for constituting a certain theatrical presence of the worker collective – a presence that in itself is anti-strategic (revolutionary strategists such as Blanqui criticize it for this). The question of knowing whether, in this, there is more than an 'analogy' with 'the aesthetic experience' crops up only if 'aesthetic experience' is isolated as something that exists separately – the experience of the Kantian subject or the contemplation of an aesthete. All the figures that I have just evoked are in fact aesthetic. All of them modify the forms of occupying time and space in which the relations between activity and inactivity are concretized. The philosophical formulation of aesthetic experience – with Kant or Schiller – is only an element of a redistribution that largely exceeds it and that is precisely manifest in forms of the aesthetics of politics as in those of the politics of aesthetics.

Oliver Davis: Following on from that question about the political valency of a certain kind of passivity, I was thinking about your analysis of the young girl Estike in Béla Tarr's film of László Krasznahorkai's novel *Sátántangó* and wondering about the potentially disruptive political (or proto-political) force of something which you call, in that analysis, 'idiocy': 'Idiocy does not designate a measure of intellectual quotient, but two structural features, two opposed and complementary features that are equally necessary for playing the lead role in Béla Tarr's films: both the capacity to absorb the environment totally and to wager against it' (A46). Within Tarr's cinematic world there is tragic potency in the stubbornly persistent imitative literalism of Estike's 'idiocy'; she and other 'idiots' who, as you suggest, play similarly prominent roles in other films by Tarr, seem to have many of the necessary psychic resources for political struggle but no sense (moral or otherwise) of a worthwhile goal. Estike, as you characterize her, is paradoxical because she is imitative to the point where this becomes disruptive. The idea of self-emancipation through the autodidactic exercise of intellectual freedom is clearly one important emphasis in your work overall but do you also see strategic political value in persisting stubbornly, 'idiotically', in not seeing or 'failing' to see the 'necessity' of the consensus, of a given *partage du sensible*? Is there a Sartrean logic here of *qui perd gagne*?

Jacques Rancière: There is a whole history of idiocy as a figure apt to blur the game of explanations and strategies. Of course Dostoyevsky comes to mind and there is something of Myshkin in the Valuska of *Werckmeister Harmonies*. Dostoyevsky constructed the figure of the idiot as an antidote to the progressivist-socialist view of history that he saw emerging. In contrast to Béla Tarr, who arrived after the historical sequence of 'real socialism', he sought in the figure of the idiot to preserve a figure of refusal, to save it from the disaster of the system. The question that traverses Béla Tarr films and is emblematized in these figures of idiocy is to know whether one draws from the communist failure a simple lesson of the nihilistic equivalence of everything with everything else, or whether one extracts figures of refusal out of nihilism. What appeared clearly at the time of the collapse of the Soviet Bloc is that the supposed 'ideological cement' linking individuals to a system of domination was nothing other than people consenting to pay lip service to the official lie. Against this consent to the lie, Béla Tarr sets figures of idiocy that do not accept that the promise of words is only consent to lying and the madman that does not renounce the promise of harmony present in the celestial system. This attitude can be defined as proto-political, in the sense that through their stubbornness these characters radicalize a decision prior to all political action – the decision to verify through one's own actions that not everything is a lie. But it scarcely makes sense to oppose this 'stupid' stubbornness to the intelligence of a strategic aim. Only things that actually stand opposed really ought to be set against one another. And the complement that both Estike and Valuska lack that would allow a real political subject to emerge is not some strategic aim. All that they stand opposed to is general cowardice and petty individual arrangements. If we leave the context of Béla Tarr's films, we come across an analogy in the arguments used by strategists of anticapitalist combat against the 'indignant', who are 'without project'. The problem is that these strategists don't have any projects either. What they do have is simply the ability to explain endlessly that a project is required. The opposition is in fact an opposition between two sorts of obstinacy: the obstinacy to turn around in the circle of explanation, which is part and parcel of the consensus; and the obstinacy to mark a distance that at least conserves the possibility of dissensus.

Oliver Davis: What do you understand by the term 'aesthetic equality'?

Jacques Rancière: Aesthetic equality takes multiple, potentially conflicting forms. First, such as it is practised by artists and writers, it is the equal capacity of every situation or of every character whatsoever to be the subject of art. Or further: it is the equality of all events of sensibility that challenge causal hierarchies. But we know that this equality of events of sensibility simultaneously stands in relation to, and in conflict with, another type of aesthetic equality: that whereby nondescript individuals claim that they are capable of participating in the forms of sensibility from which they are excluded: sensual passion, ideal love, aimless reverie, disinterested aesthetic contemplation, artistic creation, the invention of collective forms of action, and all those 'revolts fermenting in the mass of lives peopling the earth' that Charlotte Bronte evoked in the passage of *Jane Eyre* that served as a basis for Virginia Woolf's feminist reflections in *A Room of One's Own*. But at the same time, as an artist, Virginia Woolf was obliged to distinguish the 'luminous halo' of impersonal life from these 'rebellions', which remained locked in the old logic of representational intrigue. Like Flaubert, she was obliged to oppose the equality of the micro-events of sensibility to all these subjective emergences that undermined the hierarchy of forms of life. Like Proust, she was obliged to oppose to them the statement that literature alone is the 'life really lived'. This is the condition by which art maintains its difference from within its very solidarity with the forms of aesthetic equality. This is one of the aspects of the dialectic according to which inequality needs to ground itself in equality in order to deny it.

Oliver Davis: I wanted to ask you about the interiority of the modern subject (or agent, or spectator) and about the capacity of psychoanalysis to gain a hold on that. Unlike most poststructuralist thinkers you seem to have almost no time for psychoanalysis. Can you explain this aversion, if aversion it really is? Is it because, as you suggested in *The Aesthetic Unconscious*, the conceptual resources found in psychoanalysis had already been developed by the aesthetic regime of arts; or are your reservations political? Do you see psychoanalysis as intrinsically anti-egalitarian or in some other way pernicious? Even forms of psychoanalysis as practised by people like Guattari and Laing, even 'deterritorialized' and non-institutional psychoanalytic understanding of the sort theorized by Laplanche in his concept of 'wild psychoanalysis'? I ask partly because we have a contribution in this volume by a psychoanalyst and because in your recent work (in both *Aisthesis* and *Les Écarts du cinéma*, for example) you seem to be more interested than you once were in interiority, at least when you write about the affective attachment of the spectator to the work, although you choose to speak in the decidedly non-psychoanalytic terms of passion and *philia*. I ask also because it seems to me that one of the ideas in play in *The Ignorant Schoolmaster*, when you remark that it is quite possible for a student to learn useful things from even a bad teacher, is that of the unconscious (or transferential) acquisition of knowledge, the unconscious 'picking up' of attitudes and dispositions 'shed' by a subject with whom one is in some sort of proximity, things which may not at all be what the teacher is trying to teach.

Jacques Rancière: I do not think that the question of the unconscious is identical with that of interiority. But more generally, I have found little interest in questions of interiority. For me thought is always something that is exposed, written and able to be shared with, and appropriated by, others. This is my Sartrean side, if you recall Sartre's famous text on Husserl and consciousness as that which is outside, a thing among things.[1] That text shaped me a lot when I was young. The interpretation it gives of Husserl is doubtless mistaken. Little matter, it has always defined my attitude: the idea that what people have in their heads holds no interest. The only thing of interest is what they do with their thought, the way in which they conduct it materially. Naturally this links with my opposition to explanations that refer to that which lies underneath, or behind, that which holds the position of explanatory principle and gives specialists the power of explanation. And it is clear that nowadays psychoanalysis has provided a massive supply of artillery to all the mind-numbing explicators who interpret all events involving individuals and groups using a few indefinitely repeated stereotypes. But in any case, my problem doesn't lie there. I fully accept that our learning and our motivation have unconscious roots. What interests me, however, is the horizontal circulation of words and images, the way in which they become anonymous and lend themselves to multiple re-appropriations. In the passage of *The Ignorant Schoolmaster* to which you are referring, that is what stands at the centre: the fact that it is possible to treat the teacher like a book – that is to say not as a sum of authority but as a thing that one holds in one's hand, that one observes, that one dissects, and of which one appropriates this or that element. At issue here is not a phenomenon of unconscious acquisition or a phenomenon of transfer. Of course, the issue of transfer can be raised a propos of the ignorant schoolmaster. Precisely, however, the symbolic authority of the ignorant schoolmaster is one thing, and the operation that transforms the speech of the learned master into a 'thing' at one's disposal, is another.

Oliver Davis: I am struck by the prominence of bodies in *Aisthesis*, particularly the acrobatic and contorted body but also, on the part of the spectator, of the 'receptive' body; the 'serpentine' dance of Loïe Fuller, the acrobatic feats of the Hanlon-Lees brothers, the 'gestique' of Chaplin or Keaton, the truncated body of the statue of Hercules, but also the agitated bodies of the audience trembling in harmony with the extraordinary spectacle of the 'Happy Zigzags' presented by novelist Jean Richepin in *Braves gens* (1886). These bodies are all, in differently striking ways, emphatically not the 'docile bodies' of Foucault's *Discipline and Punish*, bodies shaped by disciplinary power for productive economic and other social uses. Do the 'Happy Zigzags' and their descendants point to another and less widely acknowledged dimension to embodied 'spectatorship' – 'kinesthetic empathy', so to speak – which may function in significantly different, perhaps more insidious, ways than the looking and listening of ordinary spectatorship? How far did Artaud's new theatre, for example, imply this form of empathic, corporeal, 'spectatorship' and how would you accommodate it within (or indeed exclude it from) your theorization of the aesthetic regime and emancipated spectatorship?

Jacques Rancière: As far as the question of the body is concerned, we should first take a few steps back. Modernist doxa quite readily defines the anti-representational revolution through the opposition of 'presence' to representation. But as it is essentially constructed around an artwork whose material presence is actually rather limited, namely painting, the result is that this presence is rather mystical. To criticize the 'flesh' of Merleau-Ponty, Deleuze has to use the writhing bodies of Bacon and the metaphor of the boxing ring, which, we know, theatre people in the time of Meyerhold, Eisenstein and Brecht were the first to appropriate. If we want to analyse the forms of the anti-representational revolution, we would do better to set out from the art that effectively furnished its model to the representational system, that is, drama. We can better define the aesthetic rupture by seeing it in relation to the paradigm of representational action. And that rupture can be summed up as follows: Aristotle referred dramatic action to the textual chain of causes and effects by subordinating to it what he called *opsis*, which is the disposition of bodies in the scenic space; aesthetic logic, by contrast, privileges that disposition of bodies, including under opposed figures: corporeal language of expression (Diderot, Noverre), motionless theatre (Maeterlinck), pantomime or gymnastic exercises (Meyerhold) and curative anthropological practices (Artaud). The essential thing – often forgotten by contemporary stage directors – is that the pre-eminence of bodies and of movement of bodies proceeds to the detriment of the logic of action (as the pursuit of ends and conflicts between ends). It is thus performed against the strategic model but equally against the model of the 'docile' body. From thereon in, there are two rival models: there is the model of bodies whose performance is offered as the weave on which the spectator will embroider his or her own reverie: this is the model theorized by the tradition of Gautier-Banville-Mallarmé and to which Chaplin's performances still belonged. And there is the empathic model, the model of the collective trance, theorized notably by Artaud but the effects of which Richepin had already thought through apropos of the Happy Zigzags. It is clear that the first model most conforms to aesthetic logic and that the second marks more the uncertain limits between aesthetic indetermination and ethical impregnation. But rarely can concrete figures be reduced to pure models. And the ethical model presupposes a certain pre-established harmony between a society and a form of spectacle, whereas Artaud's theatre is immediately presented as a sort of foreign body whose effects are not pre-determinable and that therefore lends itself to all sorts of appropriations.

Oliver Davis: Finally, you mentioned in London an artwork by an Indian artists' collective involving pages from your books; do you ever find yourself imagining new works, or forms of work, or indeed new forms of art criticism?

Jacques Rancière: You are doubtless referring to the Raqs Media Collective, an Indian artists' collective that has reprised elements of Gauny's texts taken from *Proletarian Nights* and has echoed them in a video called *Strikes at Time*, with elements borrowed from a contemporary Indian collective of workers who write in the evening after work, as did Gauny and the proletarians of the nineteenth century whom I discussed. As far as I am concerned, I do not project new forms of art or of critique. I merely try, on my own behalf and through my writing, to break the barriers separating work and critique, narrative and theory, meaning, in the last instance, the barriers that separate intelligence from itself in order to ensure domination.

Translated by Steven Corcoran

Notes

Editor's Introduction

1   *Les Révoltes Logiques* (1975–81) was also the title of a radical history journal produced by a collective of which Rancière was one of the leading lights; one of the others was Geneviève Fraisse, a contributor to this volume.

2   See Kristin Ross's invaluable Introduction to her translation of this text (ISvii–xxiii) and Davis, *Jacques Rancière*, pp. 25–35.

3   They are right to do so in the case of the particular creative writing pedagogies on which they mainly focus. However, I would still maintain, as I argued in an earlier article which they discuss, that François Bon's particular conception of the writing workshop can indeed be considered an example of Jacotian universal teaching. Oliver Davis, 'The Radical Pedagogies of François Bon and Jacques Rancière', *French Studies* 64, 2 (April 2010), 178–91.

4   Todd May, 'Active Equality: Democratic Politics', in *The Political Thought of Jacques Rancière: Creating Equality*, Edinburgh: Edinburgh University Press, 2008, pp. 38–77.

5   For a fuller discussion of political subjectivation see my *Jacques Rancière*, pp. 84–100.

6   Kristin Ross, 'Historicizing Untimeliness', in Rockhill and Watts (eds.), *Jacques Rancière: History, Politics, Aesthetics*, Durham NC: Duke University Press, 2009, pp. 15–29.

7   The metaphor of 'staging' is borrowed from Peter Hallward, 'Staging Equality: Rancière's Theatrocracy and the Limits of Anarchic Equality', in Rockhill and Watts (eds.), *Jacques Rancière: History, Politics, Aesthetics*, pp. 140–57.

8   On the Situationist lineage of this most famous of May's graffiti slogans see McKenzie Wark, *The Beach Beneath the Street: The Everyday Life and Glorious*

Times of the Situationist International, London: Verso, 2011, in particular pp. 149–50.

1 Rancière, Politics and the Social Question

1 See Rancière, 'Politics, Identification and Subjectivization', *October* 61 (1992), 59 where he attributes 'the current dead-end of political reflection and action' to 'the identification of politics with the *self* of a community' (italics in original).

2 This point has been made by Slavoj Žižek in *The Ticklish Subject: The Absent Centre of Political Ontology*, London: Verso, 1999, p. 230 and others, including Oliver Davis in *Jacques Rancière*, Cambridge: Polity, 2010, pp. 93–4.

3 Rancière, 'Politics, identification, subjectivization', 59.

4 Ibid., 60.

5 Ibid., 59.

6 Rancière situates his work explicitly in this context in his preface to the 1998 French edition of *Aux bords du politique*, Paris: Gallimard, p. 10.

7 Jodi Dean, 'Politics without Politics', in Paul Bowman and Richard Stamp (eds.), *Reading Rancière. Critical Dissensus*, London: Continuum, 2011, p. 76.

8 Rancière has observed ('Politics, Identification and Subjectivization', 63) that in the 1970s, there was another name for those designated by the 1990s as immigrants – the name 'workers'.

9 For example, the proportion of unemployed people in France classed as long-term unemployed rose from 12 per cent in 1974 to 39.4 per cent in 1998. Daniel Mouchard *Etre représenté. Mobilisations d'"exclus" dans la France des années 1990*, Paris: Economica, 2009, p. 27.

10 Robert Castel, *From Manual Workers to Wage Laborers: The Transformation of the Social Question*, New Brunswick, NJ: Transaction Publishers, 2003, p. 389.

11 Luc Boltanski and Eve Chiapello, *The New Spirit of Capitalism*, London: Verso, 2007, pp. 347–9. This point is also taken up by Martin O'Shaughnessy in *The New Face of Political Cinema: Commitment in French Film since 1995*, Oxford: Berghahn, 2007, pp. 8–10.

12 E.g. Nick Hewlett, *Badiou, Balibar, Rancière: Rethinking Emancipation*, London: Continuum, 2007, pp. 102–4; Kristin Ross offers a reading of the memory of May '68 informed by Rancière's critique of consensus politics in her *May '68 and its Afterlives*, Chicago: Chicago University Press, 2002.

13 Dean, 'Politics without Politics', pp. 76–7.

14 Kristin Ross, 'Historicizing Untimeliness', in Gabriel Rockhill and Philip Watts (eds.), *Jacques Rancière: History, Politics, Aesthetics*, Durham NC: Duke University Press, 2009, pp. 15–29.

15 Jacques Lévy, Juliette Rennes, David Zerbib, 'Jacques Rancière: les territoires de la pensée partagée' *Espacestemps.net*, Actuel, 8 January 2007. http:// www.espacestemps.net/document2142.html. This and all subsequent websites referenced in this volume accessed September 2012.

16 Davis, *Jacques Rancière*, p.100.

17 There have been some links with the labour movement nonetheless. On the

movements of the unemployed, for example, see Frédéric Royall, 'Politics and unemployment organisations in France', *Modern and Contemporary France* 12,1 (2004), 49–62.

18 Rancière, 'Politics, Identification, Subjectivization', 60–1.

19 Mouchard, *Etre représenté*, p.39.

20 The Occupy movement as it is known in the English-speaking world also drew on the model of the Spanish Indignados whose protests had begun in May 2011.

21 http://www.rawstory.com/rs/2011/11/17/gingrich-no-such-thing-as-99/.

22 http://the53.tumblr.com/.

23 Todd Henderson, 'Occupy Wall Street and the Myth of the 99%' *Forbes*, 12 December 2011 http://www.forbes.com/sites/realspin/2011/12/12/occupy-wall-street-and-the-myth-of-the-99/.

24 Žižek, *The Ticklish Subject*, pp. 230–2; Davis, *Jacques Rancière*, pp. 93–4.

25 For a fuller discussion of these issues see Hewlett, *Badiou, Balibar, Rancière*, pp. 17–22 and 84–95 and Davis, *Jacques Rancière*, pp. 1–35.

26 See also Chapter 3 of this volume.

27 Peter Hallward has also noted Rancière's lack of interest in the group dynamics of collective mobilization in Hallward, 'Staging Equality: Rancière's Theatocracy and the Limits of Anarchic Equality' In: Gabriel Rockhill and Philip Watts (eds.), *Jacques Rancière: History, Politics, Aesthetics*, Duke University Press, Durham NC, 2009, pp. 140–57, at p. 154.

28 Lévy, Rennes, Zerbib, 'Jacques Rancière: les territoires de la pensée partagée'.

29 The absence of affect in Rancière's account has also been discussed by Davis who raises the question of the role of indignation in the face of disrespect or injustice as a force behind the process of subjectivation. Davis, *Jacques Rancière*, pp. 97–8.

30 Mouchard, *Etre représenté*, pp. 51–2.

31 Todd May, *Contemporary Political Movements and the Thought of Jacques Rancière. Equality in Action*, Edinburgh: Edinburgh University Press, 2010, pp. 109–28.

32 This is Pierre Rosanvallon's estimate, cited by Boltanski and Chiapello, *The New Spirit of Capitalism*, p. 275. Around 20 per cent of the population was unionized in 1976, compared to around 9 per cent by the late 1990s. The factors which contributed to this collapse are discussed in Boltanski and Chiapello, *The New Spirit of Capitalism*, pp. 279–96.

33 http://www.opendemocracy.net/ourkingdom/sophie-willett/eight-months-after-english-riots-young-lives-blighted-by-punitive-sentenci

34 http://dreamofsafety.blogspot.co.uk/2011/08/paul-gilroy-speaks-on-riots-august-2011.html

35 http://www.social-europe.eu/2011/08/the-london-riots-on-consumerism-coming-home-to-roost/

36 The term was used by Secretary of State for Justice, Kenneth Clarke: http://www.guardian.co.uk/uk/2011/sep/05/kenneth-clarke-riots-penal-system

37 See, for example, the clash between Conservative Michael Gove and Labour's Harriet Harman on the BBC programme *Newsnight*: http://www.youtube.com/watch?v=UgXuX32ot8w

38 http://www.youtube.com/watch?v=mzDQCT0AJcw

39 http://dreamofsafety.blogspot.co.uk/2011/08/paul-gilroy-speaks-on-riots-a ugust-2011.html

2 Rancière and the Social Sciences

1 Nick Hewlett, *Badiou, Balibar, Rancière. Rethinking Emancipation*, London and New York: Continuum, 2007, p. 108.
2 Alberto Toscano, 'Anti-Sociology and its Limits', in Paul Bowman and Richard Stamp (eds.), *Reading Rancière*, London and New York: Continuum, pp. 217–37 (p. 232). Subsequent references to this article will be to 'Anti-Sociology' in parentheses in the text.
3 Oliver Davis, *Jacques Rancière*, Cambridge: Polity, 2010, pp. 23–4.
4 Charlotte Nordmann, *Bourdieu/Rancière. La politique entre sociologie et philosophie*, Paris: Amsterdam, 2006, p. 129.
5 Pierre Bourdieu, *Distinction: a social critique of the judgement of taste*, trans. R. Nice, London: Routledge and Kegan Paul, 1984.
6 Rancière, 'Thinking Between Disciplines: an aesthetics of knowledge', trans. J. Roffe, *Parrhesia* 1 (2006), 1–12 (at p.6). Subsequent references to this article will be to 'Disciplines' in parentheses in the text.
7 See Bourdieu, *Pascalian Meditations*, trans. R. Nice, Cambridge: Polity, 2000, pp. 9–83.
8 Plato, *The Republic*, trans. A. D. Lindsay, London: J. M. Dent, 1935, p.100.
9 Bourdieu, *Language and Symbolic Power*, trans. G. Raymond and M. Adamson, Cambridge: Polity, 1991, p. 235.
10 Bourdieu, *Pascalian Meditations*, p. 191.
11 Bourdieu, 'Questions de politique', *Actes de la recherche en sciences sociales* 16 (1977), 51–89, p. 80.
12 Ibid., pp. 71–2.
13 Bourdieu, *Si le monde social m'est supportable, c'est parce que je peux m'indigner*, La Tour d'Aigues: Éditions de l'aube, 2002, pp. 14–15, my translation.
14 Bourdieu, *Ce que parler veut dire: l'économie des échanges linguistiques*, Paris: Fayard, 1982.
15 Judith Butler, *Excitable Speech: A Politics of the Performative*, London and New York, Routledge, 1997, p. 145.
16 Rancière, 'Against an Ebbing Tide. An Interview with Jacques Rancière', in Paul Bowman and Richard Stamp (eds.), *Reading Rancière*, pp. 238–51 (at pp. 242–3).
17 G. Borio, F. Pozzi and G. Roggero, *Futuro anteriore. Dai 'Quaderni rossi' ai movimenti globali: ricchezze e limiti dell'operaismo italiano*, Rome: DeriveApprodi, 2002.

3 Emancipation versus Domination

1 Jacques Rancière, *La Leçon d'Althusser*, Foreward to the new French edition, Paris: La Fabrique, 2012, p. 12.
2 Ibid., p. 11.
3 Ibid., p. 11.

4 The collective of *Les Révoltes Logiques, L'Empire du sociologue*, Paris: La Découverte, 1984.

5 Rancière, 'Cesser de vivre dans le monde de l'ennemi', *Libération*, 17 November 2011.

6 [In my defence this was my first attempt at a translation of the title of Geneviève Fraisse's chapter from a brief abstract which gave very little indication of the weight which would subsequently come to be placed in the finished chapter on 'domination' in contradistinction to 'oppression'. The document in question was never intended for publication. – Editor's note.]

7 Geneviève Fraisse, *La Fabrique du féminisme, Textes et entretiens*, Paris: Le Passager clandestin, 2012.

8 Jean Borreil, *La Raison nomade*, Preface by Jacques Rancière, Paris: Payot, 1993.

9 Geneviève Fraisse, *Reason's Muse*, Chicago: Chicago Press, 1993.

10 'L'école de l'égalité en question', Round Table discussion on Jacques Rancière in a colloquium entitled *Le métier d'instruire*, La Rochelle, 15–16 May 1990, Centre National de Documentation Pédagogique/Collège International de Philosophie, Poitiers, 1992, p. 58.

11 See 'les amis de nos amis' [1991], article reprinted in *A côté du genre, sexe et philosophie de l'égalité*, Paris: Le Bord de l'eau, 2010, pp. 162–9.

12 Geneviève Fraisse 'Le chant des sirènes', *A côté du genre, Sexe et philosophie de l'égalité*, Le Bord de l'eau, 2010, pp. 204–14.

13 Geneviève Fraisse and Michelle Perrot (eds.), *A History of Women in the West*, Volume IV (nineteenth century), G. Duby and M. Perrot (general eds.), Cambridge, MA: Harvard University Press, 1993.

14 Jacques Rancière, 'Sur *l'histoire des femmes* au XIXème siècle', in Georges Duby and Michelle Perrot (eds.), *Femmes et histoire* (proceedings of a colloquium held at the Sorbonne, 13–14 November 1992), Paris: Plon, 1993, p. 58.

15 'De la destination au destin, histoire philosophique de la différence des sexes', pp. 57–85; reprinted as 'Les deux sexes et la philosophie au XIXème siècle', in *Les femmes et leur histoire*, Paris: Folio-Gallimard, 2010, pp. 65–122.

16 Jacques Rancière, 'Sur le devenir-sujet politique *des* femmes: réflexions historiques', *Cahiers du GEDISST*, n°11, IRESCO-CNRS, 1994, p. 34.

17 For example, Rancière, *The Emancipated Spectator,* trans. Gregory Elliot, London: Verso, 2009, p. 20.

18 Julie-Victoire Daubié, the first woman to pass the baccalaureat (1861) and the author notably of *La femme pauvre au XIXème siècle*, 1866.

19 See, *Reason's Muse*, ch. 1.

20 For example at HD60.

21 Jacques Rancière, 'Sur le devenir-sujet politique *des* femmes: réflexions historiques', *Cahiers du GEDISST*, 11, IRESCO-CNRS, 1994.

22 Joan Scott, *Only Paradoxes to Offer*, Cambridge, MA: Harvard University Press, 1996.

23 Jacques Rancière, 'Sur le devenir-sujet politique *des* femmes: réflexions historiques', *Cahiers du GEDISST* 11, IRESCO-CNRS, 1994, p. 42.

24 No reference is given here to the English translation because for some (unexplained) reason this first section of the essay on political art has been omitted from the Verso translation.

4 Reading Rancière

1 *La Nuit des prolétaires: archives du rêve ouvrier*, Fayard, Paris, 1981, appeared in
   English as *The Nights of Labor. The Workers' Dream in Nineteenth-Century
   France*, trans. John Drury, intro. Donald Reid, Temple University Press,
   Philadelphia PA, 1989.
2 'Questions from a Worker Who Reads', Bertolt Brecht, *Poems 1913–1956*,
   trans. M. Hamburger, Methuen, New York and London, 1976. 'A Worker
   Reads History', Bertolt Brecht, *Poems by Bertolt Brecht, Selected and Introduced
   by Denys Thompson*, trans. H. R. Hays, Chatto and Windus, London, 1972,
   was more widely circulated in the UK. 'Arthur Exell, 1911–1992', *History
   Workshop Journal (HWJ)* 35:1 (1993), 280–1; Arthur Exell, 'Morris Motors in
   the 1930s', *HWJ* 6 (1978), 52–78; 'Morris Motors in the 1930s, Part II', *HWJ*
   7 (1979), 45–65; 'Morris Motors in the 1940s', *HWJ* 9 (1980), 90–115.
3 For the workers' Saturday night (the Ran-dan), Carolyn Steedman, 'Cries
   Unheard, Sights Unseen: Writing the Eighteenth-Century Metropolis',
   Representations 118 (2012), 28–71.
4 Ruskin College, Oxford, is not part of Oxford University. It was founded in
   1899 to provide educational opportunities for working-class men. History
   Workshop (conferences, meetings, and Movement) was inaugurated at
   Ruskin in 1966. 'Politically, the Workshop was shaped by – and to some
   extent anticipated – a series of left-wing stirrings, common in Britain and
   Europe in the late 1960s. As a trade union college, largely recruited from
   young workers, Ruskin was particularly sensitive to . . . [a] rise of worker-
   militancy in Britain'. Raphael Samuel, 'Editorial, Introduction', *History
   Workshop. A Collectanea 1967–1991*, History Workshop, Ruskin College,
   Oxford, 1991, p.1.
5 Bishopsgate Institute, London, Raphael Samuel Archive, RS 7/037,
   Prospectus for Workshop 13. When I first consulted this archive it was
   housed at Ruskin College; it moved to the Bishopsgate Institute in May
   2011. I am extremely grateful to Valerie Moyses, Ruskin Director of Library
   and Learning Resources, for her help with my early inquiries.
6 Jacques Rancière, '"Le Social": The Lost Tradition in French Labour
   History', Raphael Samuel (ed.), *People's History and Socialist Theory*, Routledge
   and Kegan Paul, London, 1981, pp. 267–72.
7 Bishopsgate Institute, London, History Workshop, Correspondence, 7/38,
   letter from Andrew Lincoln to Raphael Samuel, 28.10.79; undated note
   from Lincoln to same. There was concern expressed about who exactly was
   going to pay for the Parisian contributors to travel to Oxford, by Lincoln and
   by Cottereau ('il y a urgence pour la question du voyage: je serai obligé de
   prendre l'avion . . .'). History Workshop, Correspondence, 7/38, Alain
   Cottereau to Raphael Samuel, 29.10.1979.
8 Martin Kettle, 'The Experience of History', *New Society* (6 Dec 1979).
9 As one Sunday afternoon participant recalled: Bishopsgate Institute, London,
   History Workshop Audio Collection RS062b.
10 Jonathan Rée, 'A Theatre of Arrogance', *The Times Higher Education
   Supplement* (2 Jun, 1995); Dennis Dworkin, *Cultural Marxism in Postwar
   Britain*, Duke University Press, Durham SC, 1997, pp. 232–45; Susan
   Magarey, 'That Hoary Old Chestnut, Free Will and Determinism: Culture

vs. Structure, or History vs. Theory in Britain. A Review Article', *Comparative Studies in Society and History,* 29:3 (2009), pp. 626–39. For a recent extended account of the deconsecrated church event, Scott Hamilton, *The Crisis of Theory. E. P. Thompson, the New Left and Postwar British Politics,* Manchester University Press, Manchester and New York, 2011, pp. 155–83.

11 Carolyn Steedman, Cathy Urwin and Valerie Walkerdine (eds.), *Language, Gender and Childhood,* Routledge and Kegan Paul, London, 1985, pp. 1–9.

12 For something of the agonistic experience of the 'linguistic turn' among Anglophone historians (especially the British ones), Bryan D. Palmer, *Descent into Discourse. The Reification of Language and the Writing of Social History,* Temple University Press, Philadelphia PA, 1990; Patrick Joyce, 'The End of Social History?', *Social History,* 20 (1995), pp. 73–91; Keith Windschuttle, *The Killing of History: How Literary Critics and Social Theorists are Murdering our Past,* Free Press, New York, 1997; Richard Evans, *In Defence of History,* Granta, London, 1997. For a historical account of 'the world of historians' and the 'much vaunted "linguistic turn"', Geoff Eley, *A Crooked Line. From Cultural History to the History of Society,* University of Michigan Press, Ann Arbor MI, 2005, pp. 123–6, 156–9, 198–200.

13 Jacques Rancière, 'Politics and Aesthetics. An Interview', trans. Forbes Morlock, intro. Peter Hallward, *Angelaki. Journal of Theoretical Humanities* 8:2 (2003), 191–211.

14 E. P. Thompson, 'The Poverty of Theory: or, An Orrery of Errors', *The Poverty of Theory and Other Essays,* Merlin, London, 1978, pp. 193–397.

15 Kettle, 'Experience of History'.

16 Samuel, *History Workshop. A Collectanea 1967–1991,* p. 97.

17 Rancière contemplates this point anew in 'Preface to the New English Edition', *Proletarian Nights. The Workers' Dream in Nineteenth-Century France,* Verso, London and New York, 2012, pp. vii–xii.

18 Annie Ernaux, *La Place,* Gallimard, Paris, 1993.

19 Kristin Ross, 'Historicizing Untimeliness', Gabriel Rockhill and Philip Watts (eds.), *Jacques Rancière. History, Politics, Aesthetics,* Duke University Press, Durham SC and London, 2009, pp.15–29.

20 Date boundaries are provided by 'The Lost Tradition in French Labour History' (1981) and the second edition of *Le Philosophe et ses pauvres* (2007).

21 Bishopsgate Institute, London, History Workshop, 7/43, Session Report; History Workshop Audio Collection RS062b.

22 Rancière, '"Le Social"', *People's History and Socialist Theory,* pp. 267–72.

23 Rancière, '"Le Social"', p. 272.

24 Laurence Sterne, *A Sentimental Journey though France and Italy* (1768), Penguin, Harmondsworth, 1968, p. 27.

25 The project of recovery was proclaimed in E. P. Thompson's Preface to *The Making of the English Working Class* (1963), Penguin, London, 1980, p. 12: 'I am seeking to rescue the poor stockinger, the Luddite cropper, the "obsolete" hand-loom weaver, the "utopian" artisan . . . from the enormous condescension of posterity'.

26 Leora Auslander, 'Archiving a Life: Post-Shoah Paradoxes of Memory Legacies', *Unsettling History. Archiving and Narrating in Historiography,* Sebastian Jobs and Alf Lüdtke (eds.), Campus Verlag GmbH, Frankfurt am Main (distributed University of Chicago Press), 2010, pp. 127–48.

27 Adam Smith, *The Theory of the Moral Sentiments*, A. Millar, London, A. Kincaid and J. Bell, Edinburgh, 1759, pp. 12–25. For 'social suffering', Pierre Bourdieu, *The Weight of the World*. *Social Suffering in Contemporary Society*, Polity, Cambridge 1999; Simon J. Charlesworth, *A Phenomenology of Working-Class Experience*, Cambridge University Press, Cambridge, 2000.

28 Marc Bloch, *The Historian's Craft*, Manchester University Press, 1992, pp. 4, 25–6; trans. *Apologie pour l'histoire; ou, Métier d'historien*, Librairie Armand Colin, Paris, 1949.

29 For example at the 21st International Congress of the Historical Sciences (Amsterdam, August 2010): Panels on 'Who Owns History? (esp. Anton de Baets, 'Posthumous Privacy') and 'The Rights of the Dead'.

30 Sebastian Jobs and Alf Lüdtke (eds.), *Unsettling History. Archiving and Narrating in Historiography*, Campus Verlag GmbH, Frankfurt am Main (distributed by the University of Chicago Press), 2010.

31 Daniel William Cohen, 'Memories of Things Future: Future Effects in "The Production of History"', Jobs and Lüdtke, *Unsettling History*, pp. 29–49; quote p.43.

32 Jules Michelet, 'Jusqu'au 18 Brumaire' (1872–4), *Oeuvres Complètes*, Tome XXI, Flammarion, Paris, 1982, p. 268. See (a not entirely serious) announcement of history as Death Studies, in Carolyn Steedman, 'After the Archive', *Comparative Critical Studies* 8, 2–3 (2011), 321–40.

33 'Noticeboard', *HWJ* 16 (1983), p.181; Jonathan Rée, 'Preface to Rancière's "Proletarian Nights"', *Radical Philosophy* 31 (1982), 10–13. The translation was by Noel Parker. Michael Sonenscher, 'Review of *La Nuit des Prolétaires: Archives du Rêve ouvrier* by Jacques Rancière; *Journal de ma vie: Jacques Louis Ménétra, Compagnon vitrier au 18e siècle* by Daniel Roche; *The French Revolution and the Poor* by Alan Forrest', *Social History* 9,1 (1984), pp. 113–16; Patrick Joyce, 'In Pursuit of Class. Recent Studies in the History of Work and Class Working-Class Formation', (review of) *Nineteenth-Century Patterns in Western Europe and the United States* by I. Katznelson; A. R. Zolberg; *Work in France: Representations, Meanings, Organization and Practice* by S. L. Kaplan; C. J. Koepp; *Money and Liberty in Modern Europe: A Critique of Historical Understanding* by W. M. Reddy', *HWJ* 25 (1988), pp. 171–7; Whitney Walton, (review of) *Work in France: Representations, Meaning, Organization, and Practice* by Steven Laurence Kaplan; Cynthia J. Koepp, *Journal of Economic History* 47,1 (1987), 232–4; Jacques Rancière, 'The Myth of the Artisan: Critical Reflections on a Category of Social History', in idem (*Work in France*), Cornell University Press, Ithaca NY, 1986, 297–316; also Jacques Rancière, 'The Myth of the Artisan', *International Labor and Working-Class History* 24 (1983), 1–16; and 'A Reply' to same, 24 (1984).

34 'We can never know for certain although Rancière sometimes writes as if he did', said Christopher H. Johnson of the interpretation of dreams in *NL*, *American Historical Review* 96, 3 (1991), 886–7.

35 Impossible to write labour history without Brecht's Worker Who Asks Questions at your elbow; he who eternally looks out at some great city, somewhere, and asks 'Who built the seven gates of Thebes?/The books are filled with names of kings./Was it kings who hauled the craggy blocks of stone?/And Babylon, so many times destroyed./Who built the city up each

time?'. For workers and windows, Carolyn Steedman, *The Stockingmaker, the Magistrate and the Law. How to Frame Everyday Life*, forthcoming.

36 Gabriel Gauny, 'Le travail à la tâche' (from *Le Tocsin des Travailleurs*, 1848) in Jacques Rancière (ed.), *Le philosophe plébéien*, Maspéro, La Découverte, Presses Universitaires de Vincennes, Paris, 1983, p. 46.

37 Joyce, 'Pursuit of Class', p. 174.

38 Eley, *Crooked Line*, p. 162.

39 A schematic bibliography of the skilled labour/labour aristocracy debate in relation to the historiography of organized labour: references in n. 33, and also Geoffrey Crossick, 'The Labour Aristocracy and its Values. A Study of mid Victorian Kentish London', *Victorian Studies* 19 (1976), pp. 301–28; H. F. Moorhouse, 'The Marxist Theory of the Labour Aristocracy', *Social History* 3,1 (1978), 61–82; Joe Melling, 'Aristocrats and Artisans', *Bulletin of the Society for the Study of Labour History* 39 (1979), 16-22; Robbie Grey, *The Aristocracy of Labour in Nineteenth-century Britain, c.1850–1900*, 1981; John Breuilly, 'The Labour Aristocracy in Britain and Germany. A Comparison', *Bulletin of the Society for the Study of Labour History* 48 (1984), 58–71; John Rule, 'The Property of Skill in the Period of Manufacture', in Patrick Joyce (ed.), *The Historical Meaning of Work*, Cambridge University Press, Cambridge, 1987, pp. 99–118; Keith McClelland, 'Some Thoughts on Masculinity and the "Representative Artisan" in Britain, 1850–1880', *Gender and History* 1 (1989), pp. 164–77; Derek Matthews, '1889 and All That. New Views on the New Unionism', *International Review of Social History* 36 (1991), 24 58.

40 'Book Reviews', *Oral History Review* 20,1/2 (1992), p. 124.

41 PN349–416; Christopher Johnson, *Utopian Communism in France. Cabet and the Icarians, 1839–1851*, Cornell University Press, Ithaca NY and London, 1974.

42 The childhoods in *Proletarian Nights* are both working-class memoir (recounted in the 1840s) and literary 'Childhoods', a sub-genre of romantic autobiography emerging across Europe in the early nineteenth century. Richard Coe, *When the Grass was Taller. Autobiography and the Experience of Childhood*, Yale University Press, New Haven CT, 1984; Carolyn Steedman, *Strange Dislocations. Childhood and the Idea of Human Interiority, 1780–1930*, Harvard University Press, Cambridge MA, 1994.

43 Carolyn Steedman, 'Maps and Polar Regions. A Note on the Presentation of Childhood Subjectivity in Fiction of the Eighteenth and Nineteenth Centuries', Steve Pile and Nigel Thrift (eds.), *Mapping the Subject. Geographies of Cultural Transformation*, Routledge, 1995, pp. 77–92; 'Enforced Narratives. Stories of Another Self', in Tess Cosslett, Celia Lury and Penny Summerfield (eds), *Feminism and Autobiography. Texts, Theories, Methods*, Routledge, 2000, pp. 25–39.

44 Which translates 'Chacun a trouvé sa voie originale pour percer le secret de ces feuilles blanches noircies, par exemple ce fragment de papier ramassé par terre que le petit ramoneur et saltimbanque Claude Genoux [. . .]' (NP63). 'So many particulars/So many questions', as the Worker Who Reads concludes . . . Questions about the altered sentence structure of the translation and the effacement of the acrobat who carried so much nineteenth-century understanding of childhood. Steedman, *Strange Dislocations*, pp. 96–111.

45 'Jacotot's New System of Universal Instruction', *Aberdeen Journal*, 9 Sep.

1829; 'Jacotot's New System of Education', *Belfast Newsletter*, 21 May 1830; 'Intellectual Emancipation', *Derby Mercury*, 16 Sep. 1829; 'La Methode Jacotot', *Freeman's Journal and Daily Commercial Advertiser*, 20 Jan 1830; 'Methode de Monsieur Jacotot', *Morning Post*, 17 Feb. 1830; 'J. Jacotot's Method', *Liverpool Mercury*, 25 June 1830, and many, many more. I have counted over eighty notices of Jacotot's work in the British press between 1829 and 1849 – and that's only in the nineteenth-century newspapers that have been digitized by the British Library (48 out of a potential 200 titles).

46 Patrick Groff, 'The New Anti-Phonics', *Elementary School Journal* 77,4 (1977), 323–32.

47 Ian Michael, *The Teaching of English. From the Sixteenth Century to 1870*, Cambridge University Press, Cambridge, 1987, pp. 17–125.

48 *Aberdeen Journal*, 9 Sep. 1829. Also 'Art. IV. 1. *A Compendious Exposition of the Principles and Practice of Professor Jacotot's System of Education*. By Joseph Payne – London: 1830. pp. 56. 2. *L'Enseigement Universel mis à la portée de tous les pères de famille, par un Disciple de Jacotot*. Paris and London: 1830. pp. 250', *Westminster Review* Vol. 17, Jul.–Oct. 1832, 63–7, which review concluded that 'M. Jacotot's ignorance of the real object of Education, is remarkable [. . .] He has carried the rote system to perfection; and his pupils are excellently trained parrots. They know many words and can say them fluently'.

49 See n. 44, above.

50 Michael, *Teaching of English*, pp. 72–130.

51 James Beattie, *The Theory of Language. In Two Parts. Of the Origin and General Nature of Speech*, Strahan, Cadell and Creech, Edinburgh, 1788, pp. 62–7, 116; *The Art of Poetry on a New Plan. Illustrated with a great Variety of Examples from the best English Poets, and of Translations from the Ancients*, two vols., J. Newbery, London, 1762, Vol. 1, pp. 8–13.

52 Beattie, *Theory of Language*, p. 61.

53 Or, 'Poetic rhythm is a heightening and exploitation of the rhythm of a particular language', in the modern scholar's terms, Derek Attridge, *Poetic Rhythm. An Introduction*, Cambridge University Press, Cambridge, 1995, p.3.

54 Robert Bloomfield, *The Farmer's Boy. A Rural Poem*, Vernor and Hood, London, 1800; B. C Bloomfield, 'The Publication of *The Farmer's Boy* by Robert Bloomfield', *The Library*. Sixth Series 15.2 (1993), pp. 75–94. The modern edition of this and other poems is Robert Bloomfield, *Selected Poems*, John Goodridge and John Lucas (eds.), intro. John Lucas, Trent, Nottingham Trent University, 1998. British Library, BL Add MS 28.266; 83–4, 85–6 for Bloomfield's syllable theory, and as quoted by B. C. Bloomfield. For British shoemaker poets see Bridget Keegan, 'Cobbling Verse. Shoemaker Poets of the Long Eighteenth Century', *The Eighteenth Century. Theory and Interpretation* 42.3 (2001), pp. 195–217.

55 Thomas Carper and Derek Attridge, *Meter and Meaning. An Introduction to Rhythm in Poetry*, Routledge, London, 2003, pp. 102–3.

5 The Paradoxical Pedagogy of Creative Writing

1 Dawson, P., *Creative Writing and the New Humanities*, London, Routledge, 2005. Freiman, M., 'Writing/Reading: Renegotiating criticism', *TEXT* 9, 1

(2005), http://www.textjournal.com.au/april05/freiman.htm (consulted August 2012); Melrose, A., 'Reading and Righting: Carrying on the 'Creative Writing Theory' Debate', *New Writing* 4.2 (2007), 109–17; McCaw, N., 'Close Reading, Writing and Culture', *New Writing* 8.1 (2011), 25–34; Smith, H., *The Writing Experiment: Strategies for Innovative Creative Writing*, Crows Nest, Allen and Unwin, 2005; Wandor, M., *The Author is Not Dead, Merely Somewhere Else: Creative Writing Reconceived*, Basingstoke, Palgrave Macmillan, 2008.

2 Bernstein, B., *Class, Codes and Control (vol 3): Towards a Theory of Educational Transmissions*, London, Routledge, 1975. Bourdieu, P., *Homo Academicus*, Stanford, Stanford University Press, 1990.

3 Rancière, J., 'The Thinking of Dissensus: Politics and Aesthetics', in Bowman and Stamp (eds.), *Reading Rancière*, London, Continuum, 2011, 1–17, at 14.

4 Kollias, H., 'Taking Sides: Jacques Rancière and Agonistic Literature', *Paragraph: A Journal of Modern Critical Theory* 30,2 (2007), 82–97.

5 Deleuze, G. and F. Guattari, *A Thousand Plateaus*, trans. B. Massumi, London, Continuum, 2004, p. 288.

6 Foucault, M., 'Of Other Spaces', trans. J. Miskowiec, *Diacritics: A Review of Contemporary Criticism* 16, 1 (1986), 22–7, at 24.

7 Ranciere, J., 'Is there a Deleuzian Aesthetics?', trans. R. Djordjevic, *Qui Parle* 14,2 (2004), 1–14, at 7.

8 Davis, O., 'The Radical Pedagogies of François Bon and Jacques Rancière', *French Studies* LXIV,2 (2010), 178–91, at 181.

9 Dawson, P., *Creative Writing and the New Humanities*; McGurl, M., *The Program Era: Postwar Fiction and the Rise of Creative Writing* (London: Harvard University Press, 2009).

10 Rancière, J., 'Sur *Le Maître ignorant*', *Multitudes Web* (2004), http://multitudes.samizdat.net/Sur-Le-maitre-ignorant (consulted August 2012).

6 *The Sharing of Uncertainty*

1 Sigmund Freud, 'The Future of an Illusion', in Peter Gay (ed.), *The Freud Reader*, New York and London: W.W. Norton and Company, 1989, p. 720.

2 Ibid., p. 715.

3 See in particular, Freud, 'On the question of a *Weltanschauung*', in *The Freud Reader*, pp. 783–96.

4 Blaise Pascal, *Pensées*, with an Introduction by T. S. Eliot, trans. W. F. Trotter, New York: E.P. Dutton and Company, 1958, pensée 78.

5 Ibid., pensée 324.

6 Daniel Arasse, *Le Détail: Pour une histoire rapprochée de la peinture*, Paris: Flammarion/Champs, 2005, pp. 248–9.

7 Ibid., p. 348.

8 Ludwig Wittgenstein, *Philosophical Investigations*, trans. G. E. M. Anscombe, Oxford: Basil Blackwell, 1963, p. 41.

9 Quoted by Claude Simon in *Quatre conférences*, Paris: Les Éditions de Minuit, 2012, p. 103.

10 Robert Bresson, *Notes on Cinematography*, trans. Jonathan Griffin, New York: Urizen Books, 1977, p. 47.

11 Ludwig Wittgenstein, *Culture and Value*, bilingual edition, Oxford: Basil Blackwell, 1980, p. 77.

12 S. Freud, 'Michelangelo's Moses', in Werner Hamacher and David E. Wellbery (General Editors), *Writings on Art and Literature,* with a Foreword by Neil Hertz, Stanford, Calif.,: Stanford University Press, 1997, p. 148.

13 Freud, 'Dissection of the Psychical Personality', in James Strachey (gen. Editor) *The Standard Edition of the Complete Psychological Works of Sigmund Freud,* Vol. XXII (32–6), *New Introductory Lectures to Psycho-analysis* and *Other Works,* London: Vintage, 2001, p.73.

14 Sabine Prokhoris, *La Psychanalyse excentrée*, Paris: PUF, 2008, pp. 35–49.

15 Freud, *The Interpretation of Dreams,* trans. and ed. James Strachey, New York: Basic Books, 1955, p. 528.

16 See Sabine Prokhoris, *The Witch's Kitchen – Freud, Faust, and the transference,* trans. G. M. Goshgarian, Cornell University Press, 1995.

17 Gilles Deleuze and Félix Guattari, *Kafka: Toward a Minor Literature,* with a Foreward by Réda Bensmaïa, trans. Dana Polan, Minneapolis: University of Minnesota Press, 1986, p. 29.

18 Cited by Hannah Arendt in her Introduction to Benjamin's *Illuminations*, with a Preface by Leon Wieseltier, trans. Harry Zohn, New York: Schocken, 2007, p. 38.

19 Freud, *The Interpretation of Dreams,* p. 281.

20 Ibid., p. 283.

21 Freud, 'Michelangelo's *Moses*', pp. 122–3.

22 Luigi Pareyson, *Esthétique – Théorie de la formativité*, Paris : Éditions de la rue d'Ulm, 2007.

23 See in particular Rancière's claim that 'The event draws its paradoxical novelty from that which is tied to something restated, to something stated out of context, inappropriately [. . .] The event has the novelty of the anachronistic' (NaH30).

24 Carlo Ginzburg, *The Enigma of Piero: Piero della Francesca*, with an Introduction by Peter Burke, trans. Martin Ryle and Kate Soper, London: Verso 1985.

25 Ginzburg, *The Cheese and the Worms: the cosmos of a sixteenth-century miller,* trans. John and Anne Tedeschi, New York: Dorset Press, 1989.

26 Notably in *The Distribution of the Sensible,* trans. Gabriel Rockhill, London: Continuum, 2004, p. 18. See our critique on this point in Simon Hecquet and Sabine Prokhoris, *Fabriques de la danse*, Paris: PUF, 2007, p. 26. See also our further comments there on Nijinsky's *L'après-midi d'un faune.*

27 Dominique Brun, *Le Faune – Un film, ou la fabrique de l'archive,* CNDP.

28 Michel Foucault, *Manet and the Object of Painting,* with an Introduction by Nicolas Bourriaud, trans. Matthew Barr, London: Tate Publishing, 2009.

29 Film by Emmanuelle Demoris, 2011, 5 DVD Edition 2012.

30 Henri Michaux, 'Danse', in *Oeuvres complètes,* vol. 1, Paris: Gallimard/ Pléiade, 1998, p. 699.

7 Why Julien Sorel Had to Be Killed

1 A11. Erich Auerbach, *Mimesis: The Representation of Reality in Western Literature*, trans. Willard R. Trask, Princeton and Oxford: Princeton University Press, 2003.

2 Auerbach, *Mimesis*, p. 555.

3 Ralph Waldo Emerson, 'The Poet', in *The Portable Emerson*, ed. Carl Bode, New York: Penguin Books, 1982, p. 247.

4 Ibid., p. 249.

5 Walt Whitman, *Complete Poetry and Selected Prose*, New York: The Library of America, 1982, p. 97.

6 Friedrich Schiller, *On the Aesthetic Education of Man*, trans. Reginald Snell, Mineola NY: Dover Publications, 2004, p. 140.

7 Whitman, *Poetry*, p. 91.

8 Ibid., p. 93.

9 James Agee and Walker Evans, *Let Us Now Praise Famous Men: Three Tenant Families*, New York: Mariner Books, 2001, p. x.

10 A295. Unanimism was a short-lived literary movement developed by Jules Romain, Georges Duhamel, and Charles Vildrac. Its ideas about the development of shared emotions are often traced to Whitman.

11 *Partisan Review*, Vol. VI, no. 4 (Summer 1939).

12 The *Partisan Review* turned down Agee's avowedly 'intemperate, inarticulate, and at times definitely foolish' response. It was reprised for *Let Us Now Praise Famous Men* as an 'Intermission', pp. 309–16.

13 For Rancière's development of the concept "modernatism" see PA26–7.

14 'Picturesque calendars' refers to one of Walker Evans' untitled images in *Let Us Now Praise Famous Men*.

15 Michel Foucault, 'Photogenic Painting', in *Gérard Fromanger: Photogenic Painting*, ed. Sarah Wilson, London: Black Dog Publishing Limited, 1999, pp. 88–9, translation modified.

16 Stendhal, *The Red and The Black: A Chronicle of 1830*, trans. Burton Raffel, New York: The Modern Library, 2003, p. 431.

17 Stendhal, *Rome, Naples and Florence*, trans. Richard N. Coe, London: John Calder Publisher, 1959, p. 302.

18 In their article 'Stendhal's Aphasic Spells: The First Report of Transient Ischenic Attacks Followed by Stroke', Julien Bogousslavsky and Gil Assal explain that the Stendhal Syndrome 'corresponds to a feeling of self-disintegration and mental decay' and that it is 'associated with an overflow of cultural or esthetic emotional stimuli (132). The essay is contained in *Neurological Disorders in Famous Artists: Part 3*, ed. J. Bogousslavsky, M. G. Hennerici, H. Bäzner, and C. Basetti, Basel: Karger Publishers, 2010.

8 Savouring the Surface

1 'Victor Hugo, créateur par la forme', in *Paul Valéry, Oeuvres*, v. 1, edited by Jean Hytier, Paris: Gallimard/Pléiade, 1957, pp. 583–9. Much in the line of Valéry, Jacques Derrida had studied the play of force and form in the initial essay of *Writing and Difference*, trans. Alan Bass, Chicago: Chicago University

Press, 1978, in which he used the title of Jean Rousset's *Forme et signification: Essais sur les structures littéraires de Corneille à Claudel*, Paris: José Corti, 1963, as a springboard to inaugurate reflections on play and difference that mobilize what is mistaken to be the static condition of 'form'.

2 In 'Le Titrier: Titre à préciser', reprinted in *Parages*, Paris: Galilée, 1986 and available in my English translation as 'Title to Be Specified' in *Parages*, Stanford: Stanford University Press, 2011, pp. 192–215, Derrida noted, a propos Francis Ponge and Maurice Blanchot, that a title carries a contractual relation with the text (or film) that follows, and vice-versa. The title is 'deferred' in the body of the material and, in one way or another, either in itself or in the imagination of the reader who makes sense of the material. Here, too, the relation of title and text is a vitally creative component of Rancière's study.

3 'Form of content' belongs to the idiolect that French philosophers and semioticians drew from Louis Hjelmslev's *Prolégomènes de linguistique générale*, Paris: Minuit, 1968. Michel Foucault applies the linguistic concept to the architecture of the penitentiary and its machinery in *Discipline and Punish*, trans. Alan Sheridan, London: Penguin, 1979, pp. 200–3, while Gilles Deleuze, in *Foucault*, trans. Seán Hand, London: Continuum, 2006, moves Foucault's 'forme-prison' in the direction of a 'diagram', an intermediate mechanism conceived to shape the future (pp. 30–1). Sharing much with both writers, Rancière enables the form of the content of his work to chart the uneasy relations of aesthetics and politics.

4 Inaugurating a concept of geo-philosophy in *What is Philosophy?* (said to be co-authored with Félix Guattari), trans. Hugh Tomlinson and Graham Burchill, London: Verso, 1994, Deleuze distinguishes a *plan d'immanence*, or ground, from concepts – which, in the context of Rancière's work, would include theory, art and politics – that move about its surface (pp. 35–6). Based on a principle of topology, in which concepts are discrete entities, Deleuze's topology of indistinct borders and overlapping divisions is close to what is given in the geography of *Les Écarts du cinéma* and other works. A *milieu* is thus a fluid field of force.

5 As stated in EC, cinema 'belongs to [*appartient à*] this aesthetic regime of art in which former criteria of representation, which distinguished the fine arts from their mechanical counterparts and set each of them among each other in its place, no longer hold. It belongs to [*appartient à*] a regime of art in which the purity of new forms often finds its models in pantomime, the circus, or commercial graphics' (EC13). Stress is placed on *appartenir* because, like what is found in *écart* and *écarter*, the action of belonging also implies 'holding apart', or away, *à part tenir*. By virtue of the verb cinema belongs to the new regime as it *draws away* or 'holds itself apart' from another; the turn of phrase performing what it states.

6 'Signifier' is used not in the binary sense associated with Ferdinand de Saussure but, rather, in a literary context in which the word has indexical agency in an audio-visual sense. Thus Montaigne, on the poetics of his writing, would like to be on a par with Plutarch who 'saw' Latin in and through the things he described: 'meaning enlightens and produces speech; not of wind, but flesh and bone. They signify more than they say.', *Essais*, ed. Pierre Villey and Verdun L. Saulnier, Paris: PUF, 1968, p. 873, my translation.

7 Rancière, *Aisthesis: Scènes du régime esthétique de l'art*, Paris: Galilée, 2011. The portion of the title following the colon echoes Auerbach's *Scenes from the Drama of European Literture* (New York: Meridian Books, 1959).

8 The history of the French reception of Auerbach is telling. Published in Berne in 1946 (written when the author was living and teaching in exile in Istanbul, after having been discharged from Nazi Germany, where he states he had little access to the many texts that he cites with meticulous precision), Williard Trask's English translation of 1953 changed the course of Comparative Literature in the Anglophone world. Why the book did not appear in French until 1968 remains an enigma. That it had been German or a study stealing from the French their celebrated tradition of the *explication de textes* may be a clue. That the book might have come with the ferment of 1968 may be another.

9 See Oliver Davis, *Jacques Rancière*, Cambridge: Polity, 2010, especially a propos commodity fetishism (pp. 14–16) in which Rancière is shown adhering with and splitting away from Althusser. Surely the spectre of commodity fetishism, incurring guilt among cinephiles, would inhabit the movie houses where Marxists of the early 1960s took refuge.

10 Antoine de Baecque plots its greater history in *La Cinéphilie: Invention d'un regard, histoire d'une culture, 1944–68*, Paris: Fayard, 2003, notably pp. 213–20.

11 It can be recalled how Jean-Paul Sartre found not only a taste for things Hollywood but also a mix of isolation and commitment, a way of being together and alone, at the movies, as noted in Michel Contat and Michel Rybalka, eds., *The Writings of Jean-Paul Sartre*, trans. Richard C. McCleary, Evanston: Northwestern University Press, 1974, vol. 1. James Tweedie notes that André Bazin, a founder of film theory built much of his work from his relation with popular culture. See 'Bazin's Bad Taste', in Dudley Andrew (ed.), *Opening Bazin*, New York: Oxford University Press, 2011, pp. 275–87, especially p. 276.

12 What Rancière calls 'a certain wisdom' [une certaine sagesse] echoes François Truffaut's 'une certaine tendance' [a certain tendency] of French cinema, the formula he applied to the suffocating effects of the high-minded French tradition of deadening literary effects, in his polemical essay of the same title, published in 1954, that became the cinephile's battle cry (reprinted in de Baecque and Lucantonio (eds.), *Vive le cinéma français: 50 ans de cinéma français*, vol. 2 of their *Petite anthologie des 'Cahiers du cinéma'*, Paris: Cahiers du cinéma, 2001, pp. 17–36).

13 For Deleuze an event is a 'nexus of prehensions', of vibrations that come from within and without the body, and that make known to those who experience the event a simultaneous subjectivation and objectivation of its qualities. Time and again Deleuze's remarks on the event offer a conceptual language adequate to what Rancière feels when seeing a close-up of a hand playing with a doorknob or hears glasses that tinkle and grey metal surface of Parisian café. Deleuze, *The Fold: Leibniz and the Baroque*, trans. Tom Conley, London: Athlone, 1993, pp. 78–82.

14 Taking this reflection a step further, Jean-Louis Comolli has shown how today's Hollywood cinema alienates its viewers from any production relation with alienation itself, in the aptly titled *Cinéma contre spectacle*, Paris: Verdier,

2009, a book that harks back to the 1960s to find critical mettle for the study of cinema here and now.

15 For geopolitics I follow Yves Lacoste, *La Géopolitique: La longue histoire d'aujourd'hui*, Paris: Larousse, 2009. The term 'designates first of all everything that concerns rivalries of powers or of influences upon territories and on the populations that inhabit them, whether being rivalries among political powers of every kind (and not only between States or nations), but also between States and political movements or more or less armed clandestine groups – all these rivalries having as objective control, conquest or defense of territories of large or small scale', p. 8, my translation.

16 The reader wonders if Rancière refers to Louis Marin's *Utopiques: Jeux d'espaces*, Paris: Minuit, 1973, a watershed study of language, space and social contradiction in both classical and contemporary France in the aftermath of the events of May 1968. Because it builds on Althusser's concept of ideology, the sense is that the two authors share a common investment in the political aesthetics of utopia.

17 See MS, especially ch. 4 on Hegel and the poetics of fragments.

18 Covered by Auerbach in *Mimesis*, pp. 400–34.

19 Rancière quotes Auerbach from the French edition at A63; cf. Auerbach, *Mimesis*, p.408.

20 Rancière, *Béla Tarr, le temps d'après*, Paris: Capriccio, 2011, p. 37.

21 In 'Beyond Subjectivity: The Film Experience' Francesco Casetti offers rich and polyvalent remarks about new tactics of viewing that can be juxtaposed to Rancière's ambivalence about the democratic nature of the medium as he had first known it, in Dominique Chateau (ed.), *Subjectivity in Film*, Amsterdam: Amsterdam University Press, 2011, pp. 53–65.

9 *The Politics of Art*

1 Ben Highmore, 'Out of Place: Unprofessional Painting, Jacques Rancière and the Distribution of the Sensible', in *Reading Rancière*, pp. 95–110, 106.

2 In Rancière's intellectual biography *le partage du sensible* could be characterized figuratively as a travel document – a passport or visa – enabling him to migrate to new terrain. The freedom to pursue his own singular 'intellectual adventure' (ES21) must be allowed to apply to Rancière and indeed there would be a paradoxical and exemplary violence in seeking to revoke that permit in his case.

3 See also my earlier discussion in Davis, *Jacques Rancière*, Cambridge: Polity, pp. 90–2.

4 Rancière, 'A Politics of Aesthetic Indetermination: An Interview with Frank Ruda and Jan Voelker', trans. Jason E. Smith, in Jason E. Smith and Annette Weiser (eds.), *Everything is in Everything: Jacques Rancière Between Intellectual Emancipation and Aesthetic Education*, pp. 1–33, at p. 10.

5 See also J. M. Bernstein's very helpful recent reformulation of *le partage du sensible*: 'Rancière's metaphysics of the everyday takes all social appearing to involve a range of exclusions, a set of those items that are not simply unsaid, unseen or unheard as such, but are so withdrawn from appearing because implicitly – without argument or contestation – deemed as unworthy or

undeserving or not entitled to appear. This entails that every act of bringing to appearance is *ipso facto* a claim to normative authority of some sort, regardless of the specific content in question.', J. M. Bernstein, 'Movies as the Great Democratic Art Form of the Modern World (Notes on Rancière)', in Deranty and Ross (eds.), *Jacques Rancière and the Contemporary Scene: The Philosophy of Radical Equality*, London: Continuum, 2012, pp. 15–42, at p. 23.

6 Peter Bürger, for example, argues that whereas collective production characterized the 'sacred' art of the High Middle Ages and collective reception characterized both that sacred art and the courtly art of the eighteenth century, both production and reception are *individual* acts in the art of the bourgeois era. See Lambert Zuidervaart, 'The Social Significance of Autonomous Art: Adorno and Bürger', *The Journal of Aesthetics and Art Criticism* 48, 1 (1990), 61–77.

7 Rancière, 'A Politics of Aesthetic Indetermination', p.19.

8 Ibid.

9 Arthur C. Danto, *The Transformation of the Commonplace. A Philosophy of Art*, Cambridge MA: Harvard University Press, 1981.

10 See also Terry Eagleton on Adorno in *The Ideology of the Aesthetic*, Oxford: Blackwell, 1990, p. 350.

11 As Gabriel Rockhill astutely observed (during a seminar on Rancière's work at the University of Bergen, November 2012) this reconstruction of the politics of art in the aesthetic regime incorporates – in its reference to an inevitable 'education' in the contingency of domination – something from the ethical regime of art, as Rancière has characterized it. However, it does only share this one single element; my reconstruction is not a tacit reversion to the ethical regime in the fuller sense.

12 Jacques Rancière and Oliver Davis, 'Re-Visions: Remarks on the Love of Cinema: An Interview with Jacques Rancière by Oliver Davis', *The Journal of Visual Culture* 10, 3 (December 2011), 294–304, at 302–3.

13 Jean-Paul Sartre, *The Transcendence of the Ego: A Sketch for a Phenomenological Description*, trans. Andrew Brown, London: Routledge, 2004.

14 Jean-François Lyotard, 'Anima Minima', in *Postmodern Fables*, trans. Georges Van Den Abbeele, Minneapolis: University of Minnesota Press, 1997, pp. 235–49. See, in particular, Rancière's discussion of Lyotard in 'Lyotard and the Aesthetics of the Sublime' (AD88–105), during which this particular essay of Lyotard's is cited (at AD93).

15 Lyotard, 'Anima Minima', pp. 242–3.

16 Ibid., p. 248.

17 Lyotard, 'Music, Mutic', in *Postmodern Fables*, trans. Georges Van Den Abbeele, Minneapolis: University of Minnesota Press, 1997, pp. 217–33, at p. 233.

18 Theodor Adorno, *Aesthetic Theory*, trans. C. Lenhardt, ed. Gretel Adorno and Rolf Tiedemann, London: Routledge, 1984, p. 347. The kinship between Lyotard and Adorno on this point can accounted for by the fact that, as Rancière has himself noted, both are reworking the Kantian sublime (AD99).

19 See Thomas Carlyle, *The Works of Thomas Carlyle*, Cambridge: Cambridge University Press, 2010, vol. 23, p. 22 n.1. It is also evident from this footnote of Carlyle's that the word was originally entangled with the histories of

German and English anti-Semitism, even if in twentieth-century usage it has shed these associations.

10 Rancière and Deleuze on Film

1 For a more extended discussion of the status of film-philosophy, see for example: J. Mullarkey, *Refractions of Reality: Philosophy and the Moving Image*, Basingstoke: Palgrave Macmillan, 2009.

2 For more detailed comment on these analyses, on *Herr Tartüff* see O. Davis, *Jacques Rancière*, Cambridge: Polity, 2010, pp. 142–6; on Mann see T. Conley, 'A Fable of film: Jacques Rancière's Anthony Mann', *SubStance* 33,1 (2004), 91–107.

3 T. Eagleton, *The Ideology of the Aesthetic*, Oxford: Blackwell, 1990.

4 For example, R. Stam and A. Raengo (eds.), *Literature and Film: A Guide to the Theory and Practice of Film Adaptation*. Oxford: Wiley-Blackwell, 2004.

5 J. M. Bernstein, 'Movies as the great democratic art form of the modern world (Notes on Rancière)', in J.-P. Deranty and A. Ross (eds.) *Jacques Rancière and the Contemporary Scene: The Philosophy of Radical Equality*, London: Continuum, 2012, pp. 15–24, at pp. 24–5.

6 T. Conley 'Fabulation and contradiction: Jacques Rancière on cinema', in T.Trifonova (ed.), *European Film Theory*, London: Routledge, 2009, pp. 137–50, at p. 149.

7 G. Deleuze, *Cinema 1: The Movement Image*, trans. H. Tomlinson and B. Haberjam, London: Continuum, 2005; Deleuze, *Cinema 2: The Time-Image*, trans. H. Tomlinson and R. Galeta, London: Continuum, 2005.

8 I. Buchanan and P. McCormack (eds.) *Deleuze and the Schizoanalysis of Cinema*, London: Continuum, 2008; P. Pisters (2003), *The Matrix of Visual Culture*, Stanford: Stanford University Press, 2003.

9 Deleuze, *The Movement-Image*, p. 117.

10 Deleuze, *The Time-Image*, p. 58.

11 Not least by D. N. Rodowick, *Gilles Deleuze's Time Machine,* Durham NC: Duke University Press, 1997, pp. xiii–xiv.

12 Deleuze, *The Time-Image,* p. 144.

13 Ibid., p. 178.

14 L. U. Marks, *The Skin of the Film: Intercultural Cinema, Embodiment and the Senses*, Durham NC: Duke University Press, 2000, p. 64.

15 For more on the phrase-image, see 'Re-visions: remarks on the love of cinema: An interview with Jacques Rancière by Oliver Davis', *Journal of Visual Culture* 10, 3 (2011), 294–304.

16 Deleuze, *The Time-Image*, pp. 207–16.

17 N. Baumbach, 'Jacques Rancière and the Fictional Capacity of Documentary', *New Review of Film and Television Studies* 8, 1 (2010), 65. My emphasis.

18 Oliver Davis is sceptical about this final emphasis of the essay on Marker, preferring 'film-essay' rather than 'documentary' as the genre appropriate to describe *The Last Bolshevik* and so rendering Marker's 'pedagogical' narration more self-reflexive and problematic. Nevertheless, the 'film-essay' is certainly not a fictional narrative as such and rejoins both the documentary's relation to the real (to be understood rather than an effect to be produced) and its

array of varied strategies (e.g. a voice-over or its absence) for achieving this.
19 For more on this issue see T. Conley, 'Cinema and its Discontents; Jacques Rancière and Film Theory', *SubStance* 34, 3 (2005), 96–106.
20 Deleuze, *The Time-Image*, p. 19.

11 Rancière and Metaphysics

1 This title is an allusion to an earlier piece by Jean-Luc Nancy entitled 'Jacques Rancière and Metaphysics', one which is mentioned in this dialogue and which can be found in Rockhill and Watts (eds.), *Jacques Rancière: History, Politics, Aesthetics* (Durham: Duke University Press, 2009), pp. 83–92.

12 On Aisthesis

1 Jean-Paul Sartre, *The Transcendence of the Ego: A Sketch for a Phenomenological Description*, trans. Andrew Brown, London: Routledge, 2004.

Index